WHO THE F*CK IS MICHAEL?!

Elyezer Shkedy

Published in the United States by Viva Editions, an imprint of Start
Midnight, LLC, 221 River Street, Ninth Floor, Hoboken, New Jersey,
07030.

Translation: Yossie Bloch
Cover design: Pini Hamou
Text design: eBookPro

First Edition.
10 9 8 7 6 5 4 3 2 1

Trade paper ISBN: 978-1-63228-115-9
E-book ISBN: 978-1-63228-101-2

Who the F*ck Is Michael?!

*An Israeli Air Force Chief's Uncompromising
Code for Acheiving Creatness*

ELYEZER SHKEDY

VIVA
EDITIONS

Who the F*ck Is Michael?!

EDITIONS

Contents

For my family.
Sending a big, strong hug
With immeasurable love.

Prologue

The Dream

When I was a child, I had a dream.

I dreamed of getting a pair of Adidas Roms, the white leather-and-suede sneakers (or as they were called in those days, "sports shoes") with three blue stripes on the side. In the 60s, they were the height of fashion. Most of my close friends at elementary school, in the Ramatayim neighborhood of what is now Hod Hasharon, wore their imported Roms with pride, while I was stuck with the black mid-tops made of canvas and with a very thin rubber sole, produced locally by Hamegaper.

One day, my mother told me that she was taking me to buy sneakers.

I said to myself: *This is it; it's finally happening. Mom probably wants to buy me the Adidas Roms I'm always fantasizing about.*

We went to the shoe store, and of course, my mother bought me...

...a fresh pair of Hamegapers.

New sneakers, but Hamegapers.

Mom immediately noticed my crestfallen look. "What's wrong?" she asked.

I didn't reply.

She repeated the question, "What's wrong? What's wrong?"

I told her, "Never mind. It doesn't matter."

"Are you disappointed?"

I hesitated for a moment and then said, "Yes." I told her how much I wanted a pair of Adidas Roms, just like all of my friends.

Then Mom asked me, "Tell me, who's the fastest runner in the whole class?"

I responded, "I am."

Mom said, "That's what really matters. What's important is what you are truly worth, who you are, and what you do. Not the shoes or the shorts."

Mom reassured and encouraged me, and she was right.

•••

Sometimes we get confused and fail to understand what is truly important.

Who the F*ck is Michael?!

(In place of a preface...)

One evening, I came home from university, opened the door, and saw my wife Anat crying bitterly.

"What happened?" I asked her gently.

No reply, just crying.

"What happened?"

No response, just more tears...

Only after the sobbing subsided a little, she was able to begin telling me.

...

Our whole family was then living in California. I had been sent there, after finishing my stint as head of the Israeli Air Force's Operations Department, to pursue a master's degree at the Naval Postgraduate School in Monterey. It meant living in America for a year and a half, so we sent our youngest son, Omer, to the Montessori school, the Harvard of early childhood education.

Omer was like the Energizer bunny: a kid with a never-ending battery and a wicked glint in his eye — when it came to being a sports freak. That's all he was interested in, and he was interested in everything: basketball, baseball, football, hockey, soccer, whatever. America, of course, is a paradise for sports fans. Even at the time, a sports junkie could find games broadcast twenty-four hours a day. If it had been up to Omer, he would have kept at it in front of the TV around the clock.

Ultimately, we reached a compromise. From 6:00 to 7:45, he could watch TV every morning. At a quarter to eight, he had to be ready with his little backpack, at the door, so I could take him to the Montessori school. My studies lasted until the evening, so Anat would pick him up at the end of his school day.

•••

"You won't believe what happened today," Anat said, her eyes still red from crying. "When I came to pick up Omer from the Montessori school, the principal, Michael, came over and said: 'Mrs. Shkedy, I don't know how to tell you this, but I have no choice. I've been running this school for twenty years. I've taught every child who's passed through these doors to read and write. I attempted to do the same with Omer, using every tool at our disposal. I truly tried, but nothing helps. He can't read or write.' And if that wasn't enough, he also said: 'In my opinion, he never will.'"

I stared at Anat and declared unblinkingly: "**Who the f*ck is this Michael?!**" I'm telling you, Omer will read in three months."

"Here we go again," Anat replied. "You and your dreams, your fantasies I know Omer is smart, but Michael has twenty years of experience, and he's convinced that Omer will never be able to read. So how can you say so assuredly that you can teach him to do it in three months?"

"I'm willing to bet you that Omer will read in three months," I answered. I believed in my son and decided that I would do anything to teach him to read. Of course, Anat believed in him too; the problem was that she believed Michael as well...

So, I conducted a debriefing, as was my wont in the Israeli Air Force. The first question I always asked was the following: **What happened?**

I placed a virtual mirror in front of my face. And what did I see? Michael, who'd been running a Montessori school for twenty years, saying that my son was a hopeless case... an utterly lost cause.

What was the first thing I wanted to do? To shatter the mirror over Michael's head. But what could I do? Michael had said what he said.

On to the second question: **Why did it happen?** Omer could not yet read or write, neither in English nor in Hebrew. Michael had tried every approach based on the Montessori method. But what was the problem with that? He'd tried teaching him in English.

Finally, the third question: **What to do differently?** We spoke Hebrew at home, so I decided to teach Omer in Hebrew — not just to instruct him, but to blaze a different trail. The best way to turn him into a reader, I told myself, had to be to forge a connection between reading — which wasn't his top priority — and his greatest passion: sports.

If I hadn't succeeded with that, I would have tried another way.

If the second method had failed too, I would have looked for a third approach.

And so on.

Regardless, I wouldn't give up.

At that time, the internet was in its infancy; we had to rely on snail mail to get our Hebrew literature, in the form of newspapers from Israel.

Omer was a Maccabi Haifa superfan. At the time, they were a formerly legendary soccer team. (Although, to our delight, as of the writing of this book, they have reclaimed their erstwhile glory...)

Alon "The Airplane" Mizrahi was still their star player, famous for spreading his arms like wings and running to and fro whenever he scored a goal.

"Forget Principal Michael. Forget the Montessori school," I told Omer. "As far as I'm concerned, you have only one mission every day: find an article in the newspaper about Maccabi Haifa. Look for words like Haifa, Maccabi, Mizrahi, Alon, airplane, goal, goalie, post, referee, ball, offside, kick.."

Three months later, Omer was regularly reading news articles written for adults, in Hebrew, without the vowelization markings schoolchildren normally use. Of course, later on, he learned English as well, but that was after we returned to Israel.

Since then, every time someone tells us that we can't, that we couldn't, that there's no way, that it's hopeless, we have a saying:

"Who the f*ck is Michael?!"

And then we charge.

In our family, these are words to live by.

Omer has since gone on to do great things, including becoming an officer and a pilot in the IAF. He has faced challenges and has come a long way relative to Michael's expectations...

I just think what might have happened if I had listened to this Michael.

Everyone has their own Michael.

In fact, there's a bit of Michael inside everybody...

• • •

Each and every one of us has our own life story.

I don't know your stories, so I'm sharing mine with you: the triumphs and the tragedies, the struggles, the successes, and the failures. Just as each and every one of us has experienced.

Every episode and insight in this book are connected, in one way or another, to all of us: young and old, women and men, secular and religious, Jewish and non-Jewish. Every time I tell one of these stories to somebody, they respond with a similar experience of their own.

I believe that you'll find meaning in these stories, even if you come from a world completely different from my own.

The true meaning of this book is what you, the readers, will find in it, based on your personal experiences and stations in life.

I hope that my words will touch your hearts and souls, bring up questions and ideas about yourselves and similar events that have happened to you, and speak to your beliefs, values, and dreams — what is right for you and what is your truth.

If the book encourages you to think about one of the things I've written about, I have done my part.

• • •

Every story in this book describes a real event in my life, as I remember it.

Naturally, each has additional perspectives and details I don't know. I have tried to present my truth, as much as possible, from my point of view, at least as I remember...

Each story stands on its own. I have deliberately arranged them associatively rather than chronologically; this means that one story leads to the next, though it may be from a different time and about a different topic. I assume that for each of you, the transitions will evoke your own associations.

Most of the events I describe involve people I love and appreciate, men and women who have been with me and by my side along the way. Unfortunately, for various reasons, not everyone can be named; but everyone in my life, whether mentioned or not, has a stake in what was accomplished, remaining a significant and integral part of my life.

All proceeds from this book will be directed to charitable ends, to advance educational, moral, and social causes in the State of Israel.

• • •

The book is dedicated with great love to my mother and father, Nechama and Moshe Shkedy.

It's all thanks to them.

Elyezer Shkedy
Tel Aviv, 2021

I.

The Pigpen

For my father Moshe, whose entire family had been murdered and burned in Auschwitz, returning to Hungary, the land of his birth, was a decades-long dream. There was a fire burning in his bones to go back — which we eventually did, the five of us: my father Moshe, my sister Yael and her eldest son Yotam, myself, and my eldest son Nimrod.

We landed in Budapest and embarked on a tour of the most significant locations in my father's young life.

We finally reached the village of Tolcsva, where Dad was born and raised. It was important to him that we pull up in a very, very big car, and that he emerge impeccably dressed, in a suit and tie.

We found the house where his family used to live. In the yard stood a heavyset woman, her brown leather shoes worn and bursting, her hair covered with a headscarf.

We got out of the car and Dad, in his fancy clothes, went over to talk to her. He was quite excited. They spoke Hungarian, and he translated for us.

A lively conversation ensued. Then he asked her: "Do you know the history of this house? Who used to live here?"

"Yes," the woman answered. "I've been living here for a few years now. Before us, another family lived here. At the end of the war, there was a pigsty here. But the worst thing is that before the swine, a Jewish family lived here..."

We didn't say a word.

WHO THE F*CK IS MICHAEL?!

We just looked at each other and understood.
She was talking about our family.

•••

Nothing has changed except one thing: we have our own country, the State of Israel... a free, Jewish, democratic, proud, amazing state. We are not dependent on anyone else's tender mercies.

2.

The Cup of Luck

Aunt Berta and Uncle Yehezkel were my father's relatives. They lived in a tiny apartment in Haifa, just above the train tracks. They spoke with a heavy Hungarian accent, and we could barely understand a word they said in Hebrew. Still, we could feel their love for us even when we couldn't grasp what they were saying. They were lovely people, Aunt Berta and Uncle Yehezkel — ultra-Orthodox Jews with big hearts.

Dad was usually preoccupied with his work running a home for troubled youth, so family travel was quite a rare event for us. Sometimes, on Saturdays, we would visit relatives — and once in a great while, we would go to Haifa to Aunt Berta and Uncle Yehezkel's home. To this day, the image of Uncle Yehezkel's long beard, huge black hat and black suit is etched in my memory, as he would accompany us to the car at the end of our stay and give us a big hug. Even though he would never travel on the Sabbath himself, it was very important to him that we came to see them. It was clear how happy he and my father were to see each other.

Once a year, we would go with them to Mount Meron: Uncle Yehezkel, Aunt Berta, Mom, Dad, my sister Yael and me. We children were most excited about the picnic on the way back: spreading a blanket on the grass climbing up to the mystical city of Safed, eating and enjoying the family outing.

One time, Uncle Yehezkel and Aunt Berta brought with them a special small goblet wrought of thick glass. They don't make them like that anymore. Unfortunately, when the time came for a little tipple, we couldn't find it. The glass had simply disappeared, as if it had been swallowed up by the earth. We searched everywhere, but we just couldn't find it.

Only after we got home, while cleaning the car, did we discover, to our surprise, that the glass had rolled under one of the seats.

We kept it, designating it "Cup of Luck." From then on, every Friday night, Dad would fill the Cup of Luck with wine to welcome the Sabbath, and we would pass it from one to another. Everyone would drink a little wine from it, close their eyes, quietly make a wish, and pass it on – until it returned to Dad at the head of the table.

It was a unique ceremony. It had more of a personal and familial meaning than a religious one. Friends and family would join us for Friday night dinner, lovingly prepared by my mother. All of us would sing Hasidic songs and drink from the Cup of Luck, wrapped in dreams and blessings. We all sat together, but everyone had their private moment, shared with no one else, just their own hopes and thoughts holding the Cup of Luck.

Dishwashing duty fell on me and Yael. One Friday, at the end of the meal, my sister was in the kitchen when, over the sound of the running water, we heard a shattering crash, followed by a terrible cry.

The Cup of Luck had simply slipped from her hands and broken. Yael was in tears and didn't know what to do.

My father was very sad.

Me too.

"Our luck is all gone," I muttered to myself.

Mom was the only one not paralyzed by the accident. Intelligent and decisive as ever, she took charge. Surveying the situation, she told us reassuringly, "Just a minute," as she rose from the table. Half a minute later she came back with a tube of extremely strong glue she kept in one of the drawers. Since the goblet was small and made of thick glass, it hadn't smashed into pieces; it had split instead diagonally into two parts — and Mom just glued them back together.

24

The re-formed glass did look a bit rough and crooked, but the Cup of Luck survived for another three or four decades. The drinking, the blessing, and the dreaming continued with the glued-together goblet, and we were happy that both the luck and the cup stayed with us. Even the grandchildren had the opportunity to drink from it.

A cup with luck.

•••

This is a little tale with a big life lesson: never give up on the important things, your dreams, what holds meaning for you. The technical problems are merely that — technical. If you're determined to overcome difficulties, you'll find the glue to put the pieces back together, even though the situation seems beyond repair.

3.

I Want Them to Salute You

When I became commander of the Israeli Air Force, I was told that my German counterpart, Lieutenant General Klaus-Peter Stieglitz, expected me to invite him to visit Israel as my guest. My predecessor, Dan Halutz, had visited Germany, and it was customary to invite the host for a reciprocal visit.

As the son of a Holocaust survivor whose entire family had been murdered, burned, and exterminated in Auschwitz, the last thing I wanted to do was meet and host the commander of the Luftwaffe.

I decided to put it off.

But the message kept coming back to me, through various channels: General Stieglitz is waiting for an invitation.

I kept ignoring it until one day some of my men came to me and said, "We understand why you wouldn't want to invite the commander of the German Air Force, but it is really putting a strain on the relations between the two militaries. We request that you reconsider inviting him for a formal visit."

I slept on it and realized that despite my personal reservations, extending the invitation was probably the right course of action.

So that's what I did, hoping he would decline...

But *Generalleutnant* Stieglitz was actually happy to accept the invitation and announced that he would come to Israel as soon as possible.

When such a high-level delegation arrives, the customary rules of the ceremony are as follows: the guest is greeted with an honor guard, invited to a formal dinner attended by all the senior IAF commanders and their spouses, and escorted on a tour of IAF bases.

I asked Avital, my secretary, to send the senior commanders of the corps an invitation to the festive dinner, but I told her to include the following caveat: "Only those who feel comfortable attending a formal dinner with the Luftwaffe commander are required to do so. Consider yourselves at liberty to decline."

Usually, officers do not like going to such events, but when the IAF commander is the one issuing the invitation, they have no choice and they come (unless they manage to find a really good excuse...)

I said to myself, "What's the worst that could happen? My wife and I will sit down to have a meal with him, his delegation, and a small cadre of senior IAF officers."

The evening arrived and to my surprise, all the commanders arrived with their spouses.

They all wanted to be there.

It was unprecedented.

General Stieglitz was genuinely thrilled. I, on the other hand, was ill at ease. His thin, tall physique; his pointed face; his slightly crooked jaw — they all raised unpleasant connotations. Images of the past ran through my mind, giving me no rest.

Standard operating procedure is for both the guest and the host to speak by heart and from the heart on such occasions, but General Stieglitz preferred to read from his notes. He said that before coming to Israel, he had toured an extermination camp and studied in depth the horrific and incomprehensible history of the Holocaust.

At the end of the meal, Stieglitz quietly told me that he wanted to invite me to Germany; he hoped to receive my response in the affirmative that evening, in front of everyone.

I didn't have to think too much. I said to him: "Thank you, General Stieglitz, but I'd rather you didn't invite me."

Despite this, after his return to Germany, General Stieglitz sent me a formal invitation to come there on an official visit as a guest of the German Air Force. I thanked him for the offer but declined.

The invitations were extended regularly. I didn't want to go, so I didn't go.

As my assignment was nearing its end, and after much deliberation and consideration, I came to the conclusion that I ought to make the visit.

I assembled my staff and set a date for the visit. Shortly before departing, I told myself that I couldn't fly to Germany without talking to my father first.

When I arrived at his home, I told him exactly what was going on. "*Abba* (Dad), I've decided to go on an official visit to Germany, at the invitation of the Luftwaffe commander. What do you say?"

For a while, he just looked at me silently, deep in thought. Finally, he said,

"Very good.

"I want you to go there.

"I want them to see the hat and insignia of our air force.

"I want them to see you in an Israeli Air Force uniform.

"I want them to see your ranks.

"I want them to see your wings.

"I want them to play *HaTikvah*," (Israel's national anthem)

"And I want them to salute you."

This put my mind at ease, and I went home to prepare for my journey.

We landed in Germany, an official Israeli Air Force delegation.

Berlin. Winter. Temperature below freezing. Everything icy.

I traveled in General Stieglitz's car, as we were being taken to review the honor guard.

Germans are accustomed to winter and their uniforms are designed accordingly: their ranks, wings, and insignia are affixed to the outside of their large, thick coats. We were coming from Israel, a warm country, and our uniforms are also designed accordingly: our ranks, wings, and insignia are affixed to the thin jackets of our dress uniforms. Our thick coats go on top and obscure everything.

What should I do? I thought to myself.

I remembered my father's words and decided that all the members of the delegation, me first and foremost, would get out of the motorcade without our coats, so our ranks, wings, and insignia would be visible to all. The way Dad wanted.

General Stieglitz asked me, "Are you crazy?"

I looked at him and said quietly, "This is what I want to do."

Rows upon rows of German soldiers, German officers, German airmen, and German air commanders stood on the parade ground in the heart of Berlin.

I reviewed the honor guard.

A German military orchestra played "Hatikvah."

And they saluted. Just as my father had dreamed.

I have never felt so warm as I did on that frigid day when the Luftwaffe's enlisted soldiers and officers smartly saluted Moshe Mendel Shkedy's son on German soil.

In Berlin.

In many ways, they were saluting all of us.

4

It All Could Have Looked Different

Before my conscription into the IDF, I took driver's ed with a teacher named Schneider in Kfar Saba.

Back in those days, the rules were a little different. On the one hand, one didn't start taking driving lessons until shortly before their eighteenth birthday. On the other hand, passing the test was all it took. A freshly minted driver could take anyone they wanted in their vehicle and go anywhere. New driver, accompanying driver, experienced driver — these terms were meaningless at the time.

In my case, the lessons went well, more or less. It didn't take me long to learn to drive stick on Schneider's already ancient and coughing Triumph. Still, it wasn't clear if I'd be able to take the test before my induction date.

Schneider, paternal and patient, went the extra mile and got me a test date right before my induction.

To improve my chances of passing the test, he informed the examiner that I was slated to join the Air Force Academy and start pilot training. If the military thought I could fly an airplane, surely I could drive a car...

Apparently, this argument made an impression on the examiner. I passed.

My father had a Ford Cortina with a manual transmission, the gearshift right by the steering wheel, with room for six passengers including the driver, three in the front and three in the rear. Right after passing the test, I came home, took the car, and picked up my good friend Yaakov and four of our buddies for our maiden trip, to make a bit of an impression.

We left Kfar Saba, heading toward Moshav Sde Hemed, east of the city.

At the wheel, I was the "experienced driver...," even though the ink was barely dry on my new license...

We drove down Weizmann Street, the main drag of Kfar Saba, eastward, stopping at the main intersection at Rothschild Street.

The road had two lanes in each direction.

I saw a vehicle idling in the right lane. Since I was in the left lane, I kept going, without hesitation. I didn't realize that the vehicle in the right lane had stopped at a crosswalk for pedestrians. And so, on the first drive of my life, with five other friends with me in the car, I missed by three feet — maybe less — a young mother pushing a stroller.

It's been a few decades since then, but to this day I remember the woman's terrified face. I cannot forget the stroller either: navy blue, a bit faded, with a shade in the front to shield the baby from the sun.

The incident left me deeply shaken, shocking me completely. I realized that it was only by a great stroke of luck that I managed not to kill a baby and a young woman.

It's just crazy.

My entire life could have looked completely different.

Since then, I've made sure to drive carefully.

Very carefully.

5.
A Kick to the Face

I was deputy commander of 101st Squadron at Hatzor Airbase, "the first combat squadron," when we reestablished it as a two-seater F-16 squadron.

The squadron commander was busy building a new house during this process. Fortunately, there were excellent people in the squadron, so we muddled through.

At some point, the commander apparently felt that the squadron was slipping out of his grasp, which caused a lot of tension between us.

One Friday, he summoned me to his office and informed me that he had decided to remove me from my position.

I was surprised.

Immediately after our conversation, he called the other deputy squadron commander and informed him that he would replace me as the primary deputy commander.

He refused to accept the promotion.

A great commotion ensued. Most of the squadron united against the move and against the squadron commander. The base commander, an officer of superior ability and character, hadn't known about the moves planned against me. Once he learned about it, he vetoed the decision.

By the skin of my teeth, I had survived. That left me with a stark choice.

• • •

I could allow myself to be pulled into a black hole of anger and resentment, turning against the entire world and deciding that I had no chance of escape.

Alternatively, I could debrief, study, understand where I'd gone wrong, change, and correct my trajectory.

I chose the latter, debriefing myself, without embellishment or assumption.

How had I gotten myself into such a situation?

I realized that professional, flight, and command abilities are imperative, but behaving like a human being is no less important.

And I had just been dead wrong.

I'd been arrogant.

I'd gotten too big for my britches.

I had acted with a basic disrespect towards my superior officer — manifested in my actions, in my direct interactions with him, in my conversations with others, and in front of the squadron personnel, even in my body language and style of speech. Whatever my personal opinion of him, it didn't really matter. In any case, I could not be allowed to disrespect him, embarrass him, insult him, or make inappropriate statements regarding him.

On a personal level, my conduct was unbecoming.

Being good or successful or popular doesn't legitimize such behavior.

On the contrary: being better requires one to do better.

As I conducted this debriefing, I totally disregarded the squadron commander's actions and attitude. They were irrelevant. I debriefed only myself and no one else. My debriefing showed me that I ought to have been much more sensitive to the dignity and status of the squadron commander, even when it came to symbolic things — especially in the presence of other people.

I have yet to see a superstar in any field who wasn't seriously kicked in the face at some point, be it personal or professional or medical or something else.

I wasn't kicked out of the IAF, nor even out of the squadron, but that smack still caught me right in the teeth.

After a person catches a kick in the head, they have two options. They can throw up their hands, say they've blown it, they have no chance, it's all over.

Or they can take stock, debrief, and try to understand what happened and why, learn their lessons, and fix their mistakes...

And to move forward.

I chose the second way.

•••

The kick to my face and the courage I found to debrief myself in an incisive and sincere way allowed me to change and course-correct.

I am convinced that it influenced my life for the better down the road, wherever I've gone.

6.

Stand Straight and Smile

Shortly after the squadron commander informed me that he had decided to "eject" me, a change-of-command party was held for a sister squadron at Hatzor Airbase. Such events are usually attended by the commander and all senior officers of the IAF.

My wife, Anat, really didn't like going to these kinds of events. I usually had to lay it on thick, so that she would agree to come. Even then, it didn't always help.

In light of the circumstances, the last thing I wanted to do was go to a party, meet with all the senior staff, and see the people around me gossiping, whispering, and looking at me with pity.

I decided not to go.

That evening I was sitting at home, reading and watching TV.

Suddenly, Anat appeared, dressed to the nines.

I looked at her in wonder and asked, "Where are you going?"

To my great surprise, she said, "We're going to the change-of-command ceremony." I never had imagined that she even knew or remembered that there was such an event...

Then she said, "Get dressed, we're going," adding, "You'll go, you'll stand up straight, and you'll smile."

I really didn't want to go. I really, really didn't want to.

But I realized she was right.

With all the mental difficulty involved, we went.

I stood straight.

I smiled.

And I broadcast that it was business as usual for us.

Anat was right.

I adopted this attitude toward life, in relation to myself and in relation to the people I love.

7.
Don't Mess with the
Depressed and Downtrodden

When I finished my role as IAF chief of operations, I was sent to pursue a master's degree at the Naval Postgraduate School in Monterey, California. NPS is a venerable institution, its student body composed of distinguished members of all branches of the US armed forces — Navy, Marines, Army, and Air Force — and of the American intelligence community as well. There is also a small but significant number of students from foreign militaries, which included me. Whatever one might be studying, Monterrey is a lovely place, and of all the places to be stationed, if you have to suffer... it's hard to think of a better one.

I signed up for a course in economics with Professor Katsuaki Terasawa, a renowned Japanese-American lecturer whose wit was razor-sharp, although one might be misled by how sparingly he spoke.

At the opening of the first lesson, Professor Terasawa told us, "You will be divided into three groups. I want you to compete against teams of your classmates."

It didn't take long for two groups of American officers to form, with not one foreign student among their ranks. We overseas students weren't a terribly hot commodity, certainly not to the impeccably dressed locals. The NPS dress code mandated jackets and ties, but many of us felt overdressed, sort of like *bar mitzvah* kids in their oversized suits — not to mention that we all kind of stuttered in awkward, heavily accented English. I looked around at my fellow depressed and downtrodden and told them:

"Let's go.

"We've got to band together.

We'll manage."

Somehow, I pulled together a motley crew of Japanese, Indonesian, Turkish, Greek, African, and Israeli officers, along with a few others.

The competition began. It was lengthy and fascinating, requiring a practical understanding of mathematics, economics, game theory, and negotiation.

When it came time to tally the score, our group blew the other two out of the water. The well-dressed American students, who looked like a million bucks, spoke perfect English and held home-court advantage, couldn't believe what had happened to them. Professor Terasawa, with his wicked smile, was pleased, and we were even happier. Our classmates, and soon the entire school, realized we were no pushovers. Quite the contrary.

Many years later, I received a phone call from the former IDF Chief of Staff, Gabi Ashkenazi, who was attending a massive airshow in Singapore at the time. "Shkedy," Gabi, who was already a civilian at the time, told me, "there is an impressive Indonesian general here named Dezi who insists on talking to you now."

It turned out that the Indonesian general was one of those foreign officers that I had gathered at the time into our group of the depressed and downtrodden, in Professor Terasawa's first class. In those days, he was still a young major with a round face and a frozen look, utterly unremarkable.

But General Dezi had not forgotten. Ashkenazi gave him the phone and we enjoyed reminiscing about experiences from that class with Professor Terasawa, in which we showed the Americans that it's not a good idea to mess with the depressed and downtrodden.

• • •

A person may appear pitiful and pathetic at first glance; their accent and vocabulary may not be impressive; their attire may not be striking — but that tells you nothing about their ability, their wit, their intelligence or their potential.

8.

Why'd You Send This Guy?

As head of the IAF's operations department, I had to send a senior officer — either a pilot or navigator — to the Northern Command, to work for a few weeks with the command staff, planning joint operations with the ground forces.

The mission was important to me, so I chose to send Danny, a man whose abilities I valued and an excellent officer whom I trusted very much.

A few hours after he showed up at regional command headquarters in the north, I received a call from a senior officer in the command staff. "Shkedy, why'd you send us this blockhead?"

I tried to understand why he would say that. Danny, the officer I'd sent to the command staff, was an individual I genuinely liked, on a personal and a professional level: he was determined, smart, assertive, possessing both operational understanding and an impressive capacity to execute. Above all, he was personable and charming, and pleasant to work with. True, he didn't look exactly like the stereotype of an Air Force pilot, tall with blue eyes, hair rustling in the wind. Apparently, the first impression of him was misleading.

I replied, "He's a serious stud. You'll see."

The senior officer from the Northern Command wasn't really convinced, but that was my decision, and so it stood.

A few weeks later, I met the same senior officer from the command staff, and he told me, "Shkedy, you really did send us a stud, he's on point, a real asset."

I said, "You're telling me all this?

"Talk to him personally.

"Tell him what you said about him when he first arrived.

"Tell him what you just told me.

"Then apologize profusely and ask for forgiveness."

I don't know how it shook out, how Danny responded, or even if he responded.

But there's a quote attributed to Albert Einstein:

"Weak people revenge.

Strong people forgive.

Smart people ignore."

Danny is a smart man...

This "blockhead," as the officer in the command staff called him even before he knew him, later became the commander of a squadron and the commander of a base. When I became commander of the Air Force, I appointed him head of the personnel division, with the rank of brigadier general.

A real stud.

9.
Want to Play Pool?

When I was a young pilot in Hatzerim, I went to Beersheba to visit Aryeh Trabelsi, a friend from when I went to school in Kfar Saba. His nickname was "Trifo" because he had a huge mane that reminded everyone of the Greek singer Trifonas.

Trifo was a talented and quick-witted guy. His family lived in Shikun Dalet, one of the rougher parts of Beersheba at the time, but he'd gotten into the boarding school for gifted students next to the Katznelson School in Kfar Saba, where we met.

I went to his house. His mother opened the door and said he wasn't there, but would come back in about an hour and a half.

This was the pre-cellphone era, so there was no way to let him know that I had arrived, so I went for a bit of a stroll until he came back.

As I was walking through the commercial center of Shikun Dalet, I saw a pool hall.

I went in. I was wearing my Air Force uniform, with my officer's bars and pilot's wings. I looked around. The place was shrouded in thick cigarette smoke (as you could smoke anywhere at the time).

Suddenly, a young man who identified the new "fresh meat" on the scene approached me. "Want to play?" he asked.

I said, "Yes."

The guy continued, "Just so you know, you've got to place a bet on every game you play here."

I said, "OK, let's bet."

He thought the fresh meat had taken the bait and started reeling me in. The game was underway and all the people in the hall at the time quickly gathered around our table, smiling and rubbing their hands with pleasure, waiting to watch the latest sucker get carved up.

But very quickly the smiles were wiped away and there was silence.

Before their very eyes, the unimaginable happened. The "blockhead" in uniform, whom they'd hoped to take to the cleaners, took their friend to the cleaners instead, right there on their home turf at the Shikun Dalet pool hall.

What they didn't know was that Hatzerim had a pool table too, and whenever we finished an exhausting day of flying, we'd get together and play.

More than that: one of the soldiers on the base was a real pool shark, and he taught us every secret of the game, all the theories, techniques, and tricks — angle calculations, shots of all kinds, backspin, sidespin, topspin, parking a cueball and even jumping it...

Thanks to him and his tutelage, we became quite good.

• • •

Never let outward appearances or features fool you.

Before each battle, you need to gather intelligence and understand who the opponent in front of you is and what their abilities are.

Even if you are a professional in the field, do not brag and do not underestimate your opponent.

Contempt can lead to a big mistake.

10.

The Air Force's "Secret"

My friend, Eyal Chomsky, is one of the owners of the Hapoel Jerusalem basketball team. Eyal, his wife Tami, and all their family live and breathe the team, with all their heart and soul, and are emotionally involved in everything that happens with it. They are addicts, pure and simple.

One day late in the season, after I finished serving as El Al's CEO, Eyal asked me to come and talk to the entire team: the coaches, the players, and the professional staff.

We met at the home of the team's CEO, Guy Harel.

I went back and forth over what to talk to them about and decided to devote the conversation to debriefing, as an excellent tool for the challenges they could expect in the short period of time remaining until the end of the season.

After my talk, I was pulled aside by the team's coach at the time, Simone Pianigiani, who had also coached the Italian national team in the past. Simone was dressed as if he had come out of an Italian fashion magazine and looked unusual in the Israeli landscape. He began to ask me questions about debriefing and wouldn't let me go. I felt that it interested him and that he wanted to study the subject in depth.

We chatted at length.

The next day, I received a message from the coach's assistant, Mody Maor, formerly a combat officer in the Air Force. It was a list of questions on various issues related to the team and the moves it needed to make in the future.

At Chomsky's request, I decided to help guide the team through the aspects of debriefing.

Although my son, Omer, was a die-hard Hapoel Jerusalem fan, my professional knowledge of basketball was unremarkable, and I certainly couldn't give advice about one player or another, nor about game tactics or professional exercises.

My forte was debriefing, and I was convinced that it could help in many areas such as interpersonal relations within the team, certain professional decisions, what to work on, what to change, how to properly prepare, and so on.

The team found itself in a difficult situation: down 0-2 in the best-of-five quarterfinal playoff series against Ironi Nahariya. Another loss would have been lights out.

They were in serious trouble and morale was low.

They asked me, "What do you suggest?"

I thought about it and came to the conclusion that it was time to carry out a debriefing in three stages:

1. What happened?
2. Why did it happen?
3. What to do differently?

The first stage: What happened? You put a "virtual mirror" in front of your face and tell yourself boldly, sharply, and clearly, without cutting corners and without bullshitting yourself, what really happened. You mustn't sugarcoat the picture so it's easier for you to digest.

The second stage: Why did it happen? You analyze yourself to understand why those things happened. What did you observe? How did you respond? What did you do? How did you do it? In other words, what could have led to the results you see in the "virtual mirror."

The third stage: What should be done differently the next time and what should be retained?

If you only go through the first and second stages, it's as if you didn't debrief at all. In such a situation, not only will you have not learned anything, but you may be left with a sense of frustration and self-flagellation.

Only once you reach the third stage, in which you decide and define for yourself what you ought to do differently next time and what you should keep, have you completed the debriefing process.

It is a circle in which each stage leads to the next. If you skip one of the steps, it disrupts the whole process.

The debriefing cycle is complete when you have a briefing before the next time. In other words, when your planning is based on the main points raised in the debriefing.

I told the leaders of the team: "You have to dramatically change the lineup, your tactics, and your style of play."

I didn't tell them what and how to change because that's their field of expertise, not mine, and everyone has to debrief themselves.

But I made it clear to them that you should not be afraid of change, even if it is extreme.

Simone, the coach, outlined a series of fundamental changes, and the team won three games in a row and advanced to the next round.

As the finals approached, they spoke to me again.

I asked, "How are you preparing for the game?"

They said, "We're studying what happened in the previous series."

I said, "The most important thing now is to plan, prepare and train for the game ahead, not the games that have already taken place. What happened in the semifinals is less relevant. You need to analyze and understand in depth your relative advantages vis-à-vis the team you will meet in the final, and impose them onto the opposing team's relative disadvantages in the most acute and aggressive way possible. Your debriefing ought to focus on the games you played against them during the season."

It was fascinating and exciting to see them listen to a person who doesn't really understand basketball but knows that real debriefing is the key to improvement and success.

They just listened to what was said, no matter who said it, and brought it to the fore on the court in the best possible way.

Hapoel Jerusalem beat Maccabi Haifa 83-76 in the finals and won the 2017 championship.

Tami and Eyal Chomsky were in heaven.

Also Omer...

Of course, my share of the success was nil. The rights are all reserved to the players and the coaching staff, but it was beautiful to see how open they were to the subject of debriefing.

• • •

The Israeli Air Force is an excellent corps, both compared to other organizations in Israel and compared to its counterparts around the world.

When you ask people why the Air Force is so good, the answer is usually: because it has excellent people, advanced aircraft, and tremendous resources.

It's always good to have excellent people and adequate resources, but in my opinion, the secret of the IAF's excellence lies in its organizational culture, of which debriefing is a central component.

When talking about debriefing, it is important to clarify what it is not.

Interrogating someone in order to "hang" them is not a debriefing.

Looking for culprits instead of learning and moving forward is not debriefing either.

People tend to confuse debriefing with investigation.

These are two completely different things.

Debriefing is a deeply structured process that is essentially about learning and making continual progress.

In a deep sense, it is a way of life for a person or an organization.

After any event of any kind, problematic or positive, the most important thing is to learn from it in order to move forward.

When you do a real debriefing, with all the difficulty involved, you embark on a positive and optimistic path of improvement and learning, even if you are in a tough situation after experiencing failure.

Usually, when something doesn't work, the first question is whose fault it is.

In most cases, people will blame someone or something else for the failure: Mom, Dad, the teacher, the CEO, the commander, the weather, an uneven floor...

And who is never to blame?

Me.

My most important piece of advice on the subject: When you "eat it," never blame anyone else for the failure.

You, and only you, are responsible for what has been done.

You, and only you, must debrief yourself.

You can improve next time by five percent, by ten percent, by thirty percent, by fifty percent, or by eighty percent.

But the debriefing is yours and the improvement and progress depends only on you and no one else.

We all make mistakes, all the time.

The important thing is not to make big mistakes, and not to make the same mistake twice.

For people who haven't come up through an organizational culture of debriefing, like the one that exists in the Air Force, it is difficult to talk about their mistakes in front of others.

Therefore, for the group you are leading to perform a real debriefing, and for this to be its organizational culture, first of all, you must demand from yourself as a leader what you demand from others. In other words, debrief yourself sincerely and incisively, with an emphasis on your mistakes. Don't just demand that others talk about their own mistakes, and certainly don't "hang" them in the public square.

Otherwise, it just won't happen.

Everything is fair game in debriefing, regardless of the subject of the event and its consequences, whether failure or success. This is true for the small things and the big things – from a Hanukkah party to attacking a nuclear reactor. At home, with family and children, with friends, in business, and in everything we do.

It's simply a way of life.

Even as I write this book, I am constantly debriefing myself.

This culture, which I believe in with every fiber of my being, has influenced and continues to influence my life, in every sphere, all along the way.

•••

I have no doubt that the IAF's organizational culture, centered on debriefing, is relevant and significant for every field — military, business, medicine, education, sports or any other issue in life — both on an organizational and personal level.

11.
I'll Never Make That
Mistake Again

When I was a young officer with the rank of captain, I went to Ben-Gurion University to study for a bachelor's degree.

Every Friday, we would meet up with Ofer and Marina, a couple of our friends who studied with Anat in medical school.

One Friday, Marina enthusiastically told us that Gadi's wife, who was also studying medicine, was the tennis champion of the South.

Without thinking too much, I said, "I'll beat her."

There was no way, I thought to myself, *that I wouldn't beat a woman at tennis.*

Marina, who was a real "Doberman," glared at me with a scorching look and said, "Really?

"We'll show you what's what.

"Play her and we'll see who wins.

"Just wait and see..."

"No problem," I answered nonchalantly. I already understood that I had gotten myself into trouble, but I couldn't back down.

I had grabbed the bull by the horns, but now I had to keep from getting gored.

I put my university studies on hold and began a regimen of intense tennis practice in front of a special training wall.

My abilities in tennis were quite limited. It was clear to me that normal volleying would guarantee a loss for me. I just didn't know how to do it well enough.

My plan to get out of my predicament was to immediately attack and rush the net (I used to be agile)... and look to end the point as quickly as possible. In other words, I intended to use the element of surprise and take advantage of the meager relative advantages that I had.

Once every few days, Marina would ask me: "What's going on? When can we schedule the match?" And I would mumble something about the overload of schoolwork, when my only burden was the intense training in front of the wall on the tennis court.

In the end, I couldn't stall anymore, and the match was scheduled.

I arrived at the court with Ofer, Marina's partner, who came to offer me moral support. I was dressed in my "luxury" tennis clothes, a particularly ugly set of military olive-colored athletic shorts with a white stripe on the side. I wore simple sneakers and military gray wool socks. I was equipped with a wooden Dunlop tennis racket which was a bit broken, a nail somehow holding it in one piece ...

And then...

The competitor appeared.

Tennis champion of the south.

Dressed like a Wimbledon champion, holding a bag with three professional tennis rackets, and a special ball holder attached to her bright white tennis skirt.

Ofer and I turned pale...

The first game ended in a completely unexpected victory. Mine.

I managed to surprise her. She was not prepared for the tactics I had developed. It turned out that my training camp helped me after all.

But it was clear to me that the next game would be a different story, and I couldn't afford to lose. So, as soon as the first game ended, I went to the net, shook her hand, and said I had to go.

I retired at my peak...

Somehow I was saved from being disgraced.

I seemingly won, but I understood perfectly well that I didn't really win. If the match had continued, she would have torn me apart. She was just a lot better than me.

WHO THE F*CK IS MICHAEL?!

•••

That day I learned an important lesson, and it had nothing to do with tennis: talent, ability and knowledge do not depend on whether you're a woman or man. My declaration that I could easily beat her was condescending, arrogant and stupid. I decided that I would never repeat such a mistake.

52

12.

You Never Get Smarter from
Listening to Yourself

"Who is smart? Whoever learns from every person."
(Ethics of Our Fathers 4:1)

One of the most important operational decisions in my life pertains
to listening.

In 2007, as commander of the Israeli Air Force, I led the preparations and planning for the attack on the nuclear reactor in Syria, and
we debated a great deal about the right course of action.

The Air Force Operations Department was headed by Amikam
Norkin, a superb man and an officer whom I trusted very much
(who would go on to become commander of the Air Force himself).
He and his team were in charge of the planning process and did so in
an excellent, professional, and in-depth manner. But alongside the
organized staff work, it was important to me that someone external,
who was not part of the planning process, challenge the operations
department. And me.

I did this through two separate channels. I turned to Gur, a per-
ceptive and sharp-witted officer known for thinking outside the box,
who was not part of the operations department, and at the same
time, I set up a "red team" — a group of people whose operational
and intelligence understanding I valued and trusted even though

they did not hold an official position. For this purpose, I recruited Aviv and Itzik, serious reservists and studs who didn't "owe" me anything and had no problem poking holes in the chosen attack plan or stepping on anyone's feet.

I listened to them very attentively, and some of my decisions were influenced by their observations and insights.

But not just them.

One of the main dilemmas was how to carry out the attack without the other side realizing what exactly had happened, so they would not be motivated to respond immediately, as one of the gravest concerns during the planning stages was to avoid a response that would lead to an all-out war.

We formulated a very good operational plan that addressed all aspects of the task. Still, we were looking for the "missing link" that would best solve this final dilemma.

I asked all the people who were secret partners in the operational planning to think of ideas that would help us crack the problem.

Norkin and I understood the operational-aviation sphere quite well, but the idea we adopted, the same component of the plan that would leave the other side in the dark, was conceived and presented to me by a relatively junior officer named Shai — a deep and serious professional who displayed inner peace and wisdom in his eyes. I listened attentively to his proposal and decided that would be the "link" to complete the operational planning.

And the rest is history...

• • •

Wisdom is not necessarily related to age, position, experience, education, or personal background.

A young person can be smarter than a senior manager.

A young officer can have more original thinking than a senior and experienced officer.

Those who hold advanced academic degrees are not always more in the right than those who barely graduated from high school.

• • •

Think about what is being said and not who is saying it.

The truth has nothing to do with the timing of the words. Is there more validity in things said in the distant past, which have since become an indisputable convention, or in innovative ideas instead?

Think about what is being said and not when it was said.

Listen carefully and with extreme openness to everything that is said.

Use your discretion.

And in the end, after you have listened and thought it over, you will decide. The decision is yours.

We all know the following template of conversation: when someone talks to you, instead of listening to them you either cut them off or think about how you will respond, waiting impatiently for your turn to speak. This is "deafness by choice."

When you lead a discussion, you have several options for how to conduct it:

The first is that you enter the discussion with a coherent opinion and sum it up exactly as you originally planned.

The second is that you enter the discussion with a coherent opinion, but at the end, after listening to the participants, you say that in light of the views and data you have heard, you need more time to think before you make a decision.

The third is that you enter the discussion with a certain opinion, but after listening to others, you change your mind and conclude accordingly.

The fourth is that you do not have a coherent opinion on the subject and use the discussion to listen, not necessarily to arrive at a decision. To really listen, you need courage — courage to think outside of your box. There's a chance you'll be convinced...

It is very worthwhile to have discussions of all kinds, not just of the first kind.

It is also worthwhile to include in these discussions not only senior officers and managers, but junior people as well.

Although they have a little less experience in the field, their minds are open. They are usually the ones who carry out the mission in practice and know what is really going on.

• • •

You never get smarter from listening to yourself.

13.
Face-to-Face with the
Prime Minister

The intelligence reports on the progress of the construction of the nuclear reactor in Syria became clearer, and it was obvious that it would become "hot" within a short period of time.

In the Air Force, in some of the general staff departments, and in the other arms of the military, we delved into and grappled with planning, training, and bringing together the operational plans for destroying the reactor before it reached completion.

The focus and tension were at their peak.

At the end of August 2007, on a Friday morning, we met in Prime Minister Ehud Olmert's home in Jerusalem to hold a final meeting on the attack on the Syrian reactor.

All of us sat there, in a room that wasn't very big: Olmert; Defense Minister Ehud Barak; IDF Chief of Staff Gabi Ashkenazi; Mossad Director Meir Dagan; Shin Bet Director Yuval Diskin; Deputy Chief of Staff Moshe Kaplinsky; Head of Military Intelligence Major General Amos Yadlin; and I, commander of the Air Force.

This was a group of very serious people who understood very well the magnitude of the responsibility on their shoulders. The faces of all the participants in the discussion and their body language testified to how seriously each of them treated the subject.

I especially loved the head of the Mossad, Dagan. I loved his way of thinking and his determined, goal-oriented personality. I loved his total commitment, the way his conduct was free of any bullshit, and the fact that his word was his bond and his handshake was worth more than a signed contract.

I always felt that we were on the same page, and on the issue of the Syrian reactor and the operational solutions for its destruction, we were in full agreement.

In general, relations at the time between the Air Force and the Mossad really flourished, reflected in important joint operations.

The meeting at the Prime Minister's Residence began. The current intelligence picture was presented there, its implications were analyzed, and an in-depth discussion was held about each of the operational alternatives and how to carry out the attack and destroy the reactor without triggering an all-out war.

Each of the participants addressed the group and voiced his opinion.

When Olmert asked for my opinion, I unequivocally recommended the IAF's plan, formulated to destroy the reactor in such a way that it would take the Syrians a relatively long time to understand what had really happened — if at all — which would greatly reduce the chances of a response on their part that could lead to war.

When the discussion ended, I asked to speak with the prime minister in private. This went far beyond the accepted protocol, but it was important to me that he be personally and directly impressed by my deep commitment to what I'd said and my confidence that the Air Force would be able to carry out the mission in the best possible way.

At the end of the meeting, we both stood alone on the far side of the room, with everyone staring at us...

I told the Prime Minister the following quietly and clearly:

The mission will be carried out by excellent pilots and navigators.

The operational plan that we have formulated is very good.

I estimate that the reactor will be destroyed and that the Syrians will not understand what has happened. The plan addresses both aspects.

In my estimation, they will not respond and will not start a war.

The destruction of the reactor is of paramount importance and must be carried out as soon as possible.

The Prime Minister looked deep into my eyes, listened very attentively, and when I finished he said: "I understood very well what you've said." We parted with a strong handshake.

I got the impression that he was determined to carry out the attack as soon as possible.

Indeed, about a week later, on September 6th, 2007, the attack was carried out in the format I had proposed.

Prime Minister Olmert very wisely led the process and made this significant decision with courage, determination and deep understanding and commitment.

• • •

I have no doubt that when the commander in chief arrives at a critical and weighty decision, there is great importance to his personal trust and confidence in the people who are supposed to carry it out.

14.
The Ofra Haza Miracle

WINTER, 1987.

Ofra Haza, who was then a huge star, came to put on a concert at the Nevatim Air Force Base in the south.

At that time, I was deputy commander of the Skyhawk squadron in Nevatim.

In the evening, before I went home to family housing at the base, I did my rounds of the squadron, meaning I went through all the rooms to see with my own eyes what was happening, as I always did.

During my inspection, I came across one of the young pilots who was wearing a G-suit. I asked him why he was dressed like that, and he answered me excitedly: "It's my first time on call for a flare illumination night flight." That meant that he was on duty in case there was an operational need to light up the night sky.

The weather that day was very cold and windy, and I thought it wasn't the right time to put a young pilot on call for the first time at night.

I said, "I'll fill in for you on call."

I didn't know if he was disappointed or relieved. Anyway, he didn't try to protest...

I put on the G-suit so that I would be ready for a scramble if necessary and went to sleep in the squadron's on-call room.

I woke up to the ear-rattling sound of a blaring siren.

Scramble.

I ran to the on-duty jeep, quickly got to the plane, and took off for the flare illumination mission. As I was flying, the controller directed me, in a very tense voice, where to place the flares in the Hebron area.

He didn't explain to me what the purpose of the illumination was, but he asked me to stay as long as possible above the area.

I continued to light up the night until the flares ran out and I was left with almost no fuel.

I flew back to the base.

Then, in accordance with tradition and Murphy's Law, the landing device that was supposed to help me touch down in bad weather didn't work.

I pulled myself together, somehow landed safely, and said to myself: *Lucky that I was the one scrambled in bad weather, replacing the young and inexperienced pilot on call.*

I quickly drove to the base's command center.

The commander of the base, Moshe Melnick, and the commander of the squadron, Amos Yadlin (who later became a major general in the IDF and head of military intelligence), both experienced commanders and serious fighters, were there. They seemed terribly worried.

You could have cut the tension in the room with a knife.

I asked what was going on.

It turned out that at the end of the performance, Ofra Haza had boarded a Cessna piloted by Yoav from our squadron, which was supposed to have taken her back to Tel Aviv. During the flight, contact with the plane was cut off and it vanished. No signals via radio or emergency instruments.

I understood what mission I had been assigned to drop flares for.

The mood was quite depressed.

There was a very high probability that the plane had crashed and that its passengers had been killed. As if that weren't enough, the commander of the Eitan unit (dedicated to locating missing persons) called up to search for the wreckage of the plane and the remains of its passengers was the father of the pilot who flew Ofra Haza and her crew.

Yoav, the pilot, had been my apprentice at a flight school. I put great stock in his skills, his professionalism, and his capability as an aviator, and I loved him as a human being too.

Even though it was against all odds, I told them that I felt he and his passengers had survived.

I had no explanation for why.

I returned to the squadron, to the on-call room, with the commanders continuing to oversee the incident.

In the morning, they woke me up and said, "You won't believe it, they found them safe and sound." It turned out that the plane had hit the mountain and overturned on its tail, but everyone managed to get out of it before it went up in flames.

They walked and reached a military base in the Hebron area.

At the entrance, they were stopped by the gate guard.

He asked them to stay out of the way because the entire base was busy with a major search operation...

15.

Just Hit Enter

My brother-in-law Naftali was, and still is, a tech and computer whiz. A man with a heart of gold as well as golden hands.

During my studies in the United States, when we lived in Monterey, California, Naftali and his wife Shiri lived in New York. One day, he decided it was time for me to upgrade my computer's operating system (which was working fine...), so he sent me a set of installation disks. That was back in the era of disks.

I said to him, "Naftali, there's no way I'm going to do this if you're not here."

"Trust me," he said, "it's very simple. You only need to insert the disks and just hit enter."

I wasn't convinced and said, "There's no way I'll do it without you."

We spoke every day, him on the East Coast and I on the West. Each conversation began with the issue of the computer. Naftali said, "Just hit enter..." and I said, "No way..."

A few months later, Naftali and Shiri came to visit us in California. The "official" reason was that they missed us and wanted to see us, but in my opinion, Naftali just couldn't bear the fact that our computer hadn't been upgraded yet — and decided to come himself.

The first thing Naftali did, after the hugs and kisses, was to run to the computer and start the installation of the upgrade.

In other words, just hit... enter...

The next morning, after pulling an all-nighter, without having slept a wink, bleary- and red-eyed, Naftali was still sitting at the computer...

• • •

The next step in "Operation Just Hit Enter" was an extensive shopping spree across California for computer parts.

To Naftali's credit, he rebuilt an excellent computer.

• • •

If it works fine, don't touch it.
If it ain't broke, don't fix it.
Or as my friend Raz says in his picturesque language, "Don't touch a dry turd..."

16.
Change of Command

Even after he moved to an assisted living facility in Kfar Saba, Dad continued to drive his battered Subaru.

At some point, his driving became dangerous for him and his surroundings. He drove in a really hair-raising way, weaving between lanes without signaling, sideswiping fences...

My sister Yael and I were very upset. The last thing we wanted was for our father to end his amazing life story with a serious accident, to hurt himself or another person. Just imagining his injuring a small child made us shudder.

But despite his condition, and despite our desperate attempts at persuasion and the weighty arguments we presented to him, he wasn't willing to give up driving under any circumstances.

For my father — we felt — giving up driving was giving up the freedom and independence that were so important to him, which he fought for with all his might throughout his life.

Then an idea came to my sister's mind. We invited Dad to join us at the Coffee Tree, his favorite café in Kfar Saba. He still didn't know why...

The three of us sat down and started talking about our childhood.

During the conversation, Yael asked my father to remember what he thought and how he reacted when I, as a high schooler, asked to buy a motorcycle.

Dad immediately unleashed a fire-breathing speech, explaining how dangerous it is to ride a motorcycle because things are not in your complete control — even if you are an outstanding rider, you are at the mercy of other drivers — and told us that he refused to allow me to buy a motorcycle under any conditions, even though I really wanted to.

My sister encouraged him to keep talking about that decision, which he had made for one reason only:

He was simply concerned about me.

I, for my part, described how hard it had been for me, how angry I had been with him, how much I had rebelled, and what I was willing to do to overturn the harsh verdict.

Dad reiterated that he had done the right thing, adding that to this day he was completely at peace with the decision.

Then Yael whispered to me:

"Go ahead, this is the moment..."

I said to my father, "Now it's our turn. We are asking you to stop driving, and we are completely at peace with that request."

We told him that if he trusted us and knew that we cared for him and loved him, then if we thought he should stop driving, that was what ought to happen, just as he decided decades ago, for the exact same reasons, not to let me buy the motorcycle I wanted so much.

And it worked.

At that moment, Dad put the keys to his Subaru on the table and never drove again.

After we had our conversation, he began taking a taxi driven by the legendary driver, Aryeh Haimi, who became a true friend of his and escorted him everywhere with all his heart and soul.

• • •

There is a stage at which a "change of command" is carried out between parents and children, from a situation in which the parents take care of their children to a situation in which the children take care of their parents. It is an integral part of the life cycle.

17.

Who Influenced You the Most?

One who thinks of the coming days sows wheat.
One who thinks of the coming years plants trees.
One who thinks of the coming generations educates people.

(*Janusz Korczak*)

As commander of the Air Force, I used to consult on various issues with Moishik Theumim, a close friend of mine. He was a man overflowing with ideas, with the Air Force in his heart and soul. In one of our meetings, we talked about education, influence, and inspiration, and during the conversation, Moshik came up with an idea: Toward the end of the pilots course, the commander of the flight school would ask each of the graduates to choose the person who influenced them the most but was not a parent or close family member.

As commander of the IAF, I would then meet with the "team of influencers" and personally invite them to the winging ceremony.

I loved the idea right off the bat. It was important to me that the younger generation of aircrew members — pilots, navigators, and flight engineers — show their appreciation and cherish these people, who helped them make it to the parade ground.

It was no less important that they understand, implicitly, their obligation to be not only excellent airmen but also guides for future generations.

I conveyed the message to the commander of the flight school, and he instructed the trainees accordingly.

A few days passed, the preparations for the winging ceremony were in full swing, and... nothing. Not a single name arrived.

I asked the flight school commander what was going on, and he replied that the graduates of the aviation course said that it didn't make sense to them for the commander of the Air Force to make such a strange request ...

I said, "Make it clear to them again that this is a personal request of mine."

This time, they made their choices.

The list reached my office, and I invited the women and men who influenced the graduates of the course to meet with me.

Most of them did not believe that the chief of the Air Force really wanted to meet them, to get to know them, to listen, and especially to say thank you to them. It was explained to them that this was precisely my intention.

It was a fascinating and very moving encounter. You could see why. There were people from the "institutional" educational world: teachers from kindergarten to high school, advisors, and principals. There were also figures from the world of informal education, from youth movement leaders to coaches, commanders, and rabbis. And also one fisherman.

I asked each and every one of them to tell me about the graduate and about themselves. The stories were inspiring.

I was particularly touched by two stories that clarified the strength and significance of the personal connection.

One of the women who participated in the meeting said, "I'm a teacher at the school where he studied, but I didn't have him in my class."

That sounded a bit strange to me.

I asked her, "Do you know him?"

"Yes," she replied, "I would talk to him during breaks."

In other words, the person who influenced him more than any other was the teacher who listened to him, sympathized with him, strengthened him, and talked to him during breaks, even though she was not officially responsible for his education.

One of the participants in the meeting, who was sitting right next to me, was trembling all over his body with excitement. I didn't say anything and waited calmly for his to turn to introduce himself.

When it was his turn to speak, he said, "You won't believe who I am. I was the kid's driving teacher..."

That says it all. Formally, he taught the guy how to move in traffic, obey road signs, and parallel park. Totally technical stuff. What made him a true educator and an influential figure was the interpersonal connection and the ability to touch the depths of a teenager's soul.

I asked my father, a man who considered education a profound mission and the purpose of his life: "What do you suggest I give to the people who were chosen?"

Father said, "Don't give them anything material, just a certificate proving that they are exemplary people and inspiring figures."

And so I did.

One day, while I was walking in Tel Aviv, a woman charged at me and started hugging me.

I looked at her surprised.

"Remember? Remember me?" she asked and continued uninterrupted, without waiting for an answer, "I was in that meeting of the most influential educators. I was so moved. It was an awesome experience. I can't stop thinking about it."

And then...

She opened her bag and took out the certificate I gave her for being an exemplary person.

It turned out that she went everywhere with it.

To my delight, the tradition continues to this day, and all the air force commanders who came after me have made sure to meet before the winging ceremony with the people who most influenced the graduates of the course. This tradition has already taken on a life of its own.

•••

One day, a few years after I retired from the IDF, I received a call from Brigadier General (res.) Rani Falk, a fighter pilot who was formerly the commander of the Ramat David and Hatzerim air bases and the attaché to the United States Air Force.

From his voice, it was evident how moved he was. Rani told me that the commander of the Air Force at the time, Major General Amir Eshel, had invited him to participate in the meeting with the people who had the greatest influence on the graduates of the course.

During the meeting, Rani said that each of the people introduced themselves and talked about their special relationship with the graduate of the course they influenced, and then the Air Force commander told those present: "Now I want to tell you who influenced me the most." He continued, "The person who influenced me the most is Brigadier General (res.) Rani Falk, and he's sitting right here with us."

I have known Rani for many years. He is truly a unique person, tough on the outside with a heart of gold, a fearless warrior, and an educator with all his soul and all his might. I've never heard him so excited.

•••

In my opinion, what makes a person a true educator is not a formal title like teacher, principal, doctor, or professor, but the ability to ignite a spark in another person's heart, touch their soul, inspire them, and influence their life. Therefore, choosing them as influential and inspiring figures is the greatest compliment a true educator can receive.

...
...
...
...
...
...

18.

I Wonder What Grandpa Said...

When my son Omer completed his pilot's course, my father made a great effort and came to his grandson's winging ceremony, even though he was no longer in the greatest of health. He loved Omer very much, and Omer loved him very much.

After the ceremony ended, my father spoke to Omer in a whisper for quite a while.

We were curious to know what Grandpa Moshe had said to his grandson, the new pilot.

As we later learned, it turned out that he told him, "Take the first salary you receive, all of it, and buy a big gift for your mom and dad."

And Omer did just that. He came through in a big way.

He spent hours cooking a family meal — for the first time in his life — and bought spectacular gifts in which a lot of thought was invested: for his mother, he bought a lovely ring, for me he bought an iPad, and for his brother and sister, he got presents as well.

It moved us a great deal.

Some of his friends who heard this jokingly said, "Don't tell our parents, they'll expect us to do it too..."

Others adopted the advice of Grandpa Moshe and did the same as Omer.

•••

The only entry in the Ten Commandments which gives you reward in this world — longevity — is the following: Honor your father and mother, so that your days will be prolonged. (Exodus 20:11).

WHO THE F*CK IS MICHAEL?!

I believe and maintain that there is an unwritten continuation of the Commandment: "and so that their days will be prolonged too."
At some point in their lives, your parents live through you.
Your success is their success.
The respect you give your parents can literally extend their lives.

19.
We Bring All of Them Back.
All of Them.

One of the most difficult decisions I've ever had to make in my life was a moral matter of the highest order.

Toward the end of the Second Lebanon War, the decision was made to launch a large-scale ground operation. This included transporting infantry in assault helicopters, CH53s, and Black Hawks, and landing them deep in enemy territory.

During the operation, one of the CH53s was hit by a Hezbollah missile and crashed. This happened a few minutes after it had unloaded dozens of paratroopers and taken off on its way back to Israel.

The price was very heavy. On board were two pilots: Nisan Shalev and Daniel Gomez; and three airborne mechanics: Sami Ben-Naim, Ron Mashiah, and Keren Tendler.

We were preparing for the rest of the flights. War is war. A short time later, the chief of staff decided to halt the entire ground operation.

As commander of the Air Force, I had to decide what to do in this situation. We had a helicopter that was shot down deep within Lebanon; it was more than likely that all the crewmembers on it had been killed. Should more soldiers be brought in to recover the bodies?

The dilemma was a difficult one.

On the one hand, this was a complex and dangerous operation

that could get complicated and end with more wounded or even more dead. On the other hand, one of the paramount values of the IDF is that no one is left behind. Any member of the Israel Defense Forces who goes into battle — aircrew, infantry, or armor, regardless — must know that the State of Israel will do everything possible to bring them home. And if, God forbid, they are killed, their bodies will be brought back to be buried on Israeli soil.

When it comes to such a decision, you are completely alone, realizing that it may have consequences for many years to come, perhaps even for generations.

After much deliberation, I decided that we would plan and carry out an operation to bring the fighters home.

The significance of the decision was clear to me, but I knew that it was the right move and that I would be at peace with myself and with my decision even if the operation went downhill.

We decided to send forces from the Air Force's commando unit, *Shaldag* (Kingfisher), and from 669, the premier pararescue unit. These are two elite units that consist of the best fighters in the IDF.

The operation was planned quickly with the units themselves, with the operations department, and with the command staff of IAF special forces.

The force arrived by helicopter at the site of the crash and found the bodies of four soldiers. That same night, they were returned to Israel by helicopter.

Sergeant First Class Keren Tendler, a true warrior, was not among them.

I decided that we would do everything to bring everyone back.

All of them.

The force remained on the ground and continued to search for Keren.

In the meantime, the morning approached and a new dilemma arose: Should the force on the ground be allowed to continue the search even in broad daylight?

On the one hand, the level of risk during the day was higher.

On the other hand, the chances of finding Keren were considerably higher in daylight, and if we stopped the searches, the soldiers would have to wait until nightfall, when they were relatively exposed inside enemy territory.

I decided to continue the search in daylight. The main thing was to do everything possible to find Keren and get the Shaldag and 669 commandos back to Israeli territory as quickly as possible.

After much effort, Keren's body was found too.

In light of the prevailing military and political situation, the force had to return to Israeli soil via a circuitous trek that lasted about twelve hours, carrying Keren's body on a stretcher.

To see the faces of the families of the fighters who had been killed; to see the faces of the Tendler family who knew they had recovered everyone but their daughter, and then to inform them that Keren had also been found — it was unimaginable and chilling even amidst the terrible reality of bereavement and war.

• • •

I have no doubt that everyone who participated in this rescue operation felt and understood that they were doing something of profound and inspiring moral significance.

We had the privilege of fulfilling our duty to bring every last fighter home.

All of them.

20.

A Belated Realization

I completed my pilot's course as outstanding cadet.

I decided not to tell my parents so that it would be a happy surprise for them at our graduation — the winging ceremony.

Most of the parents, including mine, arrived at the ceremony at Hatzerim air base on organized bus rides from the center of the country.

It was a different time...

After the ceremony, my father told me the following story:

"We were very lucky today. When we stopped for a short break, one of the parents, who knew me from the Ministry of Education, came up to me and said, 'Congratulations!'

"I said to him, 'Congratulations to you, too.'

"Then he added, 'Kudos to your son for graduating as the out-standing cadet.'

"'My son??' I looked at him surprised and asked, 'How do you know?'

"He replied, 'We have the same last name, Shkedy, and my son told me that when they call out Shkedy to be recognized as the out-standing cadet, I ought to know they don't mean him...'

"How lucky that I knew that in advance," Dad said quietly, tears in his eyes. "I don't think I would have been able to handle it."

It was only as I grew older that I realized that in light of his crazy life story, such an exciting event — even if it were joyful — could be traumatic and end badly.

But I hadn't figured it out yet.

I was wrong.

As I grew older, I realized a few more things about parents and children.

Along the way in the Air Force, every time I received a new rank, I found one excuse or another not to invite my parents to the promotion ceremony.

This, too, was a mistake that reflects a complete lack of understanding.

When I got to the positions where I was the one bestowing ranks, I corrected that.

I asked my people — to be precise, I pretty much ordered them — to invite their parents to the promotion ceremony.

• • •

There are not many things that make parents happier than seeing their children succeed, advance and fulfill themselves.

Involve your parents in the process; do not deprive them of these moments of happiness and pride.

There are things you come to understand only as you get older.

21.

They Are Just Like You

I grew up in "Givat Hod" in Ramatayim, an institution for children at risk. My father ran the place along with the adjacent school, and our family lived on the premises.

The children came from different parts of the country, and they had considerable behavioral and educational gaps. Dad saw educational work as his life's mission and went about it with all his heart and soul.

Essentially, I lived in two worlds:

The first was the school in Ramatayim, where many of the kids came from well-established families from the surrounding area. It was the world of the morning hours.

The second world was at Givat Hod, where I spent the afternoons with the children in the institution, who came from a completely different environment. We played soccer, marbles, and spud, and we also "went at it."

After those "battles," the games we played during breaks at the school in Ramatayim were easy and simple, truly a piece of cake...

My classmates from the school in Ramatayim, who came in the afternoon to play with me at the institution, were rather frightened by the encounter with children who came from a world different than their own. But I lived and felt at home in both worlds.

It was mainly thanks to my mother and father, who put in my head from a very young age some simple but important messages:

"They're just like you."

78

"Be their friend."
"Just be a human being."

And really, the children from both worlds were my friends and I felt that they were just like me: those who had the good fortune to have parents, support, hugs and affection; and those with much less luck, who had come to the institution from a challenging background. I even stayed in touch with one of them over the years.

I believe that this worldview of my parents, and the unique way in which I spent my childhood, has influenced me throughout my adult life. This period shaped the way I look at the world and see the other, wherever I am.

A human being is a human being is a human being.

• • •

These principles are a cornerstone of the Jewish conception of morality.

In the book of Leviticus, the verse "Love your fellow as yourself" appears.

The great sage Rabbi Akiva, who lived almost two thousand years ago, said, "This is a great precept in the Torah."

To me, this is not just a great precept in the Torah; this is the **greatest** rule in the Torah.

Hillel the Elder, who lived a few generations earlier, gave a practical translation of the verse "Love your fellow as yourself," stating:

Whatever you find hateful, you must not do to your fellow.

This, according to Hillel, is the entirety of the Torah "in a nutshell."

Why is this sentence so significant? Because five out of the Ten Commandments, which relate to the relationship between one person and another, are derived from this directly.

When you're debating whether to do something or not, think about whether you'd like them to do something similar to you or talk to you like that. If not, just don't do it and don't speak like that to another person.

...

Hillel the Elder had another saying of three parts, which I find marvelous:

The first part: *"If I am not for myself, who will be for me?"*
The second part: *"And when I am only for myself, what am I?"*
And the third part: *"And if not now, when?"*

This saying has been analyzed in-depth, and most interpretations see it as being focused on an individual and their personal development.

I see it a little differently.

I believe and feel that this sentence by Hillel concerns not only the personal development of an individual but also their attitude towards others.

If I am not for myself, who will be for me? You must develop yourself, face difficulties and challenges, exhaust your abilities, and advance on your own, without waiting for someone else to do it for you.

And when I am only for myself, what am I? I believe that this saying is about giving. Your personal development must not turn you into an egotistical, selfish, and apathetic person who thinks only of himself.

You've accomplished, you've evolved, you've succeeded — great. But...

If you are focused only on yourself and are not engaged in any kind of giving — of emotion, knowledge, substance, empathy, humanity, or attention and attentiveness to those around you, if you do not think about the other as well, see the other, show compassion towards them and help them — what are you? There is no real meaning and no value to your personal success.

And if not now, when? Don't postpone doing, nor postpone giving.

What you can do now, don't leave for tomorrow or next week or next year.

• • •

The greatest catastrophe in the history of the Jewish people throughout the ages, and in the history of mankind in general, was caused by insane racists who set themselves the goal of annihilating the Jewish people to the last of their sons and daughters, who formulated a systematic plan to achieve this goal, and who actually destroyed a very large part of our people.

What did my father used to say? On the way to the crematoriums in Auschwitz, no one cared about where people came from and whether they had a large *kippah* (yarmulke), a small kippah, half a kippah, a quarter of a kippah, or whether they were without any kippah.

We should understand this about ourselves and about people in general.

Where there are no people, try to be a human being.
(Hillel the Elder)

I have devoted most of my adult life to protecting and defending the State of Israel from enemy states, terrorist organizations, nuclear threats, and other external threats. I dedicated this chapter of my life to defending the great miracle in the history of the Jewish people — the state we built and the society we established.

Racism, hatred, incitement, and discrimination can undermine the foundations that have been created, can destabilize them, and lead to the destruction of our humanity, mutual responsibility, equality, and morality.

A human being is a human being is a human being.

22

Proportions

When my son, Omer, was a high school student, he was invited, together with Grandpa Moshe, my father, to a ceremony in the town we lived in, Yehud: lighting one of the six torches in memory of the six million Jews murdered in the Holocaust on the evening of Yom HaShoah.

I didn't know if I'd make it to the ceremony myself, but Omer wouldn't give up.

"Dad," he said, "you have to come. Grandpa is unpredictable..."

I managed to get organized, and the whole family came to the ceremony.

The event went as planned until Omer and Grandpa Moshe came up to light the torch. When they finished, they were supposed to leave the stage, but not Grandpa Moshe...

He motioned for Omer to go down, walked to center stage, stood in front of the microphone, and launched into an amazing, powerful, and moving speech with all his heart and soul.

The large crowd watched him, eyes watering and hair standing on end, while he told about the great catastrophe in which his entire family, except him, was murdered and incinerated. Then he spoke of the great miracle, the State of Israel.

For eight minutes, my father, who was already very old, held forth. He gave the speech spontaneously, with no notes and no preparation, until it seemed that he was about to faint.

When he finished his speech, there was silence in the audience.

Then, a few seconds later, the audience suddenly stood on their feet and clapped their hands forcefully for quite a while.

I have never seen anything like it, certainly not at the Holocaust Memorial Day ceremony.

If I hadn't been there and seen it with my own eyes, I wouldn't have believed it.

Those eight minutes, in which Grandpa Moshe stood on stage and spoke, illustrated to all of us where we had been then and where we are now.

To my delight, my father's words were recorded and posted to YouTube. In difficult moments, we hear them and understand how to put things into proportion:

In July of 1944, my mother was fifty years old and my father was fifty-one. My oldest sister, Ella, was twenty-one. My second sister, Anzi (Anna) was fourteen. My third sister, Adele, was twelve; and my kid sister, Esther, was ten. They were taken to Auschwitz, and they were murdered in cold blood.

I waited for them to come back, but no one came back. Then I decided to immigrate to Israel because it was my family's dream, my mother's, my father's, my sisters' dream.

So I immigrated to Israel.

I started a family. My eldest son, Elyezer Shkedy, named after my father Elyezer, was the commander of the Air Force for four years. And I want to remind you of just one event.

My son went through all the stages. He completed the pilot's course with honors. He was the commander of the Ramat David airbase. He was chief of staff of the Air Force.

And one fine day, my wife and I got an invitation. And in the invitation it was written that my son, Elyezer, was to receive the rank of major general.

We arrived at the hall, and I looked around. All the IDF generals were there. The commander of the Air Force, the commander of the Navy, the commander of the ground forces — everyone was there. And suddenly I asked myself: How could it be that my son is about to receive the rank of major general? After all, decades ago they murdered my mother and sisters. My four sisters. I was left alone. So I looked around and said, "How can this be?"

And suddenly I realized that it was true. That he received the rank of major general.

Then I felt like shouting, "God, open the gates of heaven! I want my mother and father who were murdered in the Holocaust to see their grandson receive the rank of major general. I want my sisters — Ella, Anzi, Adele, Esther — to listen to the chief of staff's statement, telling my son that he has made a great contribution to the security of the State of Israel. And I want them to hear the words of the Minister of Defense, who said: 'The fact that the son of a Holocaust survivor is receiving the rank of major general is a sign that we have gone from Holocaust to resurrection.'"

My daughter-in-law felt that I was not entirely OK and got me a glass of water. I drank the glass of water and recovered. I felt better.

Today, I again want to say to God, "God, open the heavens. I want my mother and my father and my sisters to see what we have here in the State of Israel. To know that we have chosen life. Let them know that the State of Israel exists. That it has a good economy. That it has a strong army. Don't dare start with us, because it won't end well.

"And especially, I want my mother and my father and sisters to know that they have a family. Hitler was unable to destroy them. They have a son. They have a wonderful grandson, Air Force Commander Elyezer Shkedy. They have a wonderful granddaughter (Yael), and we have six wonderful grandchildren. May they know, God, that we have chosen life. That we will never let what happened before, happen again."

As my son wrote there: "Remember. Never forget. Rely only on ourselves."

And I want to finish with two things.

One, the people of Israel live. That's the biggest thing. When we were in the Holocaust, we didn't know if there would be anyone left. One Jew. There were people who thought that there were no more Jews. But the people of Israel live, grow, and flourish.

And I want to end with the most beautiful prayer I know:

'May God who makes peace in heaven above bring peace to all mankind and to Israel. Amen.'

• • •

Proportions.

23.

Have You Heard Anything
from the Poles?

In 2003, as part of the collaboration between the Israeli Air Force and foreign air forces, we received an invitation to participate in an international exhibition and airshow to be held in Warsaw, marking the eighty-fifth anniversary of the founding of the Polish Air Force.

The truth is, we didn't really want to participate. It was a considerable investment, involving complex preparations and mind-boggling coordination.

But then an idea arose to give real meaning to Israeli participation in the event: Amir Eshel, who at that time was the commander of the Tel Nof airbase, suggested to the commander of the Air Force that we participate in the air show and carry out a fly-over above the Auschwitz extermination camp.

The commander of the Air Force at the time, Dan Halutz, accepted the proposal and decided to send the delegation to Poland. Halutz understood the significance of the symbolic, historical, and moral message of such a fly-over, in which IAF planes would pass over the place where more than a million women, men, and children of our people were massacred.

It was decided to send four F-15 aircraft on the mission, led by Eshel.

At the time, I was chief of staff and deputy commander of the IAF. Every day I chatted with Eshel and the main thing that interested us both was the Auschwitz fly-over. The exhibition and airshow in Warsaw interested us much less...

However, a few days before the scheduled date, Eshel told me, "The Poles won't agree to let us fly over Auschwitz. They say it's a designated peace zone." (Yeah... Sure... Obviously...)

We agreed that he would try to get permission from the Poles through the Israeli ambassador and the decision-makers in Warsaw, and that I would do everything I could from Israel. Maybe we'd be able to influence them to change course...

The air show was in full swing, our planes were already on Polish soil, but the Poles insisted, and we couldn't get them to change their minds. We realized we had a problem on our hands.

Before the planned fly-over, after which the planes were supposed to return to Israel, we spoke again. Eshel informed me that the Poles refused to let us fly at low altitudes and agreed only to allow us to fly at high altitudes, which was worthless.

I told him, "Young man, the last time the Poles told us what to do was 60 years ago. Do what needs to be done. If they have any problems, they can call me." (In the IAF, "young man" is a term of endearment.)

Indeed, the fly-over, led by Eshel, with his fellow pilots and navigators, all of whom were second-generation Holocaust survivors, was carried out at a low altitude without a hitch.

As the fly-over passed Auschwitz, Eshel said the following over the radio:

We, the pilots of the Israeli Air Force, flying in the skies above the camp of horrors, have arisen from the ashes of the millions of victims. We shoulder their silent cries, salute their courage, and promise to be the shield of the Jewish nation and its country, Israel.

Members of the IDF's "Witnesses in Uniform" delegation, led by the then-Head of the Air Division, Ido Nehushtan, stood on the soil of Auschwitz at the time, saw the Israeli jets that passed over their heads, heard Eshel's chilling words over the public-address system, understood the deep meaning of the fly-over and the meaning of standing there in the uniform of the Israel Defense Forces. They could not hold back the tears.

The planes that passed over that damned, abominable place, which symbolizes evil incarnate, represented the IAF, the IDF, the State of Israel, and the entire Jewish people, all over the world.

The message they conveyed was crystal clear.

When I finished my role as commander of the Air Force, I chose to give a framed picture of the Auschwitz fly-over to all the squadrons and units in the Air Force: to senior members of the IAF, to members of the General Staff, to the Chief of Staff, to the head of the Shin Bet, to the head of the Mossad, to the Minister of Defense, to the Prime Minister, and to the President of the State of Israel.

On each picture, I wrote in my own handwriting the extract of the will I received, without words, from my father, Moshe, whose entire family was murdered and burned in Auschwitz:

The Israeli Air Force over Auschwitz,
On behalf of the State of Israel and the Jewish people.
Remember.
Never forget.
Rely only on ourselves.

Have you heard anything from the Poles since then?
I haven't.
But they can still call...

24.
The Most Precious Thing to Lose

In recent years, I have made sure to hold talks with the younger generation, whatever secondary institutions they attend — public high schools, *yeshivot* for religious young men, *ulpanas*[1] and seminars for religious young women, pre-military preparatory academies — and in the IDF itself.

Before one of my meetings with high school students, an attorney named Odelia Shpitalni spoke to me, an impressive woman with a huge heart, who founded the nonprofit PUSH Foundation for Success, and invested all her soul in it. Through PUSH, I have come to talk to students, parents, and teachers all over the country.

"You wouldn't believe what drama there was in Pardes Katz after your talk with the schoolchildren two weeks ago," Odelia told me. "One of the boys decided that for his matriculation exams, he wanted to study five units of math instead of three units. The grade's educational adviser would not agree, under any circumstances. She said to him, 'What are you talking about? Where did you get that idea from? You can't switch to five units.'"

The reason for her refusal was clear, although no one would say it openly: such a step might lower the matriculation average or the percentage of matriculation eligibility for the school.

The boy, Odelia continued, stood his ground, would not give up, and demanded to speak with the school principal. The adviser had no choice, and both she and the student came to talk to the principal.

---

1. Ulpanas are girls-only Jewish high schools in Israel, consisting of religious education alongside the state curriculum.

The boy made it clear to the principal that this was what he wanted, that he understood the significance, and that he would invest all his efforts in the matter. He has decided to make a change, he believes in himself, and he will do anything to succeed.

Still, the adviser repeatedly explained that he could not switch from three units to five. It was just impossible...

The principal listened very attentively.

The boy would not give up.

Then an amazing thing happened.

The student, who had attended my talk two weeks earlier, said to the principal: "Who the fuck is Michael?!"

The principal, who had heard my talk as well, understood immediately. She smiled and said he could take five units of math.

I am convinced that he put in tremendous effort to succeed.

And more importantly, he managed to regain the most precious thing: belief in himself.

• • •

Those who do not believe in themselves have no chance.

Those who believe in themselves are not guaranteed success, but they are at least on the way.

When someone tells you that you are capable, they are right.

Charge forward.

When someone tells you that you can't, you can believe them or you can believe me.

I'm telling you that you can.

• • •

Don't let anyone, ever, tell you that you can't and make you believe it. Believe in yourself and people will believe in you.

25.

I Can't Talk About It...

My son, Nimo, finished the elite "Talpiot" training program — for recruits who have demonstrated outstanding academic ability in the sciences and leadership potential — which is overseen by the Air Force and the Ministry of Defense's Directorate of Defense Research and Development. Every year, there are only a few dozen accepted out of thousands of applicants. Talpiot graduates serve in very significant research and development positions in the various branches of the security forces.

Toward the end of his training, Nimo told me that he did not want to serve in the Air Force. If he succeeded, he explained, they would say it was because of his father; and if he didn't, people would say: *How come the "son of..." is a failure?*

He requested and was stationed in Unit 8200 of the Military Intelligence Directorate.

Of course, I didn't intervene.

One day Nimo came home, and we talked about his service. I asked him, "What are you doing in the unit?"

I got the following unequivocal and simple answer: "Dad, I can't talk about it."

I was very pleased with his answer. It's a great answer and that's how it should be — no matter who his mom or dad was.

And yet...

I'm his father.

I'm the commander of the Air Force.

There are very few things in the State of Israel that the Commander of the Air Force is unaware of.

There is almost no clandestine operation in which the Air Force is not a partner, involved, or contributes its capabilities.

Then I remembered that the commander of Unit 8200 had invited me several times to visit, and thus far I had not been able to come for various reasons. I decided that this time I would find a place on the schedule...

I asked my secretary to tell the Unit 8200 commander that I would come for a visit as he had requested, and after a few weeks I did arrive.

I received a comprehensive overview from the Unit 8200 commander about the unit, the people and the projects, and we went on a tour of the base together.

During the tour, he told me about a significant and singularly unique project, which in many ways was simply beyond imagination.

And who was the officer who was asked to present the project to me?

My son, Nimo.

I was thrilled.

I was proud of Nimo for not telling what he was doing, and I was proud of what he was doing.

26.

A Knife in the Stomach

My wife Anat studied medicine at Ben-Gurion University of the Negev.

Part of her training as a future doctor was studying and working in the various departments of Soroka Medical Center in Beersheba.

Each time they neared the end of a rotation in a given department, students were given a final exam as a condition for moving to the next department.

As far as Anat was concerned, everything was proceeding smoothly. She studied, advanced, and passed the tests in each of the departments calmly and successfully.

Until she reached the surgical ward.

There, for some reason, Anat felt very unsure.

There was a knowledgeable friend with her in the ward, a chubby and charming guy who studied with her in class, and when she felt unsure about the actions she was required to perform, he was pressed into service...

The test date was approaching and the pressure at home increased.

Her constant refrain was, "How am I going to pass the test? I have no chance. And this is another oral test. If it had been in writing then maybe somehow I could have passed, but in an oral exam, they'll see how frightened I am, that I'm clueless..."

I said, "You know what? I'll get you ready for the exam."

"You? How exactly? You don't understand anything about medicine in general or surgery in particular."

"That's right," I said, "but in your current situation, what do you have to lose?"

Anat agreed.

We started with training and preparations.

Every day, I asked her a few simple real-life questions about surgery. (The questions were simple, the answers really weren't...)

For example, a man comes to the hospital with a knife stuck in his stomach. You are the admitting physician. What actions do you take?

At first, her answers were stressed, disorganized and very confused.

Then an idea came to my mind: I decided to adopt the "air force method" to treat problems in flight and to "convert" it into the medical world.

It's called the PFC, preflight check.

The PFC manual has three chapters: a white chapter, a yellow chapter, and a red chapter.

The pages in each chapter are in the appropriate color.

White chapter: Normal and routine actions.

Yellow chapter: Actions carried out in a non-dramatic emergency situation, when there is enough time.

Red Chapter: Operations carried out in a substantive and urgent emergency that must be dealt with as quickly as possible.

The general idea of the PFC is:
* To identify the signs of the problem...
* To understand what the problem is and what it means...
* And to execute the correct sequence of actions to deal with the problem.

The idea of adapting the PFC to the world of medicine was to reassure Anat and allow her to express, in an orderly and systematic way, her knowledge.

For example: a knife to the stomach:

Identifying: Where exactly the knife is stuck and at what depth, what the wound looks like, what is the state of consciousness of the injured person, etc.

Significance: To determine which internal organs the knife could have hit and what such an injury would mean.

Execution: In medicine, as in flight, there are cases where you need to act very quickly; and there are cases in which time is less of a critical factor, and you ought to wait a moment and act in a more relaxed and orderly manner using the relevant aids and professionals.

Anat got the idea.

Even though from a professional point of view I really didn't know anything about the topics she talked about, I saw that her performance improved tremendously. She performed the whole process calmly and apparently also correctly, accurately and far more professionally, from identifying the problem and understanding its significance to the actions required to save the injured person's life.

Anat took the test and passed successfully. No one was happier than she was. And it was precisely the knowledgeable friend, the one who studied with her in the department, who did not pass...

Anat deserved all the kudos for her success. She had the knowledge, the ability, the skills, the attentiveness, the openness and the courage to adopt a different approach from another world.

• • •

Concepts and methods of action from one field can, with the necessary adjustments, prove themselves in other areas as well.

27.
Shkedy, I've Decided to Appoint You Leader

In the summer of 1982, I was a young captain teaching in the flight school at Hatzerim airbase. At the same time, I was also on emergency deployment to the 117th Squadron, the "First Jet Squadron," at the Ramat David airbase. In order to maintain my fitness as an F-16 pilot, I flew in my operational squadron once a week, in addition to my flights as an instructor in the flight school.

The 117th Squadron had a group of experienced pilots and a group of young, talented pilots. All of them, old and young, were excellent aircrew.

In each squadron, there are several "leaders," who are formation commanders in flight and are called "number one." One is either a "quartet leader," which is the larger formation, or a "pair leader," which is the basic formation. The rest of the pilots are "wingmen" and are designated "number two." The squadron commander is the one who determines who will lead, regardless of the pilot's rank or seniority and without the need for approval from any external commander.

When the F-16s arrived in Israel, I participated in the first conversion course held in Israel for these planes. Because of the constraints of the Israeli Air Force, I flew for a very short time in my operational squadron as a "number two" and then went on to teach at the flight school.

Sasha, Berko and I, three close friends from the squadron and later in our lives, underwent the same retraining course and served together as instructors in the flight school. On Saturday, the fifth of June, we received an urgent alert to mobilize at our operational squadron. We quickly got organized and flew in a Cessna to Ramat David in the north.

Shortly after we landed in Ramat David, the squadron commander, Zevik Raz, gave a briefing to all the pilots. Raz, a brave fighter and a fiercely intelligent man who had led the attack on the nuclear reactor in Iraq a year earlier, informed us that tomorrow war would begin in Lebanon.

After the conversation, Raz called me to his office and in his characteristically laconic tone and bereft of any unnecessary preamble, said:

"Shkedy, I've decided to appoint you leader of an interceptor pair."

You have to understand the meaning of this. A day before the war was to begin, the squadron commander decided to appoint me — a very young pilot — as commander of a combat formation, while it was highly likely that my number two would be a pilot older than me, senior to me, and more experienced than me.

It was undoubtedly a very difficult decision for him and it placed a very large responsibility on me. To me, it was more than winning a Nobel Prize...

And that's not all. A few days later, as I was sitting in the plane on the ground, waiting to be scrambled for an interception, Squadron Commander Raz hailed me on the radio to tell me he was appointing me to lead a quartet.

And so, less than a week after arriving at the squadron as a young flight school instructor, I was appointed to lead a formation of four fighter jets into battle.

The commander of a squadron has full authority and responsibility for the results of the squadron he commands, for better or for worse, and is also entitled to do things that are unacceptable in other military branches. It is deeply connected to the organizational culture in the Air Force, a culture of uncompromising excellence that does not take into account a formal hierarchy of ranks; a culture in which, at the discretion and in accordance with the decision of the squadron commander, a young pilot with the rank of captain may lead and give orders to a colonel in an attack mission or in a dogfight.

As commander of the Air Force, when I'd come once a week to fly to maintain battle fitness and feel the terrain up close, my leader in the air could have been a young and talented captain. He was also the one who briefed the members of the air formation on the ground before takeoff, led us through the air, and managed the debriefing after the flight. Senior officers outside the Air Force who see this or hear about it find it hard to believe.

It is interesting to see how the two contrasts, hierarchy and excellence, live in harmony in the Air Force.

28.
No Authorization to Do a 270

One day, while I was the commander of the Emek Squadron at Ramat David Airbase, I received mission orders from the Air Force Operations Department: deploy a quartet of two-seater F-16s to attack a target near the town of Janta in the northern Beqaa Valley in Lebanon, right on the border with Syria.

This was a period of severe confrontations with Hezbollah, and the more aggressive the organization's actions, the harsher Israel's response was, in a more painful and meaningful place for them.

The target we received was of great importance to Hezbollah and well-protected.

I decided that I myself would lead the attack and assigned pilots and navigators for the mission.

When I read the order, I came across a sentence that I had never seen for such a mission:

"No authorization to do a 270."

This meant that we could only make one pass; under no circumstances, for no reason, were we to turn around and take another swing at our target.

In other words, no subsequent offensive.

Agitated, I called the Operations Department at Air Force headquarters and spoke with the senior officer who was in charge of planning the mission.

I told him that I didn't understand why such a sentence appeared in my orders. It struck me as completely contradictory to the policy of the Air Force which had been inculcated and drummed into us: the leader of the air structure is the "Commander of the Air Force in the field," the supreme authority on the scene. The mission must be carried out at his discretion and in accordance with his decisions — whatever it takes to accomplish the task in the best possible way.

We had a heated and fierce argument. When he saw that I was determined and not going to give up, he told me, "Shkedy, do whatever you think is right…"

We launched our offensive.

The area where we were supposed to attack, very close to the Syrian border, was protected by Syrian surface-to-air missiles (e.g. SA2s, SA3s and SA6s), smaller surface-to-air missiles(e.g. SA7s) and anti-aircraft guns.

The weather on the way to Janta was harsh, with very low clouds along the way.

I decided that we would fly very close to the ground, under the low clouds, with the understanding and knowledge in advance that the weather in the target area was expected to be better and allow for an attack; and so it was.

Each of the aircraft in our quartet carried two tons of bombs, eight tons of payload in total, sufficient to utterly destroy the target.

We reached our objective, we flew in, we attacked and we left.

And then…

One of the pilots asked to "do a 270."

It turned out that he had not released his payload on the first pass, so he asked to carry out another attack run.

I quickly analyzed the situation: no heavy missiles were being fired at us, only smaller missiles whose smoke we saw curling in, along with anti-aircraft guns blazing away.

I authorized the 270, and we disengaged from the target area.

On the flight home, I realized that, in light of my decision, I was a "candidate for the gallows…"

We returned to the base and held the debriefing:

The target had been completely destroyed and the mission carried out.

But —

We carried out a 270, subject to my professional discretion and decision, contrary to what was unequivocally defined in the mission order.

A few days later, a full debriefing for the mission, headed by Commander of the Air Force Herzl Bodinger, was carried out with the aim of analyzing the attack and its results and presenting conclusions and lessons for the future — for the squadron and for the IAF as a whole.

It was clear to me that the main issue that would arise in the debriefing would be my decision to execute a 270 contrary to the mission order.

I described what had happened and explained my thought process and decision.

There was silence in the room.

The commander of the Air Force asked for the senior commanders' perspectives. They voiced various opinions.

Bodinger listened, thought it through, and decided to support my decision.

I was somehow saved...

Two years had passed. I had already completed my time as squadron commander and was the head of the Operations Department, responsible for all of the IAF's operational planning in all sectors.

At the time, Hezbollah was again escalating its activity, and it was decided to attack the organizations' most significant, sensitive, and protected location: Janta.

The area was well-known to me from the attack I had led there two years earlier.

Bodinger, who still served as commander of the Air Force, asked me to go to Jerusalem early in the morning, present the plan to Prime Minister and Defense Minister Yitzhak Rabin, and get his approval for the operation.

I arrived early in the morning at the Prime Minister's Office.

We both sat alone in his quiet room, in a rather surreal atmosphere.

Rabin, who had been chief of staff during the Six-Day War and understood the operational sphere well, seemed pensive. He looked at me for a long time, leaned forward and asked me in his quiet, slow voice to detail the goal, the mission, and how we planned to accomplish it.

I spread out a map and began to describe the operation.

Rabin, as usual, listened and delved into the details of each stage of the flight.

I felt that he was completely immersed in the planned operation.

I explained to him that we were planning to fly in a quartet at a very low altitude; I showed him where we would penetrate the air defenses; I described to him how we would execute the attack and how we would destroy the target and disengage.

I finished presenting the plan. Rabin leaned forward, held his head with both hands, thought, remained silent and said nothing.

At this point, the prime minister's military secretary entered the room, informed him of an important meeting that was scheduled, and informed him that many people were already waiting in the conference room.

"Let them wait," said Rabin, waving his hand dismissively...

Then he looked at me and said:

"Shkedy, tell me the mission again, the planning and execution from scratch."

I described the whole flight again, from start to finish.

Rabin was silent, looked down and didn't say a word. I felt that he was undecided.

Finally, he raised his head and asked, "Say, Shkedy, how long are you in missile range?"

That is, how long would the planes be under the threat of surface-to-air missiles?

I replied, "The main threat is from the moment the planes rise from a low altitude to a height that makes it possible to carry out the attack and release the bombs, until they descend back to a very low altitude and disengage from the target area. In this case, it's about a minute."

Rabin looked at me with a piercing look and said quietly, "I approve the attack on one condition — that you do one bombing run, no more."

In other words, do not do... a 270.

At that moment I understood where the prohibition of doing a 270 had originated two years earlier, when headquarters had conveyed it to me, as a squadron commander.

I understood the prime minister's perspective as a statesman who had everything on his shoulders, much broader than the relatively narrow view of the squadron commander and the aircrew who believe in their abilities and want to carry out the mission in the best possible way.

Before the Prime Minister are all the considerations and implications: the importance of the attack, on the one hand; and on the other, the danger that things might go wrong and that a pilot or navigator might be killed or captured by Hezbollah.

When I was the commander of a squadron, I didn't understand who gave the order to forbid a 270. I didn't know what was behind it, and apparently the officer in charge of planning the attack at Air Force headquarters didn't know either.

If I had known then that it was an unequivocal directive from the political echelon, which is authorized to order a deviation from the Air Force's fundamental policies of engagement, then I would have complied and that is what should have happened.

29.

Betting on Falafel

One evening, we were sitting in the yard of our house: my wife Anat, my beloved brother-in-law Naftali, and I. At one point, I got up and went to the kitchen to get something to eat.

When it comes to matters of the kitchen and cooking, I have no great skills. In fact, you could say I have no skills at all. Not in the least.

I opened several cupboards and found a bag of falafel mix in one of them.

I decided to surprise them.

I made the falafel according to the exact instructions on the bag, with the last step being to put the balls in the oven.

I put them in the oven, went back to the yard, sat with Anat and Naftali for a while, and after a while I went back to the kitchen.

I took the falafel balls out of the oven and loaded them onto a huge plate.

To my great surprise, it turned out very successfully.

They looked at me in astonishment, ate with great pleasure and with shining eyes, leaving not even a crumb.

When they finished, they asked me, "How did you make those?"

I described the process to them.

Then Anat said, "Sure, sure. You obviously did something else. There's no such thing as falafel in the oven."

A heated argument ensued.

"Want to bet?" I asked.

"Yes," said Anat, smiling from ear to ear and full of self-confidence. "What are the stakes?"

I thought for a moment and said, "If I win, I'm not doing any maintenance work at home anymore. That means changing light bulbs, plumbing, drilling (and other things I hate doing so much...). Call a professional, let him do it."

"And if you lose?"

"If I lose, I'll do all those chores immediately, no arguments."

"It's a bet," said Anat enthusiastically, as if the victory was already in her pocket.

Naftali looked stunned at what was happening and did not respond. Naïvely, he didn't realize what awaited him if Anat lost.

It was by far the most successful bet of my life.

The thing I hated doing the most, and didn't really know how to do, was removed from my plate — and was honorably transferred to Naftali. Honestly, he has golden hands and he really likes to deal with these things.

Most importantly, for years it was forbidden to bother me with issues related to the maintenance of the house.

In fact, to this very day...

Since then, Anat hasn't been willing to bet against me at all. If in the middle of the day, when the sun is shining, I were to declare that it's really night, she wouldn't agree to bet against me.

In fairness, I should note that she has since saved Naftali several times from dangerous wagers with potentially serious consequences.

• • •

Every bet has two participants: one is a shark, and the other is a mark. Before agreeing to a bet, make sure you're not the mark.

30.

The Bear Hunter and
the Wine Expert

The commander of the US Air Force, General Michael Moseley, came to pay a visit to the Israeli Air Force — a remarkable event that hadn't occurred in many years. From my knowledge of American culture after my time studying in the United States, I knew it was very unusual to invite an official guest to your home. And yet I decided to hold a completely different event than is customary in such circumstances, a completely informal dinner at my home with General Moseley, members of his delegation, and senior members of the Israeli Air Force.

My wife Anat informed me that she would cook everything on her own. This went far beyond the accepted protocol for official events, extending a personal invitation as we would to our friends.

Anat prepared for the visit for a few days and cooked the finest delicacies.

On my way home, on the evening of the dinner, I suddenly remembered that while my wife was preparing and cooking, I hadn't performed the only task assigned to me — buying wine.

I stopped at a supermarket and went to the wine section.

I had no idea about wine and never understood the field. I just knew how to say if I liked the taste or not.

I stood there quite helplessly.

Then someone came up to me and offered help; probably he saw that I was at a loss. The wine expert found me just in time. "Yes, thank you," I told him, "I want to buy a special wine."

He showed me several types of wines, and finally took off one of the shelves, a bottle of wine with a name I had never seen before: "Bazelet HaGolan."

He highly recommended the wine and told me about the fertile and rich basalt soil in which the vines grow; about the winery that is located opposite the magical landscape of the Sea of Galilee, near a spring; about the special wooden barrels in which the wine is kept to enhance its taste and aroma.

In short, he convinced me.

(Not that I had too much choice.)

I accepted his recommendation and bought a few bottles for the evening.

The guests arrived, there was a warm and cozy homey atmosphere. The food that Anat prepared was excellent (as usual...).

We drank wine, the people opened up, the conversation was easy and the feeling was great.

General Moseley was a big man with a round and smiling face. You could see at a glance that he was a people person. He told us about his hobbies:

Hunting bears... and wine.

I turned pale. I looked at him, disbelieving, and thought to myself: *How can I come out of this unscathed with the wine I bought?*

The next morning, my secretary, Avital, came into my office smiling and asked a surprising question. "What wine did you serve last night?" "I don't remember, why?" I said. I'd already forgotten...

"General Moseley would love to know," she replied.

I called my wife and asked, "Do you remember what wine we served last night?"

"No," she replied. "All I know is we finished it, and I already tossed the bottles."

"Where are the bottles?"

"In the trash can, outside."

"Do me a favor, go outside and look through the garbage," I asked.

She went and came back to me with an answer:

"Bazelet HaGolan."

It turns out that the Israeli basalt wine from the Golan Heights met with the approval of the wine expert General Moseley. He liked it so much that he took a few crates with him to America on the plane...

Since then, I remember the name of the wine very well.

• • •

Sometimes it is important that luck also shines its light on you.

31.

Impossible Landing...

I was a young Mirage pilot, a lieutenant, stationed at Eitam airbase in the Yamit region of the Sinai Peninsula, not far from El-Arish.

In those days, there was fierce competition between the Phantom and Mirage squadrons, as if every Phantom pilot had invented his own plane and every Mirage pilot had invented his own plane...

One day, we did a "doubles dogfight" exercise against a Phantom squadron — that is, two Mirages from our squadron versus two Phantoms from the other squadron.

There was a heavy haze that got worse over the course of the day, but we took off and waged the battle without heeding the weather. Landing without "shooting down" the two opposing Phantoms was out of the question.

We did win the dogfight, but we failed to leave enough fuel for landing in bad weather, which we now had to do.

As if that weren't enough, I had less fuel than my leader.

As we prepared for landing, we realized we had gotten ourselves into trouble.

We made a detour over the base; because of the weather, we couldn't see the runways well enough to allow for a normal landing. We had no choice but to carry out an "instrument landing" — touching down using the aircraft's flight instruments and the landing devices of the control tower. It's a longer process that consumes more fuel — fuel that we didn't have. And regardless of the amount of fuel, we weren't sure the bad weather and worsening haze would even permit us to carry out an instrument landing, which also has strict minimum restrictions.

In short, the situation was really not great...

The formation leader, who was fully responsible for managing the team of planes to, during, and after the battle, and who determined when to conclude the dogfight and how much fuel we needed to return for landing, asked me how much fuel I had.

I told him how much fuel I had. It wasn't much. Not much at all.

Then he told me the following sentence that I will never forget: "I'm going to land in Hatzerim."

I didn't have enough fuel to get to Hatzerim, and landing at Eitam was practically mission impossible at that point.

I realized that I had to somehow manage on my own.

I had to think quickly about how I would get out of the dire straits I was in.

Despite the heavy haze, I could see the black square of the grounds of the base, surrounded by the fence. But in no way were the runways visible.

I told the control tower of Eitam airbase, "I've run out of fuel, and I only have one pass for a landing approach. I'm going to fly towards El-Arish, turn towards the base, and descend towards the black square of the base, where the runways are. Hopefully, I'll find a runway at the last minute and manage to land."

The air control officer, Chantal, immediately realized the gravity of the situation.

I asked her to make sure to clear all the runways from vehicles and anything else with the hope that I'd be able to identify one of them at the last minute and land.

If only...

True drama.

Chantal was really outstanding. She immediately shifted the base to emergency mode, scrambled the firefighting vehicles and ambulances, and informed me in her heavy French accent:

"Everything is clear."

I decided that if I found a runway during my descent towards the black square of the base, with the wheels down and ready for landing, I would try to somehow compose myself and land on what I could see.

If I didn't identify a runway, I'd probably run out of fuel, the engines would shut off and I'd have to pull up and eject.

Luckily, the base was almost at sea level, so I could, despite the heavy haze, descend without fear of colliding with a mountain.

I slowly descended towards the black square.

Suddenly, one of the lanes appeared in front of me and I saw the control tower coming closer on my right. I immediately realized that it was a taxiway, the narrower lane for transporting planes to their takeoff position — not the main runway on which I was supposed to land.

And I was already close to the middle of the lane, not at the beginning.

Despite this, I somehow managed to land. Luckily, the weight of the plane was very low, simply because there was no fuel left in it, so I was able to brake without rolling off the taxiway.

I regulated my breathing, and only then realized that I had gotten out of it safely...

Following this event, I debriefed myself and made a simple and clear decision:

Even when I wasn't the formation leader, I still had to bear full responsibility for my aircraft. I had to see the overall picture and if necessary, in extreme situations, point things out to the leader. Even if it was against protocol.

I could not rely on someone else, in this case the leader, to do the work for me.

In the end, I am responsible for my plane.

the "Come Down to Us, Airplane," was...

32.
Our Song

When I was CEO of El Al, Israel's national carrier, we embarked on a very significant move to purchase a new aircraft, the Boeing 737-900.

We decided on a large marketing campaign to accompany the arrival of the planes in Israel.

Ongoing campaigns were planned by El Al's marketing department and were carried out through an external company. As CEO, I was presented with the marketing plans, but I generally avoided intervening and let the experts go with what they believed in.

But in this case, in view of the great importance of the move to El Al, I requested that the marketing and advertising plan be submitted for approval and presented to me in detail.

I watched the presentation they had prepared and listened attentively to everything.

There was one part that I liked in particular: the visual of a plane coming out of a huge cardboard box, wrapped in Styrofoam. But there was another part I didn't care for at all: the audio component chosen to accompany the campaign.

The song was the kids' classic "Come Down to Us, Airplane."

I didn't like the choice and felt very uncomfortable with it.

I said that I didn't approve of the selected song and asked for alternatives.

The people in our marketing department and the senior executives from the external company refused to budge. In their professional opinion, they insisted, it was the best and most appropriate option. They tried mightily to convince me that the choice conveyed innovation and creative sophistication by subverting expectations...

I told them that before I made a final decision, I would like to hear more opinions.

They suggested we run a focus group, a concentrated survey conducted among a limited number of impartial people.

I agreed.

We arrived at the place where the focus group had been assembled. In one room sat the focus group members, and in the next room sat El Al's marketing people, senior executives of the external company, and myself. There was one-way glass separating the two rooms, so we could hear and see them, but they couldn't see or hear us.

They were played several options, including the song "Come Down to Us, Airplane."

The opinion of the focus group members was unequivocal:

Almost everyone thought, like me, that the song "Come Down to Us, Airplane," was inappropriate and did not convey the intended message. Emotionally they didn't connect with it either.

At the end of the meeting, we had an in-depth discussion about the statements from the focus group.

The marketers were not convinced by what they saw and heard. In fact, they became even more entrenched in their position that "Come Down to Us, Airplane" ought to be the campaign's soundtrack.

The person who took the lead in espousing this position was an expert from the external company. From his body language and the self-important tone in which he spoke, it was clear that he held himself in high regard, and it seemed that others saw in him some kind of genius and authority in the field. He threw his full weight behind the song and repeatedly claimed that it was the most appropriate song and that it would be a mistake, an awful mistake, to use anything else.

I listened to the marketers, and when they finished presenting their arguments, I told them quietly: "Thank you. 'Come Down to Us, Airplane' won't be the song that will accompany the campaign."

Silence in the room.

The faces of the experts fell.

The face of the renowned expert became pale as chalk.

I told them that as the CEO of the company, the responsibility fell on my shoulders, come rain or shine, and therefore we would only do what I was completely at peace with.

From the list of songs presented to the focus group, we chose another song, which I liked and connected to very much. "We'll Always Wait for You" by Leah Shabbat, performed by Liran Danino:

Every plane that flies in the sky,
Every star that shines in my eyes,
Reminds me of you.

The campaign kicked off with this song, and it was one of El Al's most successful. Later on, it won the vote for favorite advertisement.

Shortly after I made the decision, I spoke with a friend who understood the field well, and he mentioned a detail that had escaped my memory, one which was not mentioned at all in the discussions that took place around the song "Come Down to Us, Airplane."

During the First Lebanon War, reserve soldiers composed an alternative version of the kids' classic, changing its lyrics to become a harsh and fierce protest song:

Come down to us, airplane,
Take us to Lebanon.
We'll fight for (Ariel) Sharon,
And come back in a coffin.

Incredible.

You can only imagine what would have happened if the song "Come Down to Us, Airplane" had been chosen to spearhead the campaign.

Although, during our deliberations, I was unaware of that shocking connotation of the song, I still felt that it was not the right choice. I insisted on this, contrary to the opinions of first-class marketing experts.

●●●

Intuitions and gut feelings are of great importance in decision-making, especially when it comes to issues of emotional significance.

With the responsibility and authority in your hands, it is important to listen to the opinions of the finest experts, but the decision is yours, and yours alone. You are the one responsible — for better or for worse.

33.
Battle Scene on a
Pastoral Campus

The Naval Postgraduate School in Monterey, California, is an institution for those pursuing master's and doctoral degrees, intended for students from all branches of the American defense establishment — army, navy, air force, marines, intelligence community and more — as well as a small number of students from foreign armies around the world.

I was one of them.

As part of my master's degree in systems management, I also decided to take several courses in the National security department focusing on the Middle East. I enrolled, among other things, in a course on the Arab-Israeli conflict, taught by Dr. Glenn Robinson.

He had no idea what was going to happen, and the truth is that I didn't either...The course was filled with dozens of students from the US military, some of them high-ranking officers. Before the course began, I asked Dr. Robinson if I could bring my wife to class as well. He agreed.

I quickly realized that Dr. Robinson, who purported to be objective, presented the conflict unilaterally and tendentiously and was hostile to the State of Israel.

I said to myself, "There's no way I'm going to let this slide."

Despite my stammering and faltering English, I decided that I would "give him a fight" that he would not forget. I would not allow him to present reality in a distorted way as he had apparently done in previous courses.

Before each lesson, I studied and researched the data and the facts as I never had before in preparation for any subject. I tried to assess in advance what Dr. Robinson would say in class and how he would try to distort reality this time. I prepared a speech in English on the subject that was supposed to come up in class and practiced it with my wife, who was just as upset and annoyed as I was.

I came to each of the classes ready for battle, and in the middle of the lesson I would stop Dr. Robinson and announce: "Now I want to tell the students here the facts and the truth about this matter."

Dr. Robinson, a tall and broad man, literally a kind of brute, would go crazy. His face turned red, and it looked like he was about to explode.

This scene was repeated in every lesson. It was a difficult struggle: he tried to stop me from speaking and I told him, in front of the whole class, that if he wouldn't let me tell the students the truth and refute his baseless statements, I would immediately appeal to the highest echelons of the university.

I left him no choice.

And so, in each lesson, I gave a fiery speech. Despite my shaky English, the students understood very well what I said with determination and passion.

I felt that I was really on an important mission: defending the State of Israel. Only instead of doing it from the cockpit of an F-16 or from the command-and-control center at Air Force headquarters, I did it from the classroom on that pastoral American campus.

For me, it was a calling in every sense of the word.

And it had consequences. At the end of each lesson, and also at the end of the course, I was approached by many students, senior military and defense officials, and they told me things like: "Now we really understand the conflict. If we'd only heard from Dr. Robinson and not from you, we would leave here with a completely different perception of reality. It's just amazing."

The minimum required of a university professor is personal and academic integrity. True learning can only happen when the facts and ideas are presented fairly and matter-of-factly and give expression to opinions on both sides.

It is disturbing and saddening to think what happens when there is no counterpoint to such "Dr. Robinsons" in other academic institutions in the Western world.

●●●

When you deeply believe in something and feel that the truth is being distorted, do not give up: investigate, learn, charge and fight – even when you are at a disadvantage.

34.
Which Fighter Jet Is Better...

As part of the reestablishment of the Emek Squadron under my command, we absorbed outstanding pilots and navigators who came from Skyhawk, Kfir, and Phantom squadrons — and trained them to fly the F-16 "Barak" and integrate into the squadron.

One of the elements of retraining and requalification was practicing dogfights. It included, among other things, a series of air battles against F-15s from another squadron.

The first stage of the series were individual dogfights — that is, one-on-one.

In those days, there was fierce competition between the F-15 and F-16 pilots.

Every pilot was sure that his plane was an incomparable wonder of the world...

One evening, during the daily debriefing, one of the retraining pilots, a nice, talented, and somewhat naïve *kibbutznik*[2] named Dror, said that he had heard that the commander of the F-15 squadron we had flown against had told his men, with great confidence, that the F-15 was better than the F-16.

I explained to the young pilots and navigators about the performance and capabilities of each type of aircraft. Together with them, I analyzed the performance graph of each aircraft at different altitudes, including stabilized turn, maximum turn, thrust-to-weight ratio, and other parameters relevant to air combat.

---

2. A person who lives on or comes from a kibbutz.

I emphasized that each aircraft had its advantages and disadvantages, telling them, "Your goal as a pilot is to learn how to make the most of the advantages of your plane versus the disadvantages of the other plane. In other words, redirect the battle to areas where your plane is better than the opposing plane."

And I made it clear that in the end, both planes were excellent.

Still, it wasn't clear and convincing enough. They were still under the harsh impression of the F-15 squadron commander's unequivocal statements.

I realized that beyond the theoretical explanation, I needed to explain it in another, clearer way.

I asked them to organize a dogfight the next day, plane versus plane, between me and the commander of the F-15 squadron who said what he said, and we would see...

It was a different time in the Air Force. Today it probably wouldn't happen.

The young guys in both squadrons were very tense in preparation for the battle of the squadron commanders.

I took Dror with me in the back seat of my plane, the same young pilot who brought back the "intelligence information" about the words of the commander of the opposing squadron.

It was an aggressive air battle, with no limitations.

It ended when we "shot down" the F-15 with cannon fire (which is considered the "ultimate treatment"...).

From that moment on, the young pilots and navigators undergoing retraining understood which aircraft was better, and most importantly — it was clear to them what I expected from them.

•••

Sometimes you have to explain things in a different way, a little clearer and a little more tangible.

35.

The Bracelet

When I took on my position as El Al's CEO, people started approaching me and telling me: The previous CEO promised us so and so...

I listened, wrote down what they had been promised, and personally checked with the previous CEO.

In the vast majority of cases, he told me that there had never been anything of the sort and that he had not made such a promise.

One day, I was approached by a woman who had a different air about her, a spot of color in the El Al landscape. She was quite upset and said in a heavy French accent that the previous CEO had promised her a rank — not a high rank — and that this had never happened, despite her many inquiries.

Then she produced a letter, signed by the previous CEO, in which it was clearly and unequivocally written that she would receive a rank.

I called the person in charge of the matter and showed him the letter. He was a little embarrassed and said, "I was told to give her that letter, but... it was hinted to me not to give her a rank."

I felt it was just wrong.

I looked at him and said:

"El Al's CEO signed the letter.

"It doesn't matter what name it is; it doesn't matter that he's no longer in the job.

"It binds me.

120

"Call her today and give her the rank."

He looked at me in astonishment, but he carried out the order.

The woman who received the rank was moved to the depths of her soul and decided to take action.

• • •

One day she came to my office unannounced. She asked Hagit and Naama, my beloved aides-de-camp, to meet with me urgently.

With their emotional intelligence, they saw that she was determined, overwrought and very excited, so they complied with her request.

I asked my secretary to come into the room with her.

The woman was holding a huge, glittering gold bracelet in her hand, an ornate piece of jewelry with my name engraved on it. She gave an emotional thank-you speech in her heavy accent and asked to give me the bracelet as a gift.

I told her I simply couldn't accept the gift.

She insisted and tried to convince me with all her might. At some point she started crying and wouldn't leave...

In the end, she placed the bracelet on my desk table and made her exit.

I told my secretary: "I am not prepared, under any circumstances, to accept the gift. Make sure it's returned to her today in person."

And so it was.

Then I remembered that a few years earlier, as commander of the Air Force, I had discovered during a visit to one of the bases that the officers had signed up to extend their service with the promise of a car as a signing bonus. However, though several months had passed since the signing, they had not yet received their cars. As soon as I returned to my office, I called the head of the personnel department and instructed him to hand out car keys the next day to all those officers who signed up, even if it meant leasing cars from a rental company. (Of course, I made sure with the Air Force's counsel that everything was legal and aboveboard.)

WHO THE F*CK IS MICHAEL?!

...

Your word is your word, and a commitment has meaning. Sometimes even doing the obvious is not obvious.

36.

Advice Worth Its Weight in Gold

When I finished my role as commander of the Haemek Squadron, I asked to go to the United States to study for my master's degree. It was important to me mainly because I wanted to close the book on my struggles with English, which made me uncomfortable and needed to be addressed. But I had no doubt that such a trip would be greatly beneficial from the perspective of our family as well.

A discussion was held, chaired by the commander of the Air Force, and it was decided that I would go to Harvard.

The move required challenging preparations on the part of our family — both for my wife, Anat, who had to leave her job as a physician, and for our three children.

We were already in the advanced stages of getting ready for the trip when I was informed that the commander of the Air Force wanted to meet me that Friday at 3:00 PM.

I came home and said to Anat: "I don't know why yet, but apparently our overseas move has gone up in smoke."

The commander of the Air Force wouldn't want to meet with me urgently on Friday afternoon for no reason.

I came to the conclusion that one of two things had happened:

Either a squadron commander had been forced to leave his position unexpectedly, and the Air Force commander would ask me to take over the squadron in trouble...

Or he needed me in the operations department.

These are the two most significant things from an operational point of view in the Air Force, and if the commander of the IAF asks, you can't say "no" to him.

I arrived at the meeting. And indeed, that's what happened.

The commander of the Air Force asked me to postpone the trip to the United States for a few years and instead fill the position of head of the combat branch in the operations department. Within a year, he said, I would become head of the operations department.

I went home.

It was not a simple situation, on a personal and family level.

I thought about it deeply, consulted with my wife and we decided: That was what needed to be done, and that's what we would do.

I informed the commander of the Air Force that I would comply with his request.

A short time later, I spoke with Brig. Gen. Moshe Melnik, who had just been discharged from the IDF after commanding the Nevatim and Hatzerim bases, and who had studied in the United States himself. Melnik, an officer and a man whose opinion I greatly appreciated, said, "Make sure you have a letter from the commander of the Air Force documenting the agreement between you" — i.e., that he had asked me to postpone the trip, that I had accepted his request, and that I would have the right to study in the United States in the future.

"Why? You think it's necessary?" I asked, surprised.

"No question," answered Melnik. "You really should have that letter from the commander of the Air Force."

I was convinced.

I called the head of the air force commander's office at the time, Sagiv Massad, who was in the know, and asked him if the IAF chief would be willing to write such a letter.

"Of course," said Massad. "I'll take care of it."

A few days later, a letter signed by the Air Force commander came to me explicitly stating that I had postponed the trip at his request and that I had the right to study in the United States later on.

Three years passed.

I finished my term as head of the Air Force Operations Department and asked to go to study in the United States in accordance with the agreement.

But agreements are one thing and reality another. The senior officer in charge of the issue in the Air Force explained to me that in light of the situation, the IDF chief of staff had laid down the law, and no one was being sent to study abroad.

It is always "in light of the situation..."

I told him exactly what happened and showed him the letter from the commander of the Air Force.

"Sorry," said the senior officer, "this is the chief of staff's decision, and I can't do anything about it."

I realized he wasn't going to lift a finger for the agreement to be honored, and I asked for a meeting with the chief of staff, Amnon Lipkin-Shahak.

I was summoned for a meeting at his office.

Lipkin-Shahak was a quiet man — serious, quick-witted, a man of his word. Without any preamble, he asked me, "Shkedy, what's the problem?"

"I don't know how it works everywhere else," I said, "but from what I know in the Air Force, a commitment by the IAF commander means something and it is customary to uphold it."

I took out the letter...

The chief of general staff read it and said to me right on the spot, "Pack your bags... You're going to America."

And so it was.

• • •

Good advice from smart and experienced people, who want the best for you, is worth its weight in gold.

37.

Approving Plans in the Masada Airport Lounge

It was shortly after Yitzhak Rabin's assassination, a difficult period of great sadness and an atmosphere of anguish.

One day, we received intelligence information about certain Hezbollah activity deep in Lebanon, far from the Israeli border.

At the time, I was the head of the IAF's operations department, the one in charge of all the operational planning for the IAF in all sectors, near and far. We concluded it would be possible to hit a large number of terrorists in one decisive operation.

Such operations are submitted for the approval of the senior military echelon, and for the approval of the political echelon: the Minister of Defense, the Prime Minister, and, if necessary, the Cabinet. After they approve, the task is assigned to the relevant squadron or squadrons.

We presented the plan to IAF Commander Herzl Bodinger and IDF Chief of Staff Amnon Lipkin-Shahak. The Air Force commander requested that after the chief of staff's approval, I would present the operation to Prime Minister and Defense Minister Shimon Peres.

Peres was about to travel abroad and asked us to show him the operation at the airport, before his departure.

We arrived at the Masada Lounge at Ben Gurion Airport, sat down, and waited for the Prime Minister.

Peres arrived, took a seat, and asked us to present the mission plan.

I unfolded a map and presented the IAF's plan for the attack.

I emphasized my personal commitment to the planning, execution, and results.

In the room were all the heads of the defense establishment: the chief of staff, the heads of the Mossad and Shin Bet, the head of military intelligence, and the head of the IDF's operations division. One by one, they explained the importance of operation to the prime minister. It would inflict serious damage on many Hezbollah terrorists and prevent future attacks both against IDF soldiers, who were still in the security zone in south Lebanon at the time, and against the State of Israel. We had waited a long time for this opportunity, and here it was.

All the senior commanders, without exception, unequivocally recommended carrying out the attack and approving the plan I had proposed.

Particularly resolute was Lipkin-Shahak, an officer and a man whom I loved. I was very appreciative of the calm and determined way in which he led the IDF. Usually he expressed himself quietly, in a reserved but clear way. This time, however, his words were particularly forceful.

The prime minister listened to us and didn't say a word.

We were done.

Peres got up and straightened his suit.

We got up too.

He went from one to the next, shook hands with each of us, and still didn't say a word...

Finally he said:

"Thank you very much. It's a great plan, but we're not going to carry it out."

Then he was gone.

Silence in the room.

We looked at each other and couldn't believe it.

In those moments, I experienced for the first time in such a tangible way the meaning of democracy. The highest military and security echelons, including the chief of general staff, unequivocally recommended carrying out the operation. But the prime minister, who headed the elected political echelon, chose not to carry it out for reasons he kept to himself.

...

The elected political echelon has the responsibility and authority to decide whether it is right to use the military option, and whether a military operation, as successful and important as it might prove to be, serves its objectives or not.

As prime minister and minister of defense, Peres had a broader view of things and had the right and authority to make the decision, provided that he had all the data he needed, understood its significance, and received a variety of opinions from all the experts on the subject first.

And so he did.

In a democratic country, this is how it should be.

38.

Democracy

I was the commander of the Air Force when the Gaza disengagement plan was devised.

The decision led to a heated public debate and fierce clashes between the plan's supporters and opponents, but in the end, the move was approved by the three branches on which Israeli democracy is based: the executive branch (the prime minister, the governing coalition, and the ministers), the legislative branch (members of the Knesset and the Knesset plenum), and the judiciary (judges of the Supreme Court that reviewed the decision and determined that it was legal).

Regardless of my personal opinion, which no one knew, it was clear to me that implementing the decision would be extremely difficult for me from a psychological perspective. How could I remove my brother from his home? It was heartbreaking and nearly inconceivable.

But my conclusion was the following, and I said it unequivocally:

We could leave Gaza and enter Gaza.

Leave Gaza and enter Gaza.

Leave Gaza and enter Gaza.

We could do this as many times as we decided was necessary, as a state, through its democratic institutions.

It would not be simple, the price would be heavy, but it would be possible.

But we could never — not even once — dismantle the democratic institutions of our country, built with our sweat and blood over many decades.

If that happened, there would be no turning back. We would lose it all.

•••

It was decided that the IDF, including the Air Force, would take part in the evacuation.

This was undoubtedly one of the most complex, difficult, and extraordinary missions I had to lead.

It was important to me that all departments and personnel in the IAF take part in this: pilots and navigators, members of the technological division, members of the administrative division, air defense command personnel, special forces troops, and combat support staff — both men and women.

All of them.

I decided to close the flight school, to the best of my knowledge, for the first time in the history of the Air Force, so that the pilot's course instructors and cadets could also participate in the evacuation. I held a special discussion in which I personally selected the commanders who would lead our soldiers.

It was important for me to choose outstanding and trustworthy commanders with the sensitivity and the ability to lead people in very complex and difficult situations.

Not against enemies.

Versus brothers.

Despite the mental and emotional difficulty, I believed and maintained that it was a critical mission for our continued existence as a free and democratic Jewish state.

Our people did not like the task, but they carried it out with wisdom, determination, tremendous sensitivity and compassion — sometimes with tears in their eyes.

They performed admirably. I was there with them and saw it with my own eyes.

ELYEZER SHKEDY

I am a great believer in our people, and I will do everything to preserve the greatest miracle in the history of the Jewish people throughout its generations – a Jewish, free, and democratic State of Israel.

39.

Whoever Rises to Kill You

The war on terror is a complex task that involves arduous challenges. One of the main ones stems from the fact that the terrorists try disguising and embedding themselves into the civilian population.

The State of Israel is in a constant and bloody struggle against murderous terrorism that uses any means to target and harm citizens: stones, knives, guns, rockets, suicide bombers, and exploding buses. The goal is the same goal — to kill Israelis indiscriminately. Men, women, and children.

One of the ways in which Israel deals with terrorism is a "preemptive strike," i.e., "targeted killings."

"Targeted killing" is not a "revenge killing" as in the underworld, but an attack on a dangerous terrorist who is planning an attack or is about to carry it out — that is, a "ticking timebomb." Targeted killings are intended to save the lives of Israeli civilians and are carried out in accordance with the highest political echelon and its authorization.

Whoever rises to kill you, kill them first.

I personally don't know a single Israeli who wants to harm women, children, and innocent people on the other side. And if there is such a person, they are the exception, not the rule.

In the homes we grew up in, in the culture we were educated in, in the ideals we received from our parents, teachers and commanders, such a thought was completely unacceptable.

Therefore, we have always done everything possible to avoid harming innocent civilians.

The terrorists, who are aware of this, deliberately operate from a crowded civilian environment and "drape" themselves with women and children wherever they go. Unlike the IDF, whose mission is to protect the citizens of Israel, the terrorists use the civilians of Gaza as human shields.

Even though we didn't want to harm innocent civilians, when I took up my position as commander of the Air Force, the ratio of terrorists to innocent people was 1:1, meaning that for every terrorist we hit, one innocent civilian was also hit.

We decided to make every effort to change the situation.

Together with other bodies of the defense establishment and the defense industry, we thought it through and invested enormous resources in developing the capabilities of the Air Force.

We have reached a point where the reality has surpassed all imagination.

When I was the commander of the Air Force, tools and capabilities developed over the years matured and became operational.

These developments were intended, first and foremost, to improve the IAF's operational capabilities and enable it to carry out its missions in the most efficient, accurate, and safe manner, but also to prevent harm to non-combatants.

Most of the developments — real-time intelligence, advanced fire and armaments systems, specialized weapons, and combat doctrines — cannot be specified for obvious reasons.

But one method we developed to prevent harming non-combatants, which I can put in writing, is called "tapping on the roof."

The terrorist organizations in the Gaza Strip used to store weapons and rockets in populated homes with the assumption — indeed, justified — that we would not want to harm civilians living there.

In order not to harm those civilians, we would inform them through the various media channels to evacuate their homes. If they had not yet evacuated for various reasons — more than once Hamas prevented them from doing so and sometimes even brought them up to the roof to deter us from attacking — we would launch a small missile at the edge of the roof of the house. Not to hurt them, but so they would understand that we're serious.

It did the job: the civilians would evacuate and then we would attack the house and destroy it along with the weapons stored there without harming the innocent civilians.

By the end of my time as commander of the Air Force, we had changed the ratio from 1:1 to 24:1. In other words, for every twenty-four terrorists we hit, one non-combatant was hit as well — whom we did not want to hurt either.

These were unprecedented results, across the globe.

People asked me, "Why is this so important to you?"

I replied, "The terrorists can't beat us through acts of terror. They can hurt us, and sometimes wound us very seriously and painfully, but they cannot beat us.

"The terrorists murder women, children, and innocent people and think it's legitimate.

"They will defeat us only if they manage to make us think like them, like the terrorists, that killing women, children, and innocent people is legitimate. And I will do everything so as not to let them beat us."

We act in this way not because of world public opinion or the International Criminal Court at The Hague, but because it is more correct, more just, more moral. Moral standards are what distinguish us from our enemies, the terrorist organizations.

We will do everything so as not to harm children, women, and innocent civilians, and we will do everything possible to harm the terrorists who are planning to murder us.

Those who know me know it is highly recommended not to find yourself in my crosshairs.

Most of those who have are no longer around to talk about it...

40.
A Call from the Prime Minister

On April 4, 2004, I was appointed commander of the Israeli Air Force.

It was in the midst of the Second Intifada and the IDF waged a constant, difficult, and uncompromising struggle against terrorist organizations in general, and Hamas in particular.

A few days after I took the command, it was decided to attack the leader of Hamas, Abdel Aziz al-Rantisi.

Taking out Rantisi was gravely considered by the heads of the defense establishment. The operation was presented to Prime Minister Ariel Sharon and approved by him personally.

I commanded the operation from the Air Force's command and control center at IDF headquarters in Tel Aviv, the "pit."

It was a sensitive and complex mission both operationally and from an intelligence-gathering perspective, but it was executed successfully and we eliminated him without harming innocent civilians.

Shortly after I got home, the phone rang.

"The Prime Minister wants to talk to you," said his secretary from the other side of the line, putting Sharon on.

"Shkedy," he said, "it is commendable that you've taken out such a murderer, who continued to plan to do everything possible to murder more people. This was very, very, very important."

I knew full well how vital this attack, on an actively cruel terrorist leader of this magnitude, was for the security of the citizens of Israel. From the determined voice of the Prime Minister, in charge of national security, I understood how essential this was for him.

41.

I Wanted to See a Parachute

During the First Lebanon War, I was a young operational leader in the 117th Squadron at Ramat David Airbase.

After several days of fighting in the air and on the ground, we, a quartet of F-16s, were scrambled to confront Syrian Air Force planes in the skies over the Beqaa Valley in Lebanon.

We had a short dogfight of less than a minute against Syrian MiG-23s, at the end of which I fired missiles at two of them. Eytan Stibbe, who was number two in the formation, also fired a missile at one of the planes. The missiles hit and both MiG-23s were shot down.

I will never forget the inconceivable sight of the huge fireball in the sky when one of the Syrian planes exploded. Apparently, a missile hit his fuel tanks, causing the huge explosion.

I remember myself in the middle of the battle, continuing to stare at the fireball and straining to see if the Syrian pilot had managed to eject from his plane.

I really wanted to see a parachute...

42.

Do You Have a Torah Scroll With You?

When Shimon Peres was President of the State of Israel, he was invited to speak at the Bundestag, the German parliament. As the CEO of El Al, I met him at Ben Gurion Airport and escorted him to his flight to Berlin.

I said that I was excited that the President of the State of Israel was going to speak at the place where the diabolical plan for the annihilation of the Jewish people was hatched. I told him I was speaking on my behalf; on behalf of my family; on behalf of my father, whose entire family was murdered in the Holocaust; on behalf of the people of El Al; on behalf of the citizens of Israel; and, I believe, also on behalf of the Jewish people all over the world.

President Peres, whom I have never seen so keyed-up and excited, told me that he intended to give his speech to the plenum in Hebrew.

I asked, "Who's accompanying you to the Bundestag?"

The president replied, "A few people from my team."

Then an idea came to my mind. "Do you want El Al personnel to come with you to the Bundestag in uniform — hats, insignias, wings and all?"

"Yes," said Peres, "That would make me very happy."

I said, "We'll make sure they come."

Then I asked, "Do you have a Torah scroll with you?"

What's more symbolic than that? I thought.

The President of the State of Israel,

WHO THE F*CK IS MICHAEL?!

In the Bundestag, in Germany,
Speaking in Hebrew,
Alongside our people in uniform,
And beside him on stage, a Torah scroll.

However, Peres told me that, unfortunately, there was no Torah scroll with him.

Consequently, we decided at El Al to have a Torah scroll written.

In my view, the meaning of this Torah scroll of ours was not religious. For me, it had a deep meaning for our people, our history, our heritage, our traditions, our values, our partnership, our unity, our character, our identity.

That's why we called it: "The El Al Torah Scroll for the Unity of Israel."

We decided that the scroll would be relatively compact, so that we could reach Jewish communities around the world with it, and so that the leaders of the country could take this Torah scroll with them to any event of significance for the State of Israel or for the Jewish people.

It was important to us that the process of writing the Torah scroll be shared by representatives of the entire Jewish people, embracing all of its segments and streams – from the heads of state through central figures in world Jewry to the "common" people like us, such as teachers and students, engineers and lawyers, drivers and laborers. Participating in the writing would be women and men; secular, traditional and religious. There was no problem with this since in most cases, the person who actually forms the letters is a trained scribe.

We decided that wherever we went to write letters in the Torah scroll, in whichever city or country, we would gather in a single centralized location only — even if there were several Jewish houses of worship and community centers in the area. This was so that all the Jews in the region would be able to meet.

This tactic proved itself: during the writing of the scroll, there were stirring meetings between those who had not seen each other in person for a very long time, those who were encountering each other for the first time, and even those who did not want to see each other for various strange reasons... The only thing that connected them was the writing of the El Al Torah Scroll for the Unity of Israel.

Among the writers of letters in the Torah scroll were the President of the State of Israel, the prime minister, cabinet ministers, Knesset members, rebbes and rabbis, the chief of general staff, the head of the Mossad, the head of the Shin Bet, the commander of the Air Force, the paratroopers who liberated the Western Wall, US senators and members of the US Congress, Jewish communal leaders from across the globe, ambassadors, Nobel Prize winners, artists, writers, athletes, El Al personnel — and, most importantly, "common" Jews, wherever in Israel and around the world we brought our Torah scroll.

We even decided to offer the possibility of virtually writing letters in the Torah scroll over the internet.

The response was so overwhelming that our website crashed...

The first and last letters were written by Rabbi Ovadia Yosef and Rabbi Yosef Shalom Elyashiv, may their memories be a blessing.

When we launched the project, I was warned that there would be communities, people, and streams of Judaism that would refuse to cooperate. However, I estimated that there would not be one Jew who would refuse to write a letter in the Torah Scroll for the Unity of Israel.

And indeed, so it was.

Everyone wrote their letter.

We reached many notable sites all over the country and the world: from the Western Wall Tunnels to the US Capitol; from the United Nations Secretariat Building, housing the General Assembly and the Security Council, to the Moscow Choral Synagogue; from the study of the Lubavitcher Rebbe in Brooklyn to the Arch of Titus in Rome; from the Auschwitz extermination camp to the Great Wall of China — and many, many more meaningful locations.

At the time of the writing of the Torah scroll, a large touring exhibition was opening in Berlin.

The thinking in El Al was that, as the company's CEO, it was very important that I participate in the exhibition.

In principle, I try very hard not to set foot on German soil, so I didn't want to go to the exhibition.

Then one of my people told me, "Come with us to the exhibition in Berlin, and then we can go write letters in our Torah scroll in the villa Wannsee — the very place where the Nazi organizers and planners of the Final Solution convened to plot the destruction of our people."

I decided that this was a good enough reason to go to Germany.

The ceremony we held at the villa at Wannsee, near Berlin, was intended to be modest and limited, but to my great surprise, large crowds of Israelis and Jews came to it.

It was an unimaginable scene: the CEO of El Al and former commander of the Israeli Air Force, along with his colleagues and members of the community, writing letters in a Torah scroll on a table in the Wannsee villa. The walls were covered with the portraits of those who had planned to carry out our genocide, gazing down at us as if in disbelief, while a Jewish child played the violin.

The embroidered mantle of the Torah scroll was a heartfelt work of art produced by the world-famous Yaacov Agam.

For Shavuot, the holiday which celebrates the giving of the Torah to our people, we inaugurated the completed Torah Scroll for the Unity of Israel at the El Al campus, located on the grounds of Ben Gurion Airport, in a ceremony that moved many to tears.

Since its writing, this Torah scroll has traveled to many places all over the world, and it has been read from by many Jews from various communities across the globe.

Long after all of us are gone, the Torah scroll we have written will continue to be a symbol of the unity and eternity of the Jewish people.

43.
Dreams Come True

As El Al's CEO, I met from time to time with Minister of Transportation Israel Katz.

In one of our meetings, alongside business matters, we discussed Ilan Ramon and his son Asaf, both of whom were killed in action as IAF pilots. Ilan, the first Israeli astronaut, perished with his crewmates aboard the Space Shuttle *Columbia*; Asaf lost his life when his F-16 crashed on a training mission.

I had known Ilan since we both flew Mirages out of Eitam airbase; later, we were in the same F-16 squadron in Ramat David airbase.

Katz and I talked about the new international airport that was being established at that time in the south, near Timna Park, meant to replace Eilat Airport in due course.

We put two and two together, and the idea of naming the new airport after them was born.

Minister Katz asked if I would speak with Rona Ramon, Ilan's widow and Asaf's mother, about the possibility of perpetuating their memory in this way — but without making any commitments in advance.

I said I would talk to Rona and suggested that he meet her face-to-face.

I spoke with Rona about the subject, which she greeted with great enthusiasm.

I told her that nothing was guaranteed yet. We would travel to Jerusalem, meet with Transportation Minister Katz, and see if he liked the idea and was indeed interested in promoting it.

WHO THE F*CK IS MICHAEL?!

We met with the minister in his office.

From my professional acquaintance with him, I can attest that Katz is not an easy person; we've had disagreements in principle on various professional issues related to the field of civil aviation.

However, I realized then from his body language and soft tone of voice that the subject had touched his heart and that he was genuinely moved by the encounter with Rona.

Still, the decision was not a simple one. There were pressures from various parties to name the new field after a political figure who had recently passed away. But Minister Katz decided to promote the move, and I became convinced that his resolve was sincere and deep.

Rona was a unique woman. After losing her husband and son, she could have sunk into mourning, but she discovered tremendous inner strength within herself and decided to devote her life to educational programs in their memory, in order to bring about change. She did it in her own special way and touched many hearts. The commemoration of Ilan and Asaf at a new airport in the south had a very deep symbolic significance in her eyes — a combination of the field of aviation, which was at the center of Ilan's and Asaf's lives, and the development and advancement of the Negev Desert.

On July 16, 2018, a ceremony was held to unveil the sign with the name: Ilan and Asaf Ramon International Airport.

Rona, who was battling cancer, had the privilege in her lifetime to dedicate the location where her loved ones were commemorated.

"This raises my spirits. This uplifts my soul. Dreams do come true," she said at the ceremony.

Five months later, she passed away.

I salute Ilan and Asaf, the best of the best of the Air Force and the State of Israel; and Rona, a brave woman who faced an unimaginable situation and chose the path of dedication, education and love.

44.
Journey of Hope

For Israel's seventy-second Independence Day, the official ceremony on Mount Herzl was held at the height of the first wave of the COVID-19 pandemic. One of the torches was lit by the CEO of Masa Israeli - I Belong Israel, Uri Cohen, a man of values and an educator at heart. Masa is his life's work. As someone who has been accompanying this wonderful project for years, I felt great pride at that moment.

"Every year, Masa Israeli leads thousands of young people, from soldiers to groups from Israel and the Diaspora, on a journey through the country's sites and landscapes. This is a journey to clarify and strengthen their connection, identity, and belonging to the people, the country, and the state," said the ceremony's moderator, Guy Zoaretz. "Masa Israeli, created by Uri and his colleagues, has already been completed by more than three-hundred-thousand participants. The experience they have gone through will shape their lives."

Since I retired from the IDF, I have been approached several times asking me to be the "father" of Masa Israeli. Since I was CEO of El Al at that point, I couldn't invest the time required for it. I told myself that when I finished my tenure at El Al, I would consider the offer.

Towards the end of his pilot's course, my son, Omer, participated with his fellow cadets in Masa Israeli. He came home excited and keyed up, telling me, "Dad, this is the most significant thing I've ever done, more than all my years in the education system. You've got to help them."

When I finished my role at El Al, I was approached again by Masa Israeli Journey. This time I replied in the affirmative, and I volunteered to serve as the president of the organization.

The expedition across Israel, which ends in Jerusalem, is in my opinion an amazing project. A fascinating study conducted by the sociologist Professor Gad Yair, published in English as *I Belong Israel: Journey of Discovery and Connection* (Yedioth Books 2021), clearly proves that Masa Israeli deepens in its participants the commitment to the State of Israel and the Jewish people; strengthens values such as tolerance, acceptance of the other and attentiveness; and also contributes to a significant reduction in the level of violence in society.

Much of this is due to the excellent Masa Israeli guides, the content chosen with deep thought, and the dynamics created during the journey. The participants are exposed to populations they have never known before, opening them up to opinions different than their own and helping them understand the importance of listening and open-mindedness. These things are not done through frontal lectures and didactic explanations, but through face-to-face conversations, meetings, and discussion circles. They are not told what is right and what isn't. The participants come to conclusions about themselves on their own, and this is much more powerful.

One of the claims against Masa Israeli is that it is some form of *hadata*, "religionization." When I hear this criticism, I have a simple answer: "Let them contact me. I am certainly not suspected of hadata. Those who have comments and suggestions, those who want to influence and are found suitable, are invited to serve as Masa Israeli guides regardless of their political opinions, religious views, or gender: religious and secular, women and men, Jews and Arabs. All of them."

Naturally, political elements try to influence the content and take Masa Israeli in certain directions. I'm not prepared to allow that, under any circumstances. My rule has been and remains simple: the decisions in principle are made by a board of directors only — which consists of accomplished people from all segments of Israeli society and the political spectrum — and finalized by the CEO and management without any political influence. When we held a large event in the Knesset, I made it clear that I would only participate if there were heads of parties on the right and left, religious and non-religious. And so it was.

In recent years, we have decided to enhance the project, expand it, and advance it in additional directions:

To significantly expand Masa Israeli for 11th graders.

To conduct a Masa Israeli program for 12th graders that emphasizes the issue of democracy and the challenges currently facing Israeli society.

To develop a Masa Israeli program for IDF commanders.

To integrate wounded IDF soldiers.

To bring in adults from companies, nonprofits, and various organizations, from groups such as "Mothers with Meaning" and others.

To integrate young Jews from the Diaspora into Masa Israeli alongside young Israelis.

To connect groups from different backgrounds, such as businessmen and wounded warriors, or young people with disabilities and high school students.

It's exciting to see the shining eyes of the wonderful younger generation we have.

To hear older women who went on Masa Israeli with great hesitation and apprehension describe the significant impact it has had on their lives...

To see the radiant faces of wounded IDF soldiers, who sacrificed almost everything for the country, after completing a joint Masa Israeli program with employees of the First International Bank...

And to hear Eyal Shamir, one of the guides who accompanied them, say in an excited voice at the end of a Masa Israeli expedition:

"Wow, there is hope for the people of Israel..."

And that says it all.

45.
Shortcuts

When I was in high school, the greatest boast was to say:

"I didn't study for the test, and I got a 100..."

I mean, that's a genius...

But I think this is the completely wrong approach, a pattern that puts you on the wrong path, based on the illusion that it is possible to succeed without training and practicing.

The right thing is to say to yourself: The subject was important to me, I planned, I studied, I practiced, I invested a lot of time and energy — and I got a 100.

Excellent. Now you are on the right path.

Michael Jordan, perhaps the greatest basketball player ever and among the greatest athletes of all time, devoted himself entirely to practice, as detailed in the documentary *The Last Dance*.

His great success was not accidental and was not based solely on his natural talent — though he had amazing talent, no doubt about it.

He understood the significance of investment, was absolutely committed, was demanding with himself, and did everything so that his teammates would also train as hard as possible.

And this is true for every area of life.

When we see a virtuoso pianist we say to ourselves: "What amazing talent," but to get where she came from, she had to practice for many hours every day, since she was a child.

To be an excellent pilot or a successful doctor, you need certain qualities, but you must also learn and train non-stop.

A lot.

I don't know of any superstar who hasn't made such an investment, dedicating their whole lives to sharpening their skills in their given field.

The first precondition for success is a huge investment.

You invested a great deal and saw great success? That's nothing to be ashamed of. Quite the contrary.

True, the ability to improvise is also of great importance — but it should be "improvisation on a solid foundation." And the solid foundation should be built through planning, study, and intensive training as a basis for action. If you have a solid foundation, it will always be possible to improvise "on the go."

• • •

The more you train, the more your skills improve.
    As well as your luck...
    As legendary golfer Arnold Palmer once said:
    "The more I practice, the luckier I get..."
    There are no shortcuts.

46.
The Competition

When I studied in the United States, we lived in Monterey, California, a charming coastal town between San Francisco and LA. Nimo, our eldest son, was in the eighth grade at the local public school.

One day, shortly after we landed there, Nimo came home from school and told us that he had been invited to take part in the most prestigious mathematics competition in California.

I asked him, "Do you want to participate?"

He said, "Yes."

I'm a big believer in my son and yet... We had just arrived in the United States, his command and knowledge of English were pretty basic, he was very young and probably hadn't learned all the material. Even I, who knew how sharp and talented he was, thought it might be a little early. I was afraid he'd get hurt.

I asked him, "How would you know the names of the basic concepts in mathematics?"

Nimo answered, "Teach me."

"And how would you know the material that is expected to be in the competition?" I asked. "It's stuff you've probably never learned."

"Then teach me," was the answer.

I felt he really wanted to, so I went with the flow.

I taught him the basic mathematical concepts in English; we went through material he'd never studied before but which I thought would come up in the competition.

Time passed, the date of the competition was approaching; and yet, I almost never saw him study or practice.

I asked, "Are you still going to participate in the competition?"

"Yes."

"But I haven't seen you studying and practicing much," I said.

He replied, "I already studied. I understood everything you explained to me."

"What do you mean? What do you understand?"

"I understand what you explained to me."

I said, "Okay then, let's see what you know." I started asking him questions about the material, and to my great surprise, he answered almost every math question I asked him, all in English. These were topics that took me, at his age, many months to learn, practice, and understand in depth.

We only had a few small things left.

I took the opportunity to talk to him about the importance of practice and training, even if you are talented.

He looked at me with big eyes, listened, didn't say a word — and went to practice.

Big time...

Nimo participated in the competition and won a medal.

The joy at the school where he studied was tremendous. The school principal and his classmates came to our house and started singing and dancing.

I think this was one of the few times that a public school student had won a medal in this competition. Most of the past winners came from California's prestigious private schools.

It's really a unique feeling of tremendous pride and great fun to see your child's special abilities, willingness, attentiveness, internalization, deep reserves of strength and courage, despite their youth, to put in the work and manage even when they are in the "underdog" position.

• • •

When your daughter or son believes in themselves and sets goals for themselves, it is right to do everything possible to support them.

Even if it doesn't work, it will make them stronger.

And that's worth everything.

47.

Hedging

One of the critical issues for the existence of an airline is the expenditure on fuel for aircraft, which could amount to one-third of total expenses. That's hundreds of millions of dollars a year, even billions of dollars, depending on the size of the company and the prices of fuel.

At certain times, El Al's fuel expenditure was over $700 million a year. During my term as CEO, the outlay reached about 35% of the company's expenses.

This isn't "just another matter." It's an existential concern. A small mistake in fuel-related policy could financially crush an airline.

Before I took on my role as El Al's CEO, I delved very deeply into the subject and realized how significant proper discipline in purchasing and consuming fuel could be, reaching the point of saving tens of millions of dollars a year.

I reached several conclusions and operative decisions in this area. El Al's management had to be made aware of the issue, ensuring that the price of fuel would be a central concern and focus of the company.

As CEO, I would deal with this personally. I would meet with the team dealing with the issue of fuel at least once a week, and I would make decisions as needed:

1. The company would recruit experts in the field of fuel procurement, hedging, and economy.
2. I would hold a comprehensive and in-depth monthly meeting

with all those dealing with the issue of fuel from different angles.

The goal was not just to take advantage of an opportunity to save money or make a profit (if we made a profit, good for us...), but to be able to plan and prepare.

And this is where we entered the field of procurement and hedging.

What exactly is a hedge?

It is possible to buy fuel at the current price or "to hedge," i.e., to buy fuel in advance according to the expected prices in the future.

This is a very complex field that raises many questions and dilemmas: Should we hedge? How much? For how long? With what tools?

There are different approaches to the subject and there is no absolute truth.

One thing was clear to me. In the past, the company had suffered heavy losses due to hedges on fuel, and these were weighty decisions: when to take a risk, what risks should be taken, and when hedging ought to be strictly forbidden. Therefore, I, as a CEO, had to be personally involved in every move carried out in the field of fuel procurement.

As it were, I got my "PhD" in hedging studies, examining the subject in depth over many weeks, even before taking on the role of CEO.

I remember sitting in a small cubicle with Nissim Malki, the company's serious and experienced CFO, and learning his perspective on hedging. I felt his relief when he realized that I was going to deal with it personally, seriously, and in collaboration with him and his people.

I read, studied and delved into mathematics and economics to understand the trends in the aircraft fuel market and everything about buying fuel or hedging on it. I also met with external experts.

Since the theory of hedging is very complex, there are companies that specialize in the field. I contacted several such companies, ordered analyses from them, heard their conclusions, and asked to see to what extent their predictions from the past had come true.

It was interesting to see the large discrepancy between the analyses and what actually happened.

A few months after I took office, I decided on a significant hedge, which seemed necessary to me in light of the external conditions and the state of the company at the time.

The day after we made the move, a member of the company's board of directors came into my office, someone I liked and whose professional opinion I appreciated. "Shkedy," he told me, "your hedge was awful."

I replied, "You appointed me CEO. With all due respect, I'll do things the way I believe they should be done, after studying the subject in depth. If that doesn't suit you, tell me now, and I'll hand you back the keys and leave."

A week later, it was already clear how important, significant, and correct the move was — and how good the precise timing had been. Without a doubt, it helped us get through a very difficult time and survive.

Another topic that I studied in depth was fuel conservation: How can you save fuel on the flight itself?

Saving as little as one percent in fuel consumption yields millions of dollars a year. Greater fuel savings can save tens of millions of dollars.

I decided to appoint an expert on the subject who would deal with this in conjunction with his role as an active pilot with the rank of captain.

There are various variables that affect the consumption of fuel in flight. For example, the lower the weight of the aircraft, the lower the fuel consumption. The altitude and speed of the flight also affect fuel consumption, and even the way air flows over the wings.

In one of the discussions, an interesting issue arose:

There are kits called wingtip devices or winglets that are installed at the end of an aircraft's wings; they increase the efficiency of fixed-wing aircraft by reducing drag. When the air resistance is less, you have to apply less engine power to fly at a given speed. This means saving two to three percent of the fuel consumption on board, which is a lot of money.

We embarked on a lightning campaign of installing winglets on all the company's aircraft that did not yet have this component. The project was led by VP of Maintenance Shmuel Kuzi, a determined and goal-oriented leader, who in the past had served as commander of the Central Maintenance Unit of the Air Force. He understood the importance of the move and led the charge with all his energy, rallying all of our people with great success.

This involved a considerable investment of funds and a complex operation, but it was clear to me from the mathematical and economic analysis that the return on our investment would be rapid and that the fuel savings would be substantial and long-lasting.

• • •

It is important to identify the "big stones" that are particularly impactful and be able to tend to them personally, even if it's difficult and the odds of success aren't high.

This is true in every area of life.

153

48.
Bullshit...???

One day, when we were re-establishing HaEmek Squadron at Ramat David Airbase as an F-16 squadron, I was approached by Yitzhak Nahum, the squadron's technical officer.

"Shkedy," he said, "in a few days the base is holding its annual Hanukkah party. Shouldn't we skip it because we're so busy getting the squadron up and running?"

"Nahum, what happens at this party?" I asked.

"Everyone on the base goes — enlisted, NCOs, officers — and they light Hanukkah candles, hold the menorah contest, hand out prizes, eat, drink, and leave."

I thought for a moment and said,

"We're going. Make sure each of our men has a shirt with the squadron's symbol in front, plain as day. Make sure we show up early, grab seats up front, and sit together."

"OK," he said.

"And one more thing," I said. "Choose the most talented and creative man we have in the squadron and tell him to build a menorah. As far as I'm concerned, our menorah should be able to do everything: sing, dance, jump, play music, whatever... The main thing is that we win first place."

Nahum looked at me surprised, "Are you serious?"

"Totally," I answered.

I knew I could trust Nahum, a serious officer that people followed with blind faith.

We embarked on our mission.

154

Hanukkah arrived. We entered the hall, all the members of the squadron wearing shirts with our symbol in bold, and we sat down together in front.

On the stage stood the menorah built by Shalom Bublil, the talented electrical officer who tended to the Barak jets.

It sang, danced, jumped, played music and...

And...

We won first place.

Why am I even telling you about this bullshit?

Because it isn't bullshit at all.

This story made clear to each and every one of the squadron's members that whatever the situation, we would do everything to be the best, to succeed, and to win.

There was no guarantee we would always succeed, but we would always give it our best. That was our approach.

There was also a message here for everyone else, and all the other units and squadrons on base understood that a baby was born — and that he would always try to be the best and win. We were not going to make anyone's life easy.

• • •

One of the most important conditions for success is your approach.

You can't be mediocre all along the way and suddenly become outstanding. You can't be a mediocre soccer player and suddenly be invited to replace Lionel Messi in the lineup.

You can't be a mediocre violinist and suddenly be invited to be a soloist at the New York Philharmonic.

You can't be a mediocre scientist and suddenly win the Nobel Prize.

Excellence is an approach and a way of life.

• • •

Almost thirty years had passed when I was invited to HaEmek Squadron to tell about its founding.

WHO THE F*CK IS MICHAEL?!

I asked the personnel, most of whom had not yet been born at that time, "What do you know about the establishment of the squadron?" I was told the story of the menorah...

156

49.
I Made a Huge Mistake

When I was a deputy squadron commander at Nevatim Airbase, I was invited, together with all the other squadron commanders and deputy commanders, to a meeting with the head of the manpower division of the Israeli Air Force, who came to visit the base.

Since the squadron commander was not at the base that day, I represented our squadron.

The meeting proceeded breezily, until the Q&A section.

"Does anyone have any questions?"

Silence in the hall.

"Questions?"

Silence in the hall.

Then the base commander turned to me, "Shkedy, don't you have a question?"

I thought about it and said, "Since you brought it up, I do have something I'd like to ask. The presentation to the head of the manpower division painted a very nice picture, but I'd still like to know why our squadron doesn't deserve coffee. It's important for the people who fly in the mornings and need to be sharp, focused, and alert."

For some reason, we do not get coffee....

Repeated appeals to the officials in charge at the base did nothing, and at some point, I didn't have the strength to fight about it anymore, so I dealt with it myself by regularly asking my wife Anat to buy coffee, out of our own pocket, at the canteen, then brought the coffee to my squadron myself.

The senior officer in charge of the matter, who was also sitting in the hall, turned red, immediately went on the defensive and said, "We always send you coffee."

I couldn't hold back and said, "How are you going to lie like that?"

But he insisted and said again, all red in the face, "Coffee is provided for your squadron."

At that point, I couldn't control myself anymore, and instead of remaining silent, I said angrily, "Not only were you lying before, you're shamelessly doubling down on it, in front of everyone."

Silence in the hall.

Somehow, the event ended...

Immediately afterward, the base commander sent me a message that I needed to apologize to that senior officer.

I said I wasn't going to apologize. The officer had lied, and I was right. What is between me and him is between me and him and had nothing to do with the commander of the base.

I thought about it quite a bit and realized I had made a big mistake.

Before Yom Kippur, the Jewish Day of Atonement, I called that officer and apologized to him from the bottom of my heart for shaming him in public. He had a very hard time with what happened, but he accepted my apology with graciousness.

This story has preoccupied me and troubled my mind for years.

I do not regret that I raised the issue. I did this out of a commitment to the care of every individual under my command; and on a factual level I was also right: we had not been getting what we deserved and needed before flying.

It is permissible to disagree, to resist, to argue — but there is a way to do it. I could have clarified the coffee issue with him face-to-face after the meeting. I could have asked him to check the issue with his people; maybe he just didn't know or wasn't aware that they had "forgotten" our squadron. But under no circumstances should I have called him a liar in front of other people, certainly not in front of the entire senior command staff of the base.

How could I not realize then that things that I thought were significant were completely insignificant in relation to the terrible act I had done to that person?

Unfortunately, it is impossible to turn back the wheel of time and no apology will help, even if it is accepted.

I made a mistake — in fact, I made a huge mistake.

What I did was something that ought not to be done.

•••

Humiliating another person in public is like spilling his blood.

50.
Who Will Lead the Pilot?

Before I was appointed commander of the combat branch at the Hatzerim flight school, an attempt was made to make a major and fundamental change to the cadets' training program. However, the move was met with fierce opposition, provoked strong antagonism, and led nowhere.

When I took on the position, I studied the matter in depth and concluded it was a correct and important step to take, and that it could catalyze organizational change and improve flight training ahead of the IAF's next challenges and future aircraft.

I tried to figure out why it didn't work.

The person spearheading the move had been a senior officer with a well-groomed beard, dressed in an ironed uniform with sharp creases in his pants, with professional knowledge of organizational systems and training theories. But he came from outside the Air Force, lacked the personality of a leader, conveyed intellectual condescension, and was unfamiliar with the world of aviation. Every time he opened his mouth, he was met with outrage from the instructors.

When I saw how the instructors perceived him, I immediately understood the problem. I decided to change two fundamental things: to choose other leaders and to define the move as a pilot program.

I chose Gil Yadlin, Amir Harpaz, and Itai "Kosta" Karin — all esteemed flight instructors valued for their personality, wisdom, determination, and professionalism. They had been my cadets; I

160

knew them well and I knew that their informal influence on the group of instructors was significant and that they could create a positive dynamic in the process.

I spoke with them about the move, its significance, and its future impact on the face of the entire Air Force, and they felt the same way I did and understood very well that this was an important and necessary measure.

I promised them that they would receive my full backing and asked them not to be afraid to do things according to their understanding. I made it clear that the only ones who would spearhead the process and talk about it with the flight school instructors would be Harpaz, Yadlin, Kosta, and myself. The external officer would continue to be involved and we would treat him with the utmost sensitivity, but he would only talk to the leaders of the pilot program and me.

To lower the flames even further, I reiterated that this was just a "pilot program." That is, we would start with a small change in a limited area, and once we succeed in creating a positive dynamic, we would advance to all the other areas of the flight school.

Indeed, the move was very successful and had a decisive impact on the training of the future generation of pilots. All of the credit goes to Kosta, Harpaz, and Yadlin, the leaders of the transformation.

When you want to make a move that is significant and complex, the best approach is to launch a "pilot program" — a small, preliminary move, a kind of promo, to reduce the tension in the group and reassure those who fear change.

Your chances of success with a pilot program will greatly increase if you keep a couple of things in mind:

1. **The group leader:** The pilot program should be led by a person who, like you, believes in the importance of the move, and is valued and accepted by the group.
2. **Your involvement as a leader:** It should be clear to everyone that you are personally watching over the process, and that you will do everything to make it successful.

When your message is clear, it simplifies things.

• • •

It is surprising to see how quickly you can lead a large-scale move after you have already achieved small success in the pilot program — all through positive dynamics, not by compulsory commands and orders.

51.
Birds of Prey

When Yoav Galant was made head of Southern Command, I felt he was frustrated to discover what the situation had been prior to his arrival. The command and its leader had only minor influence on developments in the field, and those who led the operational activity were the General Staff on the one hand and the Gaza Division on the other.

Galant, a brave warrior and resolute commander, wanted to lead the fighting in the South, and rightly so.

We met and I said to him, "Yoav, do you want to develop an operational capability that will allow you to do significant things in your command space? Or do you want to just be a pencil-pusher, as it was before you came?"

This was, of course, a rhetorical question.

I suggested something to him that would significantly enhance the Southern Command's operational scope and give him access to the Air Force's operational-intelligence capabilities and doctrines, as developed from the core lessons of the Yom Kippur War.

In the aftermath of that war, an operational research team in the Air Force was established, tasked with processing the intelligence coming from all possible sources — COMINT (communications intelligence), SIGINT (signals intelligence), and HUMINT (human intelligence) — to designate targets for attack.

Even an excellent aircraft with advanced weapons systems and daring pilots cannot fulfill its true potential without readily available, up-to-date, and accurate intelligence on the targets it needs to attack.

The decision to reveal and share with the Southern Command the "Holiest of Holies" of our intelligence-operational concept was a dramatic turning point for the Air Force, nothing less. The move was accompanied by a great deal of cynicism, passion, concerns, and objections, and I had to personally ensure that the decision was implemented.

Dozens of people from Southern Command came every morning to the Air Force's "pit" to see, learn, understand and develop this capability for themselves. Indeed, Galant fully adopted this operational concept, with the necessary adjustments, and established an intelligence-operational cell called the "Summit Cell."

The initiative paid off in spades, and in light of the success, we decided to upgrade the intelligence and operational coordination between the Air Force and the Southern Command.

Thus was born the "Birds of Prey" program — a massive attack on targets in the Gaza Strip as a preliminary stage for a comprehensive operation against the terrorist organizations, with the Southern Command responsible for the intelligence-operational side and the Air Force for the attack aspect.

The main idea was to cause complete surprise on the other side by attacking with many aircraft of all types and with a variety of munitions, to strike every target almost simultaneously, and to prevent the terrorists from "disappearing" into their underground tunnels immediately after the first bomb fell.

I presented the operational idea and capabilities that we formulated together with the Southern Command to Prime Minister Ehud Olmert at the end of a meeting we held at Hatzerim Airbase with the aircrew members who attacked the nuclear reactor in Syria. From the look in his eyes, and from the questions he asked, I got the impression that he understood the potential of the program from his broad perspective atop the political echelon.

Indeed, shortly after I was discharged from the army, the program proved itself.

The opening salvo of "Birds of Prey" on the first day of Operation Cast Lead in the Gaza Strip, led by IAF Commander Ido Nehushtan and GOC Southern Command Galant, was very successful, inflicting serious casualties on the terrorists and significant damage to Hamas within a short period of time.

•••

True partnership and open-mindedness can lead to excellent results.

52.
Preemptive Strike

As the chief of the Air Force, I commanded and controlled "Operation Density" (*Mishkal Sguli*) — the preemptive strike that was Israel's first salvo of the Second Lebanon War.

It was an operation to attack the Fajr medium-range surface-to-surface missiles hidden in dozens of homes and other hiding places in Lebanon — a project in which Hezbollah had invested a lot, seeing it as the crowning glory of its operational capability.

The feeling at that time was one of a kind.

The targeted attack, which lasted all of thirty-four minutes, was the culmination of a lengthy process in which the IAF's operational and intelligence apparatuses took part alongside Military Intelligence and other bodies of the defense establishment.

I remember the intricate and in-depth intelligence research, the meticulous intelligence and operational planning, and the drills and target models of the squadrons that participated in the operation. This was undoubtedly the product of extraordinary preparation and impressive teamwork by the best of our people.

When going into battle, the correct tactic is to attack the enemy's most significant assets with a preemptive strike.

The main advantage of such a move is the mobilization and concentration of forces with proper timing, surprise, purposefulness, and aggression against the enemy's critical power points.

The preemptive strike must be prepared well. It must not be a last-minute improvisation.

ELYEZER SHKEDY

• • •

On the face of it, this is true only in the military sphere.
But a "preemptive strike" is not solely a military concept, and it is
undoubtedly also relevant to other fields and worlds.

53.

You're Making the Biggest
Mistake of Your Life

When I finished my role as commander of the Air Force and retired from the IDF, my wife Anat and I planned to travel to twenty destinations around the world, rent an apartment in each place and live there for a long period of time — not as tourists, but as locals. At the end of each such episode, we would return to Israel for a certain period of time, then hit the road again.

I wanted to take a significant break, to think, to consider things calmly, and see what spoke to me and in which direction I might choose to turn.

I met with Rafi Peleg, a consultant and personal mentor for retirees from the IDF and the defense establishment and for people who are facing a second career. Rafi heard my plan, and despite it being very different from the conventional approach after retirement, he listened and accompanied me very openly and wisely.

We started implementing the plan, with the first stop being Paris. At the same time, I started receiving various offers for senior management positions. Most of them sounded interesting, but not enough for me to change my plans. I replied to all of them politely and appreciatively, but in the negative.

On one of our visits to Israel, I was approached by the former chief of staff of the IDF, Amnon Lipkin-Shahak, who was on El Al's board of directors, and asked what I thought of being the company's CEO.

The dilemma was a thorny one. The field of civil aviation is very tough and complex. There is an axiom that goes like this: "The surest way to become a millionaire is to start as a billionaire and buy an airline..." But El Al is not just another airline. There is something significant and symbolic about it that goes beyond the business world. In many ways, El Al acts as the "civilian wings" of the State of Israel and the Jewish people.

It is no coincidence that the Israeli flag is emblazoned on its planes.

This led me to think: Maybe I should change my plans after all.

I met with the company's controlling shareholder, Tamar (Tami) Mozes Borovitz, with whom I had no prior acquaintance. We chatted for a while, as Tami tested my willingness to serve as El Al's CEO.

At the end of the meeting, I told her, "Think about it, and decide what seems to you to be the best thing for El Al. In the meantime, I'll learn all about the company and decide if I'm willing and ready to take it on my shoulders. If you let me know that you want me as CEO, I promise to give you an answer within three days. And if you decide you're not interested, that's fine."

I told myself that even if nothing came of it, learning in depth about El Al would be an interesting and relevant project for whatever I might do in the civilian world.

At Tami's request, I held talks with the board members and the company's chairman, Amikam Cohen, a genuine, direct man who said everything in his heart without embellishing things. From the first moment, I felt that I would find a common language with him.

At the same time, I began to learn about the company independently, as an autodidact. More specifically: I wrote a book about El Al, thirty-seven chapters long, from different angles. I studied and delved into the economic issues with the accountant Uzi Messinger, a true professional and a wise man who was of great help to me; and into the legal issues with my sister-in-law, attorney Nily Kally, a real legal eagle who has been and remains by my side, assisting me with all her heart in everything I do. I met with serious people whose opinions I appreciated; I listened and I deliberated.

WHO THE F*CK IS MICHAEL?!

All my friends told me that I was crazy and that I shouldn't dare do it and destroy the reputation I had built for myself during my thirty-three years of service in the Air Force. No, there's no chance of success at El Al, they warned me.

In other words: you're making the biggest mistake of your life.

The person who encouraged me to take the position anyway was Brigadier General (res.) Rafi Harlev, who served as El Al's CEO for fourteen years, including during its hardest times, when it was in receivership; a true professional, under the stiff outer shell, he had a heart of gold. "It's really crazy, but it's just right for you," he said.

A few weeks later, while I was abroad, the phone call came from Tami . "The board wants you to come and serve as CEO of El Al," she told me.

I thanked her and said I would give her an answer within three days.

I thought, deliberated, and came to the conclusion that despite the warnings of most of the people with whom I had consulted, people whose opinions I respected and who I knew wanted the best for me, I could do important things at El Al and pilot the national airline to bluer skies.

I told Tami "yes" and was invited to the board meeting, where my appointment was officially approved.

I am happy and proud to have had the privilege of leading El Al for more than four years, which were challenging and complex. The company coped with its difficulties, got on the right business path, and towards the end of my tenure was even chosen by a leading aviation magazine as one of the twenty best airlines in the world.

Here, in Israel, we were privileged to be among the three companies that won the title of "brand of brands."

•••

Even when things seem crazy, difficult and hopeless, you must study, analyze, deliberate, understand the risks and prospects, truly listen, and then decide.

In the end, the decision is yours.

170

54.

Go Forward

Over the past few years, I have done my best to meet with the young generation — in public high schools, *yeshivas* for religious young men and *ulpanas* and seminars for religious young women, pre-military prep academies, and in the IDF itself.

In these conversations, I talk to them about life, not necessarily about the army. I feel it's important for them — and for me.

One day, while I was sitting with friends in a restaurant, a girl who worked there as a waitress came up to us and asked me with bright eyes and an embarrassed smile, "Can I talk to you?"

"Of course," I said.

We moved aside and she said, "My name is Or. You were at our school in Hadassim and talked to all the students. I listened to what you said, and I'd like your advice."

"Gladly," I said, and she continued.

"I've been invited to screen for the Naval Officers Course, but some of the people around me think it's a bad idea. They tell me I have no chance of making it. I don't know what to do. What do you say?"

I was impressed by her determined body language and the way she spoke and replied:

"Don't be afraid of anyone.

"Go forward.

"When you finish the course, I will come to your graduation ceremony. I promise."

Or decided to go through the intense screening process, passed

171

the trials, and embarked on the actual course to become a naval officer, one of the most difficult and highly regarded training programs in the IDF.

A few months later, her grandmother invited me, on her behalf, to the graduation ceremony for the first stage of the course, which includes boot camp and basic seamanship training.

I told her, "The goal is not to finish basic training but to finish the entire Naval Officers Course. I promised to come to the graduation ceremony — and I'll come."

Two years later, I received an SMS from Or: "I am finishing the Naval Officers Course, and you promised that you would come. Will you come?"

"Of course," I answered. "I promised to come, and I'll come."

As fate would have it, on the day of the graduation ceremony I had a fever of a hundred-and-two and had lost my voice.

I said to myself, "There's no way I'm not going." A promise is a promise.

I downed a few tablets and drove off.

I was with Or and her family at the ceremony, and I shared their excitement and their pride at her accomplishment.

After a while, she called me, "I want to invite you to meet and talk to the officers in my Advanced Naval Command Course."

Obviously, I went.

Years passed, and one day I got a phone call from a girl named Gal.

She introduced herself and said, "I was there when you spoke with the students at my high school in Sderot,[3] and I would very much like to consult with you."

"Gladly," I said.

"I've been invited to screen for the Naval Officers Course," Gal continued, "and people around me say it's a waste of time, that I have no chance of getting through... What do you say?"

She said the matter was extremely important to her, so she worked hard to get my phone number, overcame her inhibitions,

---

3. Sderot is a small city in southern Israel, located less than a mile from the Gaza Strip.

and did everything possible to seek my advice. Her determination was evident in her voice and words.

I told her:

"Don't be afraid of anyone. Charge ahead.

"I promise you: When you finish the Naval Officers Course, I'll come to the graduation ceremony."

And I gave her Or's cell phone number...

55.
"Shmbm"

My good friend, Professor Moti Mark, is smart and sensitive, a
psychiatrist whom I love and appreciate very much, in part because
of the courage to follow his truth to the end.

In addition to being a psychiatrist, Moti also got a Ph.D. in law.

Together with Israel Prize laureate Professor Shlomo Giora
Shoham, Moti took it upon himself to lead a course for an
interdisciplinary master's degree in psychiatry and law at Tel Aviv
University.

When Moti began planning the course, he and his wife Sary came
to consult with Anat and me. Moti told us about the idea behind
the course: to develop synergy, attentiveness, and understanding
between the two worlds.

I asked him who, in his estimation, would likely want to participate in such a course, and he replied, "Serious and formidable
people from both fields: psychiatrists, therapists, nurses, lawyers,
judges, and families of patients who have these issues burning in
their bones."

I realized that the key to success lay in the teaching method. I told
him that in my opinion, the course material should not be conveyed
in the conventional academic format of frontal lectures, but rather
in discussion circles that could create a dynamic of attentiveness,
openness, and understanding instead of oppositional fixation, with
everyone entrenched in their positions.

My idea was that each meeting would be attended by a person
of stature from every field, who would speak for ten to fifteen

minutes about topics fundamental to them, and then there would be a discussion between the students sitting in a circle led by Moti and Shlomo, the professors leading the course. During the conversation, the lecturers would sit in a circle with the other people. They would not speak during the evolving discussion but would only listen.

Moti listened earnestly and the idea appealed to him, but he had two main concerns:

One, what serious expert would be willing to come and talk for ten or fifteen minutes and then just sit and listen?

Second, could a valuable learning process really emerge from the students themselves and not from the lecturers — experts in their fields?

I said, "Whoever agrees to come, great. And those who don't, they'll miss out. Explain calmly to the lecturers and experts that the opening lecture is an important trigger for discussion and learning among the students, who themselves have knowledge and significant experience in these areas." The attentiveness, openness, and creative thinking of the students themselves, who are less bound by prior conventions, held the key.

In preparation for the opening of the course, Moti and I spoke again, and I realized that it was going to be the other way around: at the last minute, Moti decided to go back to the seemingly "safe" frontal approach.

I said, "Let's meet again."

We met.

I understood his concern about the unconventional approach I proposed, but to his credit, he was brave and open to listening to someone who came from a completely different field and a completely different background. He listened and he was convinced.

What was there to lose?

Superb lecturers would have the opportunity to participate in something innovative and different, and students with potential would be at the forefront of interdisciplinary development and knowledge.

At the same time, it became clear that this approach had a

"cousin" called the Balint Method — a discussion and support group for doctors and therapists that focuses on the doctor-patient relationship.

The Balint method focused on only one area, whereas we were dealing with two areas that had a deep conflict between them. But despite the fundamental distinction, we decided to adopt this approach as the title of the teaching method in the course.

We came to the first lesson — Sary, Anat and I — to get an impression.

Every week, Moti kept me updated on what was happening in class. I was happy to hear from him that the method was working well and that excellent dynamics had been created.

We agreed that at the end of the semester, I would conduct a debriefing in the Israeli Air Force style.

All the students in the course and many of the lecturers took part in the debriefing.

It was exciting to hear about their feelings and interactions, the insights they had formed, and how each of them had been affected.

It was also beautiful to see the hosts, guest lecturers, and students be open enough to honestly convey what they had learned.

Indeed, the following year the main lessons from the previous year's course were adopted.

In the debriefing, I realized, specifically as an outsider and layperson in these subjects, that they had actually developed an "on-the-go" method of study suitable for many other areas, particularly multidisciplinary subjects with a deep conflict between the fields.

It's basically an evolution of the Balint method. I call it the "Shmbm method," an acronym for Shoham, Mark, Berliner, and Munitz. Retired Justice Shmuel Berliner and the psychiatrist Professor Hanan Munitz were invited to speak in the course as renowned experts, each in his own field, thus creating a real and deep integration between the white lab coat and the black robe.

They enjoyed it so much that they wanted to come to the next classes as participants and not necessarily as lecturers. Thus they informally became part of the course's leading team. In the debriefing, they excitedly told me that this was the only course in which they themselves, as lecturers, felt that they were really learning.

This approach was attempted in a multidisciplinary academic course combining the worlds of medicine and law, but in my view, its value extends to many other fields and can make a real difference.

56.

"Over My Dead Body"

The excellent technical officer of HaEmek squadron at Ramat David Airbase, Yizik Nahum, was about to complete his tenure, and in light of the great importance of the position, I began an intensive search for a suitable and worthy candidate.

The candidate I chose was an officer from Tel Nof Airbase named Yossi Meir. Although his background and professional experience were in a slightly different field, I concluded that he was the most suitable person to lead the technical section of the squadron thanks to his unique personality, approach to people, professional expertise, and organizational skills.

At a meeting with the base commander, I announced my intention to appoint Yossi as the squadron's technical officer. Also participating in the meeting was the commander of the maintenance squadron, the highest professional authority at the base in the technical field, who thought of himself (erroneously...) as responsible for appointing technical officers within the operational squadrons, even though he was not their commander. The technical officer of each squadron was subordinate to the commander of that squadron and not to the commander of the maintenance squadron, just as the armament officer in an armored battalion is subordinate to the battalion commander and not to the brigade ordnance officer.

The commander of the maintenance squadron, a man who took himself painfully seriously, leaned towards me with his head tilted forward, his body language threatening, and said:

"Over my dead body would I let you do that."

I replied: "You can lie down right now..."

The base commander felt very uncomfortable in this situation, since the commander of the maintenance squadron held a very central role, rightly so, and his view usually carried a great deal of weight when it came to staffing technical officers in the squadrons. It was very unconventional to do anything in these areas contrary to his opinion.

I spoke with the base commander and insisted, as the technical officer's direct commander, that Yossi Meir would come to our squadron.

And so it was.

Yossi led the technical section of the squadron impressively. He continued to advance up the IAF's technical ladder and became the commander of the maintenance squadron at Ramat David airbase, commander of the Israeli Air Force Technical School, and head of the aircraft and helicopters department of the Equipment Group, which is responsible for the maintenance and operational fitness of all aircraft in the IAF.

Yossi's fingerprints are all over the air force, even today.

Not surprisingly, when it had already become clear that Yossi Meir was a very talented officer and a true professional, the person who had strongly opposed the appointment said that Yossi was his choice...

57.

I Really Want You

When Lieutenant Colonel Ram Moshe Ravad entered the position of Air Force Chief Rabbi, I called him in for a conversation and asked him what he was in charge of.

Rabbi Ravad answered, "Sabbath observance and kosher food."

I said, "You are relieved from your duty."

"Why?" he asked.

I replied, "We are the Air Force of the State of Israel. On Shabbat, we will do what needs to be done, and we will not do whatever is unnecessary. As for kosher food, that's all we eat right now on our bases, and it will stay that way. So, why do I need you?"

Rabbi Ravad, who had studied at the prestigious Hebron Yeshiva and was the epitome of a *haredi* (ultra-Orthodox Jew), was a terrific guy with a prodigious roguish streak, and he responded, "Then what do you want from me?"

I replied, "It's important to me that you deal with something completely different, much more meaningful. I want you to invest in the joining of hearts — bring people closer together."

"What do you mean?" he asked.

I said, "I want you to bring *haredim*[4] to the Air Force."

After all, the *haredim* have somewhat of a stereotypical reputation: that they do not want to work and do not want the State of Israel to exist.

I am a heretic when it comes to these two statements.

---

4. "Haredim" is the plural form of the Hebrew word for ultra-Orthodox Jews, the singular form being "haredi."

I've never met parents who don't want to support their children and their families. This is human nature.

And when you talk to *haredim* one-on-one, without other people around — and I've spoken with quite a lot of *haredim* one-on-one — you find that they are no different. They want to make a living and love the country just as much as non-*haredim* do.

After all, who is a *haredi*?

There is a high probability that the grandfather or great-grandfather of each and every one of us was *haredi*.

They didn't fall from the moon...

We chose the path that suits us, and they chose their own path.

Rabbi Ravad asked, "How can we get *haredim*?"

I said, "We can, we can... go get them..."

I promised him that I, personally, as commander of the Air Force, would do everything possible to help the process succeed. Wherever I was needed, I would be at the disposal of the project.

We were off.

I accompanied Rabbi Ravad to see all the great rebbes and rabbis, and they became convinced that my intentions were genuine. There was a win-win-win-win situation here: for these young folks individually, for the *haredi* community, for the Air Force, and for the State of Israel.

Air Force personnel, who had already begun tending to the issue a few months earlier, tackled the project enthusiastically alongside Rabbi Ravad.

We called the program Blue Dawn.

The inaugural class, consisting of seventeen people, was set to report to the IAF Technical School in Haifa to undergo training and be assigned to technological positions in the Air Force.

I decided I would come and meet them on their first day.

Normally, a visit from an IAF chief is a fairly dramatic event and tremendously exciting for the soldiers and officers involved, and not because my name is Shkedy... However, the *haredim* who had just enlisted had no idea who I was.

I told them, "I came here as commander of the Air Force to tell you only one thing: **I really want you.**

"We will make sure that you can integrate and continue to maintain your lifestyle — whether it is in food, prayers, living environment, or anything else. If you need a higher standard of kosher food, that's what you'll get. If you want all of your instructors to be male rather than female, that's how it'll be."

They successfully completed the course and were sent to Palmachim Airbase.

After a short while, the commanders there told me, "Only send us soldiers like these — dedicated, professional, with sky-high motivation."

We continued full throttle.

A few months later, I called Rabbi Ravad and told him, "The project is progressing nicely. Now I want you to bring Harvard, Yale, and Princeton graduates to the Air Force as well."

"What do you mean?" Rabbi Ravad asked, not really understanding what I wanted from him. What did *haredi* recruitment have to do with the most prestigious universities in the United States?

"I want you to bring to the Air Force the graduates of the best *yeshivas* in Israel such as Hebron, Ponevezh — the *haredi* Harvard,'" I explained.

"Sir, that mission is really impossible," the rabbi answered.

I said, "We can, we can... go get them... I trust you."

The move did not arouse much enthusiasm in the General Staff, to say the least.

We presented our plan to the Manpower Directorate, which is in charge of all IDF recruitment.

A very senior officer there, who didn't like the idea, glared at me in the most unfriendly manner and said, "Over my dead body will I let you do this."

I replied without blinking:

"You can lie down right now..."

Our ancestor Abraham couldn't find one righteous man in Sodom, but I was more fortunate. Major General Ami Shafran, a pleasant, determined, and principled man, was then the head of the IDF's Computer and Information Technology Directorate.

I said to him: "Ami, what's it to you? We'll get excellent people who, despite not knowing English and mathematics, are exceptionally bright and able to study Talmud twelve hours a day. We'll teach them English, math, and computers, and then the sky's the limit."

"I'm with you," said Ami.

And so it was.

Rabbi Ravad found twenty-five graduates of leading *yeshivot*. I went to meet them. They were all married men, each with a child or two or even three.

I told them, "I really want you. We will make sure you learn English, math, and computers, and we will do everything to make you successful."

In the hall were plaques with simple arithmetic exercises and with basic English words used for programming alongside their translation into Hebrew. These were things they had never encountered in yeshiva, but it turns out that those who can study Talmud can also learn mathematics, English, and computers at a high level. The motivation with which they came, and the logical thought processes they had imbued in them after years in yeshiva, covered the gaps in their general knowledge. Indeed, they completed the course, most of them with honors, and integrated into central positions in the IAF in the field of computing, such as Ofek, our technological-operational unit. They served with graduates of the Talpiot program for gifted people, with graduates of the Atuda program for academics, and with other talented people.

Bringing us all closer and a joining of hearts, in every sense.

Their contribution to the Air Force, and to the security of the state in general, was significant. Some of them later won the most important awards of the defense establishment, such as the Israel Defense Prize, the Air Force Commander's Award, and more.

It was exciting to see how far they had come.

Every Memorial Day, I go to Pilots' Mountain near Jerusalem, the memorial site for the fallen soldiers of the IAF. One of the things that touches me most is that after the ceremony, *haredi* soldiers approach me and tell me about their work and integration into the Air Force. They even organized a special Memorial Day ceremony attended by *haredim* — people who previously never stopped for the siren that sounds on that day.

Ultimately, the rest of the IDF realized their excellent potential and began to introduce *haredim* into other branches as well: the Intelligence Directorate, the Navy, and more.

Some years later, the head of the Air Force Equipment Group invited me to participate in a rank ceremony. This was quite a while after my retirement, so it seemed strange to me.

Then I realized that the recipient of the rank was a *haredi* officer.

I asked Rabbi Ravad who it was, and he told me that the individual in question had gone from a prestigious yeshiva to enlist in Blue Dawn. He went on to become an officer and was about to take on a very significant position: a project officer overseeing the IT, information systems, and cybertechnology of the F-35, the most advanced fighter aircraft in the world. His name was Meir and he personally asked me to come to the rank ceremony.

Of course, I went.

The ceremony was held in a large hall in the presence of a large audience, including a large group of *haredim* who came with their families — with black suits, big black hats and shining eyes. The event was one of true inspiration, real excitement, and tremendous pride.

One day, when I was already serving as CEO of El Al, the phone rang early in the morning, while I was on my way to work. On the line was Rabbi Ravad.

I answered the phone and asked, "Rabbi Ravad, why are you calling so early in the morning? Sure, I have to get to work, but you?"

"I couldn't resist," the rabbi answered. "I had to call you. Do you remember we were at the Manpower Directorate?"

"I remember it well."

"Do you remember the senior officer from the Manpower Directorate who told you, 'Over my dead body...?' And you said, 'You can lie down right now?'"

"Sure, I remember."

"He was just interviewed on the radio and said it was his idea..."

I said to him, "You, Rabbi Ravad, have a reserved seat in heaven. If our biggest opponent is claiming the idea, you can rest assured that Blue Dawn is a great success.

"More than that: it could be that our one-time opponent has really forgotten or repressed the fact that he was dead set against it. He has since undergone a metamorphosis and now he really believes in the idea. It means that we have new partners in good faith and good deeds, which is a great thing."

Rabbi Ravad of the Air Force and Rabbi Aryeh Frenkel of El Al are two wonderful people whom I love very dearly. They have been at my side for years, and I have never encountered a problem or challenge — however complex it might be — that they have not found a solution for. Never. They know that I look for solutions, not explanations as to why something is impossible.

Saying "no" or "you can't" is the easy way out.

• • •

When you embark on an unconventional endeavor and go against the flow, usually only you — and maybe one more person, on a good day — think it's a good idea. At least ninety percent of the people will oppose the move, openly or beneath the surface, summoning signs and wonders to show that the initiative is a waste of time and money with zero chance of success. Another, smaller group, will adopt a wait-and-see attitude, watching which way the wind blows from the veranda.

If the move has some success and the results are reasonable, some of this latter group will declare it a good idea, while some of the larger group of vehement opponents will come out to the veranda, as it were, to see which way the wind is blowing. If the initial success fizzles out, they can always do an about-face and return to the camp of hardened opposition.

And what is the best proof that a certain move has finally been deemed an unambiguous success, that a farfetched idea turned out to be brilliant?

When the biggest opponent claims it is his idea...

58.

The Audition

When I was in the first phase of my pilot's course, a rumor circulated among the cadets that it had been decided to make a movie about the Israeli Air Force and that some of us would participate in it.

There was great excitement.

The rumor turned out to be true, and one day all the cadets in the pilot's course were taken out to the parade ground, so that the director could choose those of us who looked like future pilots and would be suitable to participate in the film.

The flight school's master sergeant — who scared us all to death — and the director, who was a famous filmmaker and whose face was familiar to us from the newspapers, walked up and down the ranks, looking at each of us.

We stood excited and tense, and each of us hoped with all our hearts that he would be chosen, assuming that it said something about his skills, abilities, and future as a pilot in the IAF.

There were cadets who were asked to leave formation and wait on the sidelines. They were the lucky ones who had passed the audition.

There were cadets whom they lingered by for a moment, examining their appearance meticulously but then moving on. That is, they vacillated but decided no...

And there were cadets whom they walked past in a hurry; they didn't look, didn't examine, didn't hesitate. In other words, there was nothing to talk about, they just didn't fit the role.

I was one of the latter. They breezed past me without blinking and without lingering even for a second.

At that moment, the thought struck me: I'm not fit to be a pilot. It's only a matter of time before I'm kicked out of the course.

In retrospect, quite a few cadets who were skipped by the director and the master sergeant and were not found suitable to star in the film ended up standing on the parade ground and receiving their pilot's wings.

Appearance matters for cinematic purposes, and perhaps some others.

Not for aviation.

59.
Attacking the Enemy's Rear

The Second Lebanon War was raging.

The General Staff discussed the execution of a commando operation deep in enemy territory.

The objective was to launch a ground attack in the area of Baalbek in Lebanon's Beqaa Valley, a Hezbollah stronghold where its men were supposed to feel safe. It was an operation with the potential to harm terrorists, take prisoners, destroy weapons, gather intelligence, and have a profound psychological impact that could undermine the enemy's security. These were not easy days for the IDF in particular and for the State of Israel in general.

The ground forces fought fierce battles in southern Lebanon, with many dead and wounded. Hezbollah's barrages of missiles and rockets caused heavy casualties and damage to the home front as well. The criticism of the way the fighting was conducted was harsh. The feeling was that everything was stuck; that chaos and disorder reigned.

In this reality, I also thought that a commando operation deep in Hezbollah-controlled territory could have a considerable impact, imagining what it would do to Hezbollah terrorists on the front lines when they realize their safe space, their home front, has been raided.

Although it was unprecedented, I suggested to IDF Chief of Staff Dan Halutz that the IAF plan and command the operation.

Halutz accepted my offer and appointed me to lead the attack.

Ordinarily, it would have taken several months to a year to plan such an operation and train for it. This time, we only had two weeks.

This was the first time that the IAF, during wartime, planned and directed such a complex combined ground and air operation. Together with the operational units, the planning was led by Colonel Yoram Yoffe, commander of the IAF's Special Air Forces, an experienced officer and professional expert in ground combat; and by Colonel Oded, an excellent man and an officer whom I trusted very much. Oded, formerly the head of the IAF's Operations Department, had been serving as the army's attaché in Switzerland, and he returned to Israel when the war broke out, so I assigned him to plan the complex air mission.

With us was Brigadier General (later Major General) Tal Russo, an expert in the field of commando operations, who was tasked by Halutz to coordinate special operations during the war.

Colonel Nitzan Alon was appointed commander of the ground force. Alon was formerly the commander of Sayeret Matkal,[5] and later became a Major General as well.

It was one of the largest and most complex commando operations in the history of the IDF, with dozens of aircraft and about one hundred and eighty fighters from the elite of our military, led by the commanders of the units themselves:

- Shaldag — the commando unit of the Air Force, under the command of Itai Yehudai;
- Sayeret Matkal — the commando unit of the Intelligence Directorate, commanded by Oded Rauer;
- 669 — the IAF's Combat Rescue and Airborne Evacuation Unit, under the command of Boaz Hershkovitz.

Every IAF participated in the aerial part of the operation: helicopters, transport aircraft, fighter jets, and unmanned aerial vehicles.

The tasks assigned to them included transporting and inserting the commandos, providing support fire, and gathering intelligence, as

---

5. Sayeret Matkal is roughly similar to the US military's Delta Force.

well as command and control. The operation was conducted at a time when the enemy was on high alert, the area was ablaze, and everyone had their finger on the trigger, so it was very sensitive and risky.

I felt that I and the entire Air Force had a heavy responsibility on our shoulders.

I fully understood the implications in the event that things got messy, both in terms of human life and in terms of the impact on the war and on the State of Israel.

Because of the unique situation, my main emphasis as IAF commander was on planning and carrying out the operation like a dogfight, with no compromise: reaching the target zone, carrying out the mission in a purposeful and aggressive manner, and disengaging as quickly as possible.

Command and control of the operation was conducted from two adjacent control rooms: one for the phase of aerial activity, and the other for the commando operation on the ground. As overall commander of the operation, I moved between the two rooms accordingly, along with the head of the air division at the time, Johanan Locker, as well as Tal Russo and many other good people who specialized in planning, intelligence, and command and control.

The tension was enormous.

Despite the high risk and the considerable potential for entanglement, the operation ended successfully and without casualties on our side. Its results were eliminating terrorists, taking prisoners, destroying and collecting weapons, and gathering intelligence information. It's all thanks to the excellent troops on the ground and in the air, proper organization and implementation, and an impressive integration of ground and air forces.

• • •

In hindsight, analyzing the outcome, the operation did not change the campaign. But I think it had long-term significance for our enemies and not only in Lebanon. We sent them a clear message: We will reach you, wherever you are — from the air, from the sea, and from the ground. Even in the most unexpected places.

60.

Samson's Foxes

I met Danny Stapleton when he was head of the security division at El Al. A tall and handsome man, impressive in appearance, but no less so in his soulfulness and great sensitivity.

One day we met at a wedding. "I want you to come and see a place I'm sure you'll love," Danny told me.

We set it up, met, and drove together to Kibbutz[6] Tzuba in the Jerusalem corridor. When we arrived at the kibbutz, Danny took me to meet Jumba (Alon Grinbaum), a special person who is all heart. Jumba told me his difficult life story, described his path through learning difficulties and disappointments and how he learned to read, with difficulty, at a really late age.

In the army, he served in the reconnaissance unit of the Nahal Brigade, of which Danny Stapleton was the commander. Following a circuitous path, Jumba finally made it to officer school, graduated, and became the weapons officer of the reconnaissance unit.

Danny said that Jumba performed his role commendably.

A few years after being discharged, Jumba decided to devote his time to people with special needs: children on the autistic spectrum; the blind; those with other disabilities, physical and mental. One of the projects he initiated was an accessible grove offering challenging and educational activities for children with special needs. This complex in Kibbutz Tzuba, the "Children's

---

6. A kibbutz is a type of settlement that is unique to Israel. A collective community, traditionally agrarian.

Island Grove," was established by the kibbutz's farmers and young people, featuring accessible facilities such as a carousel and swings, a shooting gallery with paintballs, soccer goals, an arts-and-crafts corner, a tabun for baking pita bread and more. The children who went there experienced real moments of happiness.

During the tour of the grove, I told myself that I had to help them. I still didn't know how...

Later on, we met with the young men and women who were doing a year of national volunteer service before enlistment, who told us with excitement and enthusiasm about the things they were doing as part of Jumba's project for children with special needs. True giving, wholeheartedly.

At the end of the tour, we arrived at the "activity house," from where the activities for the children and youth with special needs are coordinated. To my surprise, the place was full of wooden benches.

Lots of benches.

"What are these?" I asked.

It turned out this was the special handiwork of the "Samson's Foxes" group, which consisted of youth on the autistic spectrum. The benches were built as part of the carpentry club, with the assistance of the volunteers doing their year of national service; and selling them helped finance the activities there.

I looked at the benches and sat down on some of them. They were comfortable and there seemed to be a lot of attention and love put into making each of them.

When I saw these wonderful young people and their lovely project, I knew what I wanted to do. But at that point, I didn't say a word.

The next day, I told Danny that I wanted to buy all the benches I'd seen and have them make more, which I'd purchase as well.

I had two requests:

One, that the Foxes knew that all the benches they had built had been sold and that they had created something valuable.

Two, that each of them would sign their name on the bench they built, just like an artist's signature.

This caused a lot of excitement for them and the volunteers.

I decided that I would distribute the benches to family and friends and tell them the special story about the teenagers who built them.

We picked a day, we commandeered a huge truck, we loaded the benches on it, and we left — Danny, Jumba and I — to distribute them.

Anyone who received a bench and heard the story behind it was moved to the depths of their soul.

Some decided to purchase extra benches to give to their friends.

One of the families decided that the bench would not be on the balcony but in the center of the living room, with the signatures of the artists visible. That warmed my heart.

It is a great privilege to sit on such a bench.

61.

Words That Still Ring in My Ears

I was a young officer with the rank of captain, commander of the Advanced Combat Course at flight school, the final phase of training for fighter pilots.

Toward the end of the course, I was invited to the final committee meeting headed by the commander of the flight school, where decisions are made regarding the graduates on all the tracks.

The commander of the Hatzerim Airbase at the time, Brigadier General Asher Snir, was also invited to the same discussion, and I greatly appreciated his wisdom, his composure, and his inner strength.

There was a long, in-depth, and substantive discussion about each of the cadets, and then the following issues were discussed: Who would be the outstanding cadet of the course?

There were a number of candidates, of whom two were particularly worthy and notable.

They asked my opinion.

I thought that one of them was more suitable both in terms of his personality and from the perspective of his abilities as an aviator and a professional.

I gave an impassioned speech in which I explained why he was suitable, and with the same fervor, I explained why the other candidate was not suitable.

When the hearing ended, Snir came up to me and told me words that ring in my ear until today:

"Never, but never, put down one person to raise up another."
How right he was.

62.

The Mikveh

When I was commander of the Air Force, I received a somewhat strange and unusual request: to establish a *mikveh*, or ritual bath, at the Ovda Airbase in the south.

Jewish tradition dictates that married women immerse themselves in a mikveh once a month to maintain family purity. It requires collecting a large amount of naturally occurring water.

There were housing units in the bases where career officers and aircrew members lived with their families, but there was no mikveh at any Air Force base.

I tried to understand what the request meant, why it was so important, and whether it was right to make such a decision.

Since I didn't understand anything about it, I consulted with the Air Force Chief Rabbi, Lieutenant Colonel Ram Moshe Ravad, and with the head of the Manpower Directorate, Major General Elazar Stern — ethical people with a broad perspective who understand the subject well.

I learned from them about the importance of a mikveh for a religious person in general, and about the significance of its absence in a remote place such as Ovda Airbase in particular.

I found out that women who kept this tradition and lived in family housing were forced to immerse themselves in a mikveh in Eilat — almost an hour's drive in each direction.

I realized that to a large extent, for traditional Jews, a mikveh is more important than a synagogue.

I felt that this was genuinely distressing for people with a worldview and lifestyle different from mine, in a field I didn't know and wasn't connected to.

After much deliberation, and despite great opposition, I decided that a mikveh would be established at Ovda, and I concluded that it would be issued as a decision of the commander of the Air Force.

A mikveh is not something that can be built from one day to the next, and in the meantime, I finished my tenure and was discharged from the army.

It took time, but in the organizational culture of the Air Force, an official decision of the commander of the Air Force will be carried out even if the individual who issued it is no longer in uniform.

After I retired, the commander of the Ovda Airbase took on the task. As a leader, he saw it as his duty and mission to take care of the people of the base whoever they were, as the father of everyone, and he went above and beyond to establish the mikveh.

He and his wife, a charming couple whom I love very much, had a tragic family story. My heart cried with them, and I found myself deeply shaken by their misfortune.

They dreamed of having healthy children, but their health situation and genetic background posed immense challenges, as they had learned from bitter experience over the years. This is not the place to elaborate on the matter but let us say that it was essential that they undergo a special series of extremely expensive tests before attempting to bring a child into the world. It was clear that it would be difficult, if not impossible, for them to deal with the issue financially. But then they learned that there was a nonprofit that subsidized these tests.

They asked for the organization's assistance, but they were told that it was a *haredi* charity and that with sincere regret, in light of the huge costs and limited resources, the assistance was available only to *haredi* families.

The base commander and his wife said nothing.

After a while, the heads of the association somehow learned about the establishment of the mikveh at Ovda, and about the significant role played by the base commander in its construction.

Following this, the nonprofit decided to pay for their tests, and the end of this tale is a happy one, filled with lovely children.

The commander of the base built the mikveh with the purest of intentions, in order to take care of his people and implement the decision of the commander of the Air Force, and not for any reason otherwise — revealed or hidden.

The work of the righteous is done by others.

63.

I Have to Talk to You

This amazing story happened when I was a deputy squadron commander, and we lived in family housing at Nevatim Airbase.

One evening, my wife went to an enrichment class she was taking on the base and I was at home.

There was a knock at the door.

I opened the door and there was a woman standing in front of me. She looked confused, with a strange look in her eyes, dressed untidily and her hair unkempt. It took me some time to figure out where I knew her from: she lived in the family housing complex and worked in my son Nimo's kindergarten.

The woman just came into our house without asking, turned off the light with the switch next to the door — luckily there was still a light on in the kitchen — and said, "I have to talk to you."

I looked at her in astonishment and said, "Okay, sit down."

I sat down as far as possible from her and said, "I'm listening."

Then she dropped a bomb:

"The base commander got me pregnant, and he abandoned me and the child in my belly. I have no one to talk to; I'm asking you to help me."

I looked at her, unable to believe my ears.

I said, "I got it. I'll take care of it."

I didn't hesitate for a second and didn't wait for my wife to come back from class. I got dressed quickly and headed to the house of the base commander, who lived opposite me.

I knocked on the door. His wife, whom I liked very much, opened the door with a big smile on her pleasant, round face.

I asked her in a serious tone if I could talk to the base commander.

The commander arrived and I started talking...

Then he told me the following incredible thing:

The woman who had come to my house had decided she was pregnant by him.

We never locked our doors in family housing at the base, like on a kibbutz, and she would come into their home, enter without invitation, walk down the long hallway to their bedroom, lie on the bed, caress her belly, and talk loudly about the child she and the base commander were expecting.

She did it every day, even when they were at home.

She was not pregnant, neither from the base commander nor from anyone else. She was simply ill, and eventually was hospitalized in a psychiatric ward and received treatment.

It was a very complex situation on the base in general and in the family housing in particular. The sensitivity with which the base commander and his wife handled the situation aroused in me a great appreciation for them, which I still feel to this day.

•••

When something seems delusional and incomprehensible to you, reality can be even more delusional.

It is very possible that there are things you do not know...

64.

The Essence of the 'Great Trip'

When I was the CEO at El Al, a young officer from the Duvdevan anti-terrorist unit named Gili Cohen approached me and told me that he had an idea. He wanted to set up a meeting with me.

We met.

Gili, a tall and impressive guy, began to tell me with bright eyes and tremendous passion about the idea born while traveling with his wife in the Far East.

The "Great Trip" had become almost a mandatory rite of passage in the lives of young Israelis after their discharge from the IDF. Gili's dream was for these young men and women to incorporate an element of volunteering with local children and teenagers into their globetrotting post-military travels. He asked me to be the "father" of the project.

I immediately fell in love with the idea. I was excited to see a man at the beginning of his career and adult life, amid arduous service in an elite unit, dreaming of giving back to others from a pure and sincere place.

I didn't hesitate for a second and decided to accept the challenge.

And that's how the "Heroes for Life"[7] project was launched.

To promote the project and make it a reality, we made several important decisions:

    1.   The program would be open to anyone after their military or

---

7. In Hebrew: "Lohamim Lelo Gvulot."

national service, regardless of religion, race, or gender.

2. Every year, delegations would go to several locations around the world, and each delegation would be named after one of the IDF's fallen soldiers.

3. The following year, we would return to the same places to continue accompanying the children and helping them progress, but we would also reach new places. Follow-up missions would keep the names of the fallen soldiers so that their memories would be perpetuated for years.

4. Before their trips abroad, members of the delegation would volunteer for a few days in youth villages in Israel.

5. All graduates of the program who participated in delegations abroad would become part of an ongoing club of sorts, allowing them to continue to give, contribute, and volunteer.

Our message was that the volunteering and giving element ought to be the most important and significant part of the Great Trip. After being discharged from military or national service, young people want to "discharge" too: travel, see the world, drink, smoke — and especially to unburden, let loose, and clear their heads, with the focus being on themselves. Volunteering is giving to others, and therefore it is fundamentally different.

The first delegation, which left for India, consisted of seventeen people. Since there were no volunteers yet, most of them were from the project's founding team. But the news quickly passed by word of mouth, and almost everyone who heard about the idea asked to join.

We developed additional ways to spread the word—from hanging a huge sign alongside the Jerusalem-Tel Aviv highway through social media advertising to meetings with recently discharged soldiers. But the most important ambassadors for the project were those who participated in the program and enthusiastically told their friends about it.

Indeed, in short order, the demand reached enormous proportions. We had thirty applicants for each available spot. In other words, when we put together a delegation of twenty, we had six-hundred people vying for it. We had to turn applicants away at a certain point, as otherwise, we might have had two thousand trying to get into a program for thirty.

Some of the volunteers based their Great Trip itineraries on where they would be going within the framework of the program. Most of them did their volunteering activities at the beginning of the trip, while others did so at later stages. Clearly, combining the two was feasible. Moreover, some departed with their delegations, volunteered, and then returned to Israel without another stop on their Great Trip...

Within five years, we were sending fifteen delegations a year to countries in Asia, South America, and Africa, including India, Nepal, Vietnam, Myanmar, Ethiopia, South Africa, Uganda, Brazil, Argentina, Guatemala, Mexico, Peru, Chile, and Ecuador. Each delegation consisted of between twenty and thirty-five volunteers. There were places we reached five times in a row, year after year.

Even when the COVID-19 pandemic was at its height, we continued the project — but in Israel instead of abroad, and instead of integrating it into the Great Trip, it was combined with a trek along the Israel National Trail. Young men and women, backpackers who had completed their military service, volunteered in Beit Shean, Kiryat Shmona, Ramle, Ashkelon, and other places.

Bishvil Israel,[8] **in both senses of the term — on the Israel National Trail** (bishvil), **and on behalf of the people of Israel** (bishvil).

As expected, political elements tried to hitch a ride on the project and appropriate the hard work and success. Not on my watch. I do not consent in any way that these young people be labeled politically or that politicians "take them for a spin."

To this day, I meet and talk to each delegation before it embarks. I

---

8. In Hebrew, the Israel National Trail is called "Shvil Yisrael." Meanwhile, "on behalf of" in Hebrew is "bishvil."

feel that I have a great privilege, and this brings me incredible joy. It's a thrill every single time to see these wonderful young men and women, people with huge hearts and wonderful souls, acting out of a sense of purpose and a genuine desire to give. First and foremost, they represent themselves as human beings, as well as the State of Israel and the Jewish people. They are exemplars of virtue, morality, and unconditional giving to every single person, regardless of religion, race, or gender.

They are the beautiful face of Israel, a "light unto the nations" in the deepest sense.

65.
The Volcanic Ash Cloud

When I was appointed CEO of El Al in early 2010, I decided to visit each of the company's destinations around the world, more than thirty cities. My goal was to get to know the company's representatives and people abroad and learn in-depth about what was happening in those places and the issues relevant to each country from El Al's perspective.

The president of the country at the time, Shimon Peres, whom I knew from the time I was commander of the Israel Air Force, was just about to fly to Paris and invited me to join and attend several ceremonies and events with him.

Since I planned to go to Paris anyway, one of El Al's main destinations, this was an opportunity to combine the two.

So I went.

It was a very important trip for El Al and fascinating on a personal level as well. It was a special experience to go with the president of Israel to Élysée Palace, the official residence of the president of France, to see the admiration and respect with which he was greeted and to hear him speak in fluent French.

On one of the days, Peres and I walked the streets of Paris and chatted. It was always interesting to hear his perspective on what was happening in Israel and around the world.

Suddenly, while we were walking down the street, an El Al official came running, panting and gasping, and said he needed to talk to me urgently.

I asked what happened and he said there had been a huge volcanic eruption in Iceland; the ash cloud was spreading rapidly toward the European mainland and there was a real fear that it might shut down civil aviation. The airports in Paris, the representative said, were expected to close that night.

It was clear to me that we were facing a complex event necessitating centralized management and coordination from the company's headquarters in Israel, so I had to return to Israel immediately on the next flight.

One can decide when to shut down an airport, but knowing when it will reopen is another story — especially in such a situation, when a volcanic ash cloud threatens to cover the skies of Europe.

Israel's Memorial Day and Independence Day were days away, and it was clear to everyone that the president ought to be in the country at such a time. He could not be stuck in Paris.

I recommended that he cut short his visit to France and return to Israel with me.

Peres was very reluctant, but he consulted with his staff and eventually decided to return with me.

We took care of the necessary arrangements and quickly left for Charles de Gaulle Airport.

At the entrance to the airport, we were greeted by El Al's station manager in Paris, Rani Omer, a true professional, a man with a heart of gold and graying hair. It was hard to miss the considerable commotion. Crowds of people stood next to El Al's check-in stand, shouting and crying.

"Shkedy, don't go over there. They'll kill you," Rani told me.

"Why? What's the issue?" I asked.

Rani replied, "The airport in London is closed. We told the people stuck there to try to get to Paris by car, through the Channel Tunnel (La Manche) or any other way, and we'd try to get them on a flight to Israel from here. And now that they've arrived here, they realize there's no guarantee that everyone will have a place on the flight."

I told Rani, "Of course I have to be here, with the people. A leader is a leader and that is what is expected of me. This is very important for both El Al personnel and passengers. People have tried to kill me quite a few times in the past and failed... Don't worry, let's go over to them."

We walked toward the passengers who had gathered in front of the check-in stand. They really were very upset. People were crying, shouting, and accusing us: "Why did you make us travel by car from England? You screwed this up!"

I listened to their claims and told them:

"Do you know the difference between us and other airlines?

"The other companies, once they realized the situation, took the keys and threw them into the ocean. They actually told their passengers: 'You're on your own. Go figure out alone what to do.'

"We, at El Al, have not left, are not leaving, and will not leave you, no matter how complex the situation is. We will search for solutions and find them.

"I promise you that we will do everything to get you on a flight to Israel as fast as we can."

The atmosphere calmed down a bit, but in the meantime, a new problem arose: It turned out that there was great chaos in Paris, and it was impossible to secure overnight accommodations. There was a real fear that they would be stuck in Paris for a very long time without a place to sleep.

Drama.

What to do?...

Then Rani approached me together with Dror Levy, El Al's security officer in Paris, who clearly had the weight of keeping us all safe resting on his firm shoulders.

"Tell them we won't leave anyone at the airport," they told me. "If we can't get them on a flight, they'll be hosted and accommodated in the homes of El Al personnel. We'll manage."

I was thrilled.

I gathered all the passengers and told them, "If we can't get you on board a flight today, we'll put you up in the homes of El Al personnel."

Silence.

At that moment they realized that our slogan was not just advertising: El Al really is "The most at home in the world." It's not something you can find anywhere else.

In the end, Rani managed to get everyone on flights, to this day I don't know how...

We all flew to Israel before the airport closed.

The volcanic ash cloud continued to spread. Airports across Europe were shut down and air transport was almost completely paralyzed. We had long discussions about how to deal with the complex situation.

All the other airlines simply "closed shop," canceled flights, and left their passengers to fend for themselves.

We, at El Al, decided to open five hubs from airports in Europe that had not been closed. We informed all our passengers who had a plane ticket to Israel from anywhere in Europe to drive or ride to one of the five open airports, and from there we would fly them to Israel.

We conducted it like a military operation: thousands of people, who traveled hundreds or even thousands of miles to reach the five open airports, were returned to Israel by an "airlift" of El Al planes. No one was left behind.

It was very moving to see them and hear their reactions. "My father, a Holocaust survivor who traveled to Germany with a number of friends for the Holocaust Day ceremony, also found themselves trapped in Germany and were so happy to return home last night," wrote Sherry, the daughter of one of the passengers.

As expected in such cases, I received a call from several well-known people, influential people with connections and finances, who asked us to put them on our flights. At first, I didn't understand why they were calling. I explained to them the format of the airlift we were carrying out and assured them that the matter was being dealt with; that we would make sure to return all El Al passengers to Israel.

Then it turned out that most of the people who called me were not El Al passengers at all and that they had tickets from other companies. Some of them offered huge sums of money for us to put them on our flights.

I listened thoughtfully and answered calmly, "Anyone who has an El Al ticket, from anywhere in Europe, is the first priority. I promise you that if any seats remain, we will gladly accommodate you too."

El Al and its people are truly the most at home in the world. You can see it, particularly during crises.

66.

May I Wish You a Happy Holiday?

My father had a custom that my sister Yael and I really liked.

Twice a year, before Rosh Hashanah[9] and before Passover, we'd
take a ride with him in the car for a "Happy Holiday Tour."

It was a regular circuit of friends whom Dad loved and who
loved him, and it was important for him to greet them personally,
face-to-face.

My parents had a circle of good friends, a loving, happy, and
cheerful group. I remembered each and every one of them very well,
as well as their children.

And there was another circle of people who knew my father from
a completely different place, whom I also remember very well.

I remember Shifra and Avraham Friedler, for whom my father
harbored a special place in his heart. When he was lonely in Israel,
without a family or anything else to his name, they took care of him
and helped him get settled in Ramatayim, find work in a children's
institute, and get on the right path.

I remember Bracha and Avri Vardi, Holocaust survivors from
Hungary, like Dad, who together with their children Noam and
Shimon were our "family" in the deepest sense of the word, even
though we had no biological connection. Avri was a lovely man who
was always willing to help wholeheartedly; Bracha was a woman
whose warmth was enveloping, with a heavy Hungarian accent.

---

9. The Jewish New Year.

An excellent cook, she prepared, especially for Dad, Hungarian delicacies which reminded him of home, like stuffed peppers, lecsó (vegetable stew), and more.

In every home we went to, we were greeted with great joy and genuine interest. Before Passover, they would give Yael and me nuts; and before Rosh Hashanah, they would give us sweets.

We eagerly looked forward to this tour.

Also, about a week before the holiday, Dad would get in touch with wider circles of friends and acquaintances.

There was something lovely about what Dad did intuitively.

He met them, listened to them, or called them specifically. Dad felt that there was no substitute for a face-to-face meeting — or at least ear-to-ear through the phone.

Growing up, I adopted my father's custom, at least partially...

Before the holidays, I make sure to call friends, colleagues, and people dear to me from different circles.

There is something powerful about hearing a person's voice and listening to it. It is possible to feel people and read them between the lines, even without speaking at great length.

This is fundamentally different from "technical" correspondence via WhatsApp or SMS, and it indicates a deep connection and empathy.

In these conversations, I take great care not to talk to them about work, business, and the like, but instead to show interest in how they feel, how the family and children are doing, and their plans and dreams for the future. The things that really matter.

These conversations put things in proportion, providing reasons for optimism while strengthening the relationship.

I know there are many who await these calls. Me too.

Some of my friends say they simply can't start the holiday without this conversation...

I never wait for them to call me; rather, I call everyone I want to hear myself. And I do it early, long before the holiday. The call in and of itself is important, no matter what is said in it.

Who the F*ck Is Michael?!

It makes me happy to see my children also continuing the tradition.

So... may I wish you a happy holiday?

67.
Elijah the Prophet in Budapest

My father's life story is an amazing and unimaginable one.

He was born in Hungary in a village called Tolcsva and moved alone to Budapest.

In 1944, when he was nineteen, he jumped off the death train. "I jumped into complete darkness and after catching my breath, I heard the shouts of soldiers guarding another transport," he later said. "There was a brakeman's cabin on an empty wagon, and that's where I sought shelter for the night. Still, it was so cold I had to jump on one leg all night so I'd be able to walk the next morning."

When day broke and he made his way to town, he was surprised by an old man with a wagon who suddenly popped up from one of the alleys. "I asked him if I could help him, and he was happy to accept my offer. We each grabbed a handle of his cart, and as we walked, I saw that there were millions of leaflets scattered on the ground... All the streets were full of Nazi soldiers, and on every corner, the soldiers asked the old man I was escorting for his papers.

"Luckily, I didn't look Jewish, which helped me get out of about twenty inspections by the soldiers, who thought I was just a grandson helping my grandfather. When I said goodbye to him, he asked what he could pay me for the help. I said in my heart: 'You saved my life, and now you want to pay me too?' Omer, my grandson, says it wasn't just an old man, but it was Elijah the prophet with a cart."

So, through quite a circuitous route, Dad made his way to the Glass House in Budapest, which the Swiss consulate used to provide shelter for some three thousand Jews. In light of his appearance, as a blond boy with curls and a jutting nose, Dad's job in the Glass House was to go out every day to hand out *Schutzpass* documents (forged Swiss certificates) to Jews throughout Budapest, with the hope that it might help and save them.

Every day he went out, he didn't know if he would come back.

When the war ended, my father returned to his village and waited for someone from his family to return.

Almost two years passed.

Then he realized:

"I've been left alone in the world."

He decided to immigrate to Israel.

Since then, and throughout his life, he was accompanied by one open question; a question that remained unanswered, which would not let him go and would not let him rest; a question he asked himself all the time and asked us too, his children:

"Why did I survive while my whole family was murdered and burned in Auschwitz?"

I said, "Dad, you weren't with your family. You jumped off the train when they were not with you. What could you have done?"

It didn't help.

In 2007, when I was commander of the IAF, we attacked and destroyed the Syrian nuclear reactor. At the end of the operation, I received a personal letter from Prime Minister Ehud Olmert. He wrote warm and moving words about the Air Force and its men, about the impressive determination, planning, and execution, and about the significance of attacking the reactor for the continued existence of the State of Israel and the Jewish people.

Olmert, who knew my father's life story, added in his own handwriting at the end of the letter:

"Warm regards to Dad."

For more than a decade, the State of Israel did not officially admit that it was behind the attack on the reactor, so the issue remained very secret, and I could not talk about it with anyone, not even with myself...

I decided not to show the letter to my father.

• • •

The years passed, and at the beginning of 2015, I realized that my father, this beloved, brave, and resolute man, was at the end of his path in life. He didn't speak, but from the deep look in his eyes and from his body language, it was clear that he understood everything.

I felt it was the right time.

I came to him, showed him Olmert's letter, and read it to him.

Dad didn't say a word, but tears trickled down from his deep blue eyes.

I saw that he was relieved.

He passed away a short time later.

I don't know if it's true or not, but I felt that for the first time in his life, he got an answer to the unanswered question that had accompanied him all his life: Why did he survive?

●●●

Dad was involved in education all his life, and not by chance.

He was a man for whom freedom was the essence of his life and in whom existed a deep tension between that freedom, on the one hand, and his deep commitment and belonging, on the other — to his family, his country, and his people.

A Jew who grew up and studied in the Diaspora, but for whom the Diaspora did not subdue his character, his inner strength, and his mental fortitude, and he never effaced himself in front of another person.

He was entirely a Hebrew man, a free Jew, everywhere and in his country, Israel.

This special combination, and his ability to allow contrasts to dwell harmoniously within him, gave him inner strength, enhanced his ability to touch every person he encountered, and instilled deep meaning in his life.

The family of people whom Dad loved and who loved him, wherever he went, was large and unique.

It was fascinating to see how Dad managed to make people, at any age and in any place, feel good about themselves first.

As someone who managed to escape a terrible abyss, he gave

people the feeling that life was beautiful, taught them that one should always look forward but never forget what was; that everything is possible, and that you don't have to be afraid of anything.

He was a hopeless optimist, sensitive, determined, and full of *joie de vivre*, and always saw life in proportion. "There are problems and there are difficult and complex struggles," he used to say, "but when you think about where we were then and where we are now, you have to look at things in proportion."

Everything in proportion.

We are in the midst of a great miracle — the resurrection of the State of Israel.

The fact that I am alive is a miracle.

The fact that we are all alive is a miracle.

Some of us have a family story similar to my father's. Others have a different story, but it is also a miracle. And there are those whose miracle was greater, because the Nazis and their accomplices simply did not have time to reach the countries where their families lived; like my mother, Nechama, who was born in Egypt.

Let's not confuse the matter: if they had reached those places, the same thing would have happened.

One fate awaited us all.

● ● ●

My sister Yael and I had the privilege of being the children of our father Moshe and our mother Nechama. To follow the path they outlined for us. To believe, to dream, to do, not to be afraid, to love.

Maybe we managed to make Dad happy with what we were able to accomplish and do.

We certainly managed to bring him joy and happiness with wonderful and amazing grandchildren: Nimo, Maya, Omer, Yotam, Gal, and Ben, each of whom follows in the footsteps of Grandpa Moshe in their own way.

Unfortunately, Dad is no longer with us, but I believe he looks down at us and watches over us from the heavens.

68.

What Is Important, Not What Is Considered Important

Our basketball team, which consisted of students from the STEM and humanities tracks, reached the finals of the basketball championships at Katznelson High School in Kfar Saba, a rather impressive achievement in light of our meager abilities in basketball.

There was no doubt at all that the opposing team was far superior to ours. We had a large but agile point guard named Danny Horowitz; and we had a very good player named Amos "Kopla" Kopolovitz, not very tall but athletic, quiet but sharp and goal-oriented, with a deceptively shy smile. Everyone else, including myself, were mediocre players and below. Really nothing to write home about...

The team that came to play against us in the finals had a superb roster and above all a big star whose reputation preceded him in our high school, Pinny Biton — a skinny kid who was loved by everyone, including us, quick as a cat and able to snipe from anywhere on the court.

In preparation for the final game, we debated what to do.

We planned the "battle" and decided on two significant things:

Offensively, we needed to clear a path for Kopla to get to his favorite spots on the floor; he just knew how to score much better than all of us.

Whereas defensively, because I was quite good at soccer (far better than basketball...), I assumed the task of locking Pinny down in "any way possible." In other words, to kick his ass.

The game was emotionally charged, back-and-forth, and quite violent.

Due to our aggressive style of play, we had few fans, so the loud crowd mostly cheered for the other team.

We fought as a team with all our might. Luckily for us, Kopla was at his peak that day, and we were able to knock Pinny off of his game just enough.

We won.

∙∙∙

In teamwork — and it doesn't matter if it's a basketball game or some other group assignment — everyone must do their part with all their heart and soul, contributing what is important and not what others consider important.

Sometimes you are the star and sometimes you do the dirty work. The victory belongs to the team.

69.
When There's a Doubt,
There's No Doubt...

Hanukkah was approaching and we decided to hold an event at the squadron's clubhouse.

The squadron had several sections, with enlisted soldiers, NCOs, and officers serving in a variety of positions: flight, technical and administrative. These are great people and professionals, each in their field, and their importance to the squadron is tremendous — no matter if their work is done on the ground or in the air.

On the very first day of the establishment of HaEmek squadron, I decided that everyone, from our enlisted men and women to NCOs and officers, would be invited to each event, and that no events would be held for separate groups.

The message was easy to understand. I made it clear without words to each and every member of the squadron how important and significant they were to me, and how each and every one of them was an integral part of the group.

And the same went for the Hanukkah party.

That evening, I arrived early at the squadron. It was a rainy winter day, but nothing seemed particularly unusual to me.

An hour later, while I was sitting in my office, Alex Gan, one of the squadron's reserve pilots who was formerly a squadron commander at Ramat David Airbase, a resident of the nearby community of Timrat, burst through the door.

"Shkedy," he said without unnecessary preamble, "there's a crazy storm. It's raining cats and dogs. There may be flooding."

I left the room and saw that Alex was right: The rain was coming down at a crazy rate. A true deluge.

I "jetted" to the clubhouse, where the squadron members were already gathering for the event, festively dressed, and I said: "We're all leaving right now, getting into cars and driving as quickly as possible to the HASs (hardened aircraft shelters) and the planes. Get into your planes as you are; we don't have time to put flight suits on. Technical section crew must quickly get the planes out of the HASs so we can start them up. The pilots will then drive them to Concourse Seven (situated beyond our squadron's territory, but on reliably high ground). The second you park a plane out there, double back to the HAS for the next one until we've gotten every last aircraft onto that high ground."

Our squadron used two types of hardened aircraft shelters:

The American HAS stores the planes more or less at runway level, meaning they can be taxied around fairly easily, without any special procedures.

The French HAS is dug deep into the ground. To extract the planes, they must be towed to a place from where they can be moved, requiring intensive and integrated work. These shelters were vulnerable to extreme weather, such as a flash flood, which could submerge the HAS and all the aircraft inside it in short order — even if the drainage system was functioning relatively well.

A torrential downpour.

All of us, technical personnel and aircrew, were soaked to the bones. We got all the planes out of the HASs, revved them up, and taxied to higher ground as quickly as we could. Then we returned to the squadron barracks to dry out and take a breather.

Shortly after we removed the planes, the HASs were completely flooded.

Alex's memory from previous flooding events on the base was essential, and there's no doubt that the deep personal connections throughout the entire squadron — from the technical wing and the

220

aviation wing — enabled us to carry out such a coordinated, concentrated, swift, and significant operation.

After we finished the aircraft rescue operation, I updated the commander of Ramat David Airbase, Avner Naveh, who was busy at the time uncorking a bottleneck at a culvert in the wadi running through the base. I told him what we had done and that things had ended well.

It was the day before Avner's wedding, which would have doubtlessly been overshadowed if our planes had turned into submarines.

Nowadays, information arrives instantaneously, but back then we had no way of knowing what was happening at other airbases.

The next day we celebrated the nuptials of Avner and the love of his life Lily — a joyous and moving affair, with the people we loved.

I noticed that a good friend of Avner's, another base commander, hadn't come to the wedding.

It turned out that he had still been busy dealing with flooding at his base, so he couldn't make it.

Got it...

• • •

When there's a doubt, there's no doubt at all — it's better to be safe than sorry.

The most important thing is to act purposefully and quickly. Worst case scenario, you've overreacted, but then you can course correct. It is better to exaggerate in the name of caution, certainly when it comes to an event with the potential for significant damage and a colossal error.

Luck is an important element in life, but it's worth giving it a helping hand...

70.
Blue Steel

One of the most significant components of the IAF's strength and capability is its technical branch. The majority of air force personnel — in the field and at headquarters — belong to it, and they have a tremendous impact on both force buildup and operational activity. Every squadron commander knows full well that their squadron's capabilities largely depend on its technical section and the support of the maintenance squadrons and headquarters.

Unfortunately, the technical sector does not always receive the great appreciation it deserves.

Technical training in the Israeli Air Force is closely related to technical education in the State of Israel, and unfortunately, the investment in technical training in Israeli schools has declined significantly over the years.

In the IAF, we decided to deal with the issue independently by launching the "Blue Steel" project.

The main idea was to open classes in high schools all over the country, from Eilat in the south to the Golan Heights in the north. In every school that was interested in it, a class of girls and boys would be established to study these subjects, with IAF personnel accompanying them. The chosen schools would be designated and branded with the IAF emblem, and the students in the program would wear uniforms. The project would draw from the knowledge base of the Air Force Technical School and its affiliates across the country.

I believe that Israel's younger generation — in the periphery and main cities, women and men, secular and religious, new immigrants and native-born — must be given a real opportunity to learn a technical profession, enlist in the Air Force, and embark on a path of accomplishment and success.

I defined the project simply and clearly:

There would be no limitations.

There would be no justifications or excuses for why it is impossible.

There would be no "Why us?" and there would be no "Why now?"

Formulate a plan, then implement it as quickly and decisively as possible.

So it was.

We embarked on a comprehensive program throughout the country. Colonel Ilan Avishai — head of the relevant department at Air Force Headquarters — and Lieutenant Colonel Ofer Atia led the charge, directing a select group of our best and brightest, displaying wisdom, resolve, and commitment with all their hearts and souls. And the results speak for themselves: dozens of schools have embraced the project, and more than fifty percent of the IAF's technicians are Blue Steel graduates. Just fantastic.

It was thrilling to see our people and their ability to promote such an important enterprise for the Air Force, for Israeli society, and for the country as a whole. The success of the project led additional branches of the IDF to pursue similar programs.

• • •

One of the places where we opened a Blue Steel class was in the periphery, in the northern town of Hatzor HaGlilit.

I arrived with IAF personnel at the Ort School there, and we met with the students, the teachers, and the principal, Alik Avner.

Alik told me with great excitement and beaming eyes that decades ago he had been a student of my mother Nechama at the school in Kfar Malal.

My mother was born in Alexandria, to a family that immigrated to Israel from what is now the country of Georgia and later moved to

Egypt. She'd had difficult experiences throughout her life and her motto was: "They are just like you." Through her actions and the way she led her life, she taught and conveyed this message to us, her children, her students, and everyone who knew her.

Alik was just carrying on her mission.

71.
Skewer

It is customary to think that the excellence of a group depends on the quality of its people and the resources at its disposal.

Of course, having excellent people and sufficient resources is a good thing.

These are necessary conditions, but they are not enough.

There are three additional prerequisites that are pivotal for group excellence.

The first condition is that the group truly functions as a group.

We know organizations that have great people and great resources, but their people are constantly busy justifying and explaining, in words or actions:

Why their job or profession is the most important,

Why the others are much less important,

Why when something succeeds it is only because of them,

And why when something doesn't pan out, everyone else is to blame...

Such an organization, despite the professional quality of its personnel and despite its many resources, will not achieve collective excellence.

On the other hand, an organization that functions as a group, whose people understand the great importance of collaborating and supporting each other, who share a common goal, who are not busy amplifying why each is more significant or more important than the other, who have respect and true appreciation for the work of each member of the group — such an organization is on the right path. The paramount task of the group leader, in their messages and actions, is to make the group's whole greater than the sum of its parts.

The second condition is that the group leader must give his or her people confidence, support, and inspiration so they can express and realize their talents and abilities, encouraging them to initiate, act, take flight, and be fearless.

The leader's messages and statements are of immense importance. "The successes are yours, the failure is mine," is a dictum that is always important for me to convey and to say to my people.

It's amazing to see what it does to people — to their commitment, their energy, their willingness to charge forward, and their sense of pride.

Your greatest accomplishment as a leader is that your people feel and know that the achievement is due to the work of each and every one of them. Success is theirs.

The third condition is that the group leader believes in his or her people and their joint ability to reach the sky — and delivers this message in a variety of ways. If that doesn't happen, they just won't get there.

If the group leader believes in his or her people, shares a dream with them, and makes them believe in the idea, in themselves and the group, they will charge forward. There is no guarantee they'll make it to the destination, but they are already on their way...

• • •

In early 1992, when we were in the midst of establishing the HaEmek Squadron as an F-16 squadron, the Skewer Competition was held. At the time, it was considered the most significant competition among the IAF's fighter squadrons. When I received the message detailing the launch of the competition, I was shocked to discover that our squadron had not been invited to participate.

I immediately called the head of the training department at Air Force Headquarters, who was in charge of the issue, and asked him why we weren't participating.

"Because you are not an operational squadron," he answered. "You're a work in progress. You've only got eight planes, not even one to spare. I don't know if you even have munitions. So how would you participate? It doesn't make sense to me. You'll just be embarrassed."

I said, "I request that we be allowed to participate. We will compete against everyone, under exactly the same conditions, even though we have only eight planes and none to spare, and even though we are not yet an operational squadron. We will cope."

He sounded skeptical but somehow agreed...

I called the squadron's technical officer, Yitzhak Nahum, a professional and a true leader.

I told him, "Nahum, I've decided we will compete, despite the odds. I'm asking you to do everything, absolutely everything, to make sure every plane we have is functional. That they'll take off, release the munitions, that everything will work one hundred percent, and that all our bombs will blow up."

Nahum looked at me with a determined glint in his eye and said, "We'll do what it takes."

We prepared for the competition — both aircrew and technical personnel — like we were training for the Olympics. Years later, Nahum told me what our people in the technical section did to prepare: how they checked each and every bomb, how they aligned all the fins of the bombs with a level, how they worked on and prepared each jet as if it were the most important plane in the world, etc...

I remember how we transported our planes from the HAS (hardened aircraft shelter) to the takeoff position with our technical crew riding in vehicles alongside us. I really remember the look in their eyes, as if watching their infants, ensuring nothing bad would happen.

All the planes took off; all the air missions were carried out well; all the bombs were released, hit the targets, and exploded.

We beat the other IAF squadrons by a huge margin. The difference between us and second place was the same as between second place and last place.

This victory was thanks to all the members of the squadron, on the ground and in the air, and thanks to the character, commitment, collaboration, and deep and true partnership among them.

"I'm counting on you.

"I believe in you.

"I'm convinced of your ability.

"And I'm proud of you, as usual..."

72.
Don't Tell the Commander...

As a young pilot with the rank of lieutenant, I was stationed at Hatzerim Airbase. I was an instructor in the Advanced Combat Course at the flight school, the final stage of training for fighter pilots.

The flights with an instructor were carried out in a two-seater Skyhawk, with the cadet sitting in the front and the instructor in the back.

One day, a young technician, an efficient go-getter named Yossi Barazani, who had recently arrived at the squadron and was liked by everyone, was preparing me for a flight.

The technician was the one who fastened the cadet and the instructor to their ejector chairs, taking out the safety pins so the aircrew could trigger their escape should it become necessary.

The technician was supposed to show the security pins to the pilot and then put them in special compartments at the front and back of the cockpit.

Barazani finished fastening the cadet and me, we started the engine, we taxied out of the hangar where the planes were stored — and suddenly I saw Barazani and Eli Dabach, the team leader, signaling me with quick and nervous movements to turn off the engine.

I shut it off.

What was wrong?

The safety pins of my ejector chair, with the red ribbon tied to it, fluttered over the air intake.

What happened was that I had taken the safety pins instead of the technician and placed them, with the red ribbon, over the air intake, and Barazani had not put them into their designated compartments. Thanks to the vigilance of the soldiers who noticed the red ribbon — Barazani among them — the pins were not sucked into the engine, which could have caused the blades of the engine to be shredded, even leading to a crash if it happened while we were aloft.

It was definitely a very big screw-up, for both me and the technician.

We put the pins in their compartments, turned the engine back on, and took off.

After the flight, some of the technical staff came up to me and asked me not to report what had happened. They were afraid that Barazani, the young and beloved technician of the team, would go to prison.

I told them there was no way.

We had messed up, we had made a mistake, and we would report it.

I made one thing clear to them: The screw-up was mine and Barazani's equally. I unequivocally will tell the squadron commander that I needed to be punished with exactly the same severity. Were it decided that Barazani ought to be sent to prison, I ought to be sent to prison.

And that's exactly what I told the squadron commander when I reported the incident to him.

I don't remember what punishment we got. But they didn't put us in prison...

Barazani, a man for whom I have utmost appreciation and affection, advanced in the IAF and went on to become a technical officer, commander of a maintenance squadron, and eventually also the commander of the Air Force Technical School, who is responsible for training the IAF's entire technical sector. He performed all his duties admirably. He was later appointed vice president of maintenance at El Al.

I have no doubt that this formative event in our youth affected both of us throughout our lives.

73.

Just You Wait...

Aunt Tamar, my mother Nechama's sister, was loved by us very much. She was a considerate woman, clever, understanding, and generous. She was married to Nitzan, and they had three children — Smadar, Michal, and Yoav — whom we also loved very much.

Smadar and Michal, who were more or less the ages of my sister Yael and me, would sleep at our house often, and we at theirs. They felt at home with us and vice versa.

The Halevi family home was literally our second home. It was always fun going over there and being with them.

The night of the Passover Seder came, and every year the entire tribe gathered in Petah Tikva with Grandpa David and Grandma Hannah — who was full of heart and soul — their five children as well as us, a battalion of wide-awake, noisy and active grand-daughters and grandsons. We wouldn't rest for a moment and weren't really interested in what was going on at the Seder itself...

Grandpa David, a proud and upstanding man, had a regular cus-tom: He would give each of us grandchildren nuts so that the Seder could go on undisturbed, and our "nutty" games filled the time before, during, and after the Seder, with each of us trying to win the other cousins' nuts.

There were several types of games, but our favorite was the following:

We would lean a large cutting board for bread against the wall diagonally, and each of us, in turn, would roll a nut from its top. If the nut you rolled hit one of the nuts that were already lying on the floor, you won all the nuts.

As a child, I was a bit of a rascal, and the Seder night would usually end with most of the nuts in my bag.

The same was true this time.

At the end of the evening, it was decided that we would go to sleep at Aunt Tamar's for a few days during the Passover holiday break.

On our first morning there, Tamar went to buy nuts. She handed them out to Smadar, Michal and Yael — who remained impoverished from the Seder the night before — and we started a new and suspenseful game with the cutting board leaning on the wall.

Tamar closely followed the game, like a soccer fan in the stands. She cheered on from the kitchen, providing us with a running color commentary.

Not surprisingly, the game ended with all the nuts in my bag, which had swelled to impressive proportions.

Aunt Tamar was getting a little hot around the collar...

Suddenly, she left the house and disappeared.

A few minutes later, she stormed in with a huge bag of nuts.

This time, she didn't distribute them to anyone but said in an annoyed tone:

"Now I'm playing against Eli, and I'll show him what's what."

She looked at me and mumbled: "Just you wait..."

It was a wild game with everyone watching on the edge of their seats. It ended after all the nuts from the huge bag that Aunt Tamar had bought found their way into my bag, which was now more like a sack...

• • •

Sometimes even the most considerate, the most mature, the most generous, the most loving, and the most beloved person cannot hold back and is drawn into an emotional and aggressive game, with fire in their eyes, against a ten-year-old child.

In some ways, in the end, we are all children...

74.

The Promising Watermelon

During one of our summer vacations, we played host to young Nurit and Iris Wolf, the delightful daughters of family friends.

At the time, we lived in an educational institution in Ramatayim that my father managed.

We all went for a short trip with Mom and Dad, and on the way back home we did some shopping. We stopped at the roadside stand where we'd regularly buy a watermelon *(avatiach)*. One struck us as particularly promising *(mavtiach)*.

We got home with our *avatiach mavtiach* (promising watermelon). From the parking lot, a path led to the backdoor of the house, straight to the kitchen. Each of us took a few bags from the car.

Iris took the *avatiach mavtiach*.

First my mother went, after her Iris walked with the watermelon, followed by her sister Nurit and my sister Yael, each with her hands full of bags. I brought up the rear, well behind everyone else.

Just in front of the kitchen door, the watermelon fell from Iris's hands, crashed to the ground, and exploded with a loud noise.

My mother let out a scream, "Eli, what have you done? Why are you always messing around?!"

I wasn't even there, and certainly not guilty.

I was so shocked, I couldn't get a word out of my mouth.

• • •

Who can you get angry at?
Only those you feel at ease with and close to.

75.
Now You Tell Me?!

At the end of my first year as CEO of El Al — which was quite suc-cessful — we decided to hold a festive gala to pay tribute to the company's staff and its loyal customers.

We held discussions about the nature of the event and where it should be held. The meetings were attended by officials from inside and outside the company whose opinions I greatly valued. I summed up the discussions and decided that we would hold the event at the Tel Aviv Fairgrounds, a sprawling expo center.

The day after I made the decision, I received a phone call from public relations consultant Rani Rahav, who was El Al's spokesman.

"Shkedy," he said, "you shouldn't hold the event where you decided to. This is significant in terms of El Al's image as the national airline."

It's usually hard to annoy me, but this time Rani made me very angry. I could literally imagine his face on the other side of the line. I was steaming and said to him angrily and impatiently, as if we were talking face to face.

"Rani, now you tell me?! Your senior officials sat in all those meetings and participated in forming that decision. How can you be telling me this now?"

"Shkedy," answered Rani, "you can get as angry with me as you want, it's even justified, but you need to relocate the gala. Hold the event on the company's premises, even if it costs just as much; this is a significant statement both internally and externally."

I kept quiet and told myself it didn't matter how furious I was or how much Rani was pissing me off. I couldn't let anger be my guide. I had to take a breath.. drink some water.. count to ten... and think quietly and matter-of-factly about what he said.

El Al is Israel's national airline, so its appearance, outwardly and internally, is of great importance. Every action it takes is under the public spotlight, unlike many other companies.

In terms of the internal and external message, it was correct to hold such an important event on the company's premises, at home, and not some glamorous outdoor location.

I came to the conclusion that Rani was right.

I changed my decision.

Rani, who had a strong intuition, spoke his truth despite the consequences. It was important for him to voice his professional opinion, even in a very uncomfortable situation before me and his people.

●●●

I could have made a big mistake. I'm glad I had the courage to think about it in a businesslike way, overcome the anger, really listen to him, and change my own decision despite the price it entailed.

76.
The Neglected Figurine

While we were living in the United States, we decided to embrace an American tradition we wanted to experience for ourselves: holding a garage sale. This was very common in Monterey, where we lived, and allowed us to get rid of a lot of unnecessary things that in Israel we probably would've just thrown away. We'd gone to such sales as buyers and thoroughly enjoyed the experience.

The idea was that our children would take part in the experience and learn lessons relevant to other areas of life, so we asked each of them to choose some of their own things that they were willing to sell. In any case, large sums of money wouldn't be on the table.

The kids were very excited ahead of the big day. They actively participated in the preparations for the event and debated which items to sell, where and how to display them, and how to convince people to buy them.

One of the fascinating things for them was to set the asking price of each and every item.

I didn't intervene.

I let them have the full experience.

My eldest son Nimo had a wooden figurine that was small and neglected, extremely ugly, and also a bit cracked. It had been purchased during a cruise that Nimo went on with Grandma Renia and Grandfather Jakob, while their ship was docked in Egypt.

Nimo realized that the figurine was not worth anything and debated with himself how to sell such a thing and what price to write on it.

In the end, he decided to consult with me.

I said, "Maybe try something interesting? Make it the highest-priced item at the garage sale and just see what happens."

And so he did. The day of the sale arrived, and the first item that was easily snatched up was the figurine.

It turned out that the high price made people think that it was something valuable, a real bargain.

77.

A Fish on the Hook?

I don't like shopping, but when it comes to a real *shuk*, or Middle Eastern bazaar, I like to walk around and enjoy the lively atmosphere, colors, and aromas.

And what can I say? You cannot go to the shuk without engaging in the experience of commerce.

In stores and malls, the prices are quite consistent; what remains is to choose a product and pay. It's different in the shuk.

Choosing a product and buying it is secondary to the real thing: negotiating the price.

Haggling is an action-packed experience, and the traders in the market are undoubtedly master negotiators.

Our tour of the shuk goes like this:

I stroll among the stalls, becoming interested in a not-very-expensive product. My wife, rightly so, tells me, "What do you need it for?"

I really don't need it. Not at all.

But what about the experience?

I start aggressively negotiating, with all the methods I've acquired in other areas, where the sums are quite different: making myself appear offended, announcing that the product is worth much less, declaring that I have seen it elsewhere at a much lower price; I begin to move away from the stand so that the seller calls me back; I tell them how much I am willing to pay, that is: an extremely low amount. In short, trying to bring the price down through the floor, however I can.

In the end, after tough negotiations, an agreement is reached on the price.

And then —

I give the seller the amount they asked for at the beginning.

They look at me puzzled and incredulous...

And pretty soon they realize I'm not a fish on the hook.

I am satisfied because I reveled in the bargaining and happily paid a fair price for the enjoyment and experience, regardless of the product; and the seller is satisfied because they had an unfamiliar experience with a surprising ending, along the way earning more money than they ever expected...

78.

The Gifted Musician

At some point in my childhood, my parents decided that I should have a "musical education" and enrolled me in recorder lessons with Shoshana Hazor, a teacher whose reputation preceded her throughout the region.

The class was held in a type of shed in the yard of her home in Ramatayim, around a table in a U-shaped formation, with her sitting in the center of the U.

I had an assigned seat in the room, right by the front door, which was always open. Through the doorway, I would watch with great heartbreak as my friends, the children of the neighborhood, played soccer in the field on the other side.

I really liked soccer; I dreamed of soccer. That's what I wanted to do, and I was not bad at it either.

To learn the recorder and get better at it, you need to practice, at least a little. Of course, I didn't practice at all and didn't touch the thing when I was at home. I only played the instrument during the lessons themselves, when I had no choice.

And that's exactly what my musical performances sounded like.

At the end of the year, Mom and Dad received an unequivocal verdict from Shoshana Hazor:

This is a waste of time.

The boy really does not want to play the recorder; it's pretty clear it's not for him and he has no talent for it anyway.

I was delighted. I thought this meant my suffering was at an end and that I could finally enjoy soccer with my friends instead of enduring the misery of recorder lessons.

But it wasn't that simple...

In the school that my father ran, there was a teacher named Lutz — thin, bespectacled, nice — and, as it turned out, Shoshana Hazor's husband.

And so, with the help of "friends in high places," we arranged a talk to persuade Shoshana to reconsider the musical future of "the child."

With me sitting on his knee, my father negotiated with Shoshana, promising her that next year, the child — that is, I — would start practicing properly, convincing her that I ought to stay in her class.

That's how I advanced to the next "grade" of recorder lessons.

It's hard to believe, but this ritual was repeated three years in a row. Each time, I came with my father to talk to Shoshana Hazor, and each time he somehow persuaded her to keep me in the class for another year.

All the other children in the class made progress, while I simply marched in place.

After three years of practicing with a small recorder, we moved on to learning about the alto recorder, which is larger and designed for advanced students.

You already know how advanced I was...

Of course, nothing changed, even when I was holding the alto recorder in my hand.

I saw the soccer field and dreamed.

At the end of the fourth year, a large celebratory concert was to be held at the prestigious Beit HaAm concert hall in nearby Ramot Hashavim. Parents and friends were invited to watch, listen, and be impressed by our skills and achievements.

My parents and sister came in their best clothes, sitting down alongside the other proud and happy parents of the young musicians.

All the children in the class sat excitedly on stage.

In light of how impressive my skills and achievements were, I was benched, at the end of the last row on the stage.

Just don't muck things up.

During the concert, which was really quite impressive, I honked a bit from time to time with my recorder.

The show was over, and we were on our way home.

Silence in the car.

My father looked at me in the rearview mirror and remained quiet.

Then Mom, who couldn't hold herself back any longer, turned around and asked... "Eli, tell me, is that all you've learned in four years???"

•••

Parents direct their children to develop along different paths, with the best of intentions.

Sometimes they're right, sometimes less so...

That's fine too.

79.

Between Shlomo Scharf and
Erika Landau

I went to primary school in Ramatayim and then attended Brenner elementary school in Kfar Saba.

Soccer filled my whole world at the time; academic pursuits interested me much less.

My friends and I played soccer almost every spare minute we had during recess and after school.

I played for the Hapoel Kfar Saba soccer team when the coach was Shlomo Scharf, and Yitzhak Shum his assistant. Later on, once we had put them through their paces coaching the youth team, Scharf and Shum went on to coach Israel's national team. Not a bad promotion...

My parents, who envisioned a slightly different future for their son, didn't care for my pastime. But they didn't say anything to me.

One day, two other Brenner pupils and I were informed that we were being sent, in addition to the regular studies, to Erika Landau's school for gifted students in Tel Aviv.

It didn't exactly make me happy, especially after I found out that the supplementary studies in Tel Aviv took place in the afternoon, exactly on the days and at the times of soccer practice for Hapoel Kfar Saba.

But it definitely pleased Mom and Dad, who killed two birds with one stone: The new schedule kept me from the soccer field, and sent me to the gifted kids' class...

• • •

One advantage I saw, however, had nothing to do with studies that really didn't interest me: it was that the school for gifted students was located in Ramat Aviv's Eretz Israel Museum, and on the way back home we would pass through the Central Bus Station in Tel Aviv.

To coax me — and my two classmates — to attend, they gave us pocket money to buy hot corn and falafel there. It was definitely nice bait in those days.

I finished high school and began my pilot's course in the air force.

In the first stage of the course, we flew in light, single-engine Pipers to weed out those who just weren't meant for flying, and I didn't exactly establish myself as an outstanding aviator.

After I had a string of five not-very-successful selection flights, which I barely passed, they replaced our instructor.

The new instructor was a reservist, a fatherly figure from an entirely different mold than his rigid predecessor. He delved into my personal file and read that I had studied at Erika Landau's school for gifted students.

He was interested and asked me about it.

I don't know this for a fact, but I feel that my history spoke to him and impressed him in some way — much more than soccer.

Perhaps it even impressed him enough that he allowed me to pass the stage of selection flights in Pipers, under his guidance.

As I advanced in the pilot's course, I managed to get by on my own.

• • •

You never know when a certain thing you have done or gone through will resurface and affect the course of your life.

80.

Dad, I Want a Tutor, Too

My son Omer was a very good student in middle school. But when he reached high school, he came back one day with a remarkable 40 on a math test.

He said to me resolutely, "Dad, I want you to get me a math tutor."

"Sorry," I said, "but why do you need a private tutor?"

He replied, "All my friends have one, and they passed the test. If I had had one, I would have passed too."

I knew his friends. It was perhaps more convenient for them or their parents, but none of them really needed a private tutor. They could have gotten along just fine on their own.

So could Omer.

I said, "There's no way I'm going to hire a tutor for you. You can excel in math on your own. It's up to you.

"Take the textbook and the workbook.

"Review all the theoretical material. Alone.

"Go through all the examples. Alone.

"Solve all the exercises. Alone.

"Do all the tests. Alone.

"If there's something you can't do, go over it again.

"If you try very hard and still don't succeed, then, if you want, we'll do it together at night when I get home from the army."

Omer responded with a sour face. He didn't like it very much, but he didn't have a choice.

I informed him without blinking that he would not be able to touch the television or computer until further notice. It would be just math, all the time. But I gave him special permission for basketball practice so that he'd have a reason to smile despite it all and have energy...

He studied alone, solved the exercises on his own, and committed on his own. From time to time, when I got off duty late at night, Omer asked to go over a math topic or another, and we did.

By the time the year ended, he got a 97 on his report card. (Not bad compared to the 40 he started with...)

Omer successfully completed the advanced mathematics track for his matriculation exams, all credit to him.

What Omer did not know at the time and only discovered years later — on our joint trip to Peru — was that the period during which we occasionally solved math exercises together was exactly the time I was prepping the attack on the nuclear reactor in Syria.

There's no contradiction.

When I was there, I was there.

And when I was with him, I was with him.

All in.

81.

The Aspic Test

The relationship between me and my then-girlfriend Anat was developing nicely, and things seemed to be trending in a serious direction.

But Anat's father, Jakob, who came from Poland — a brilliant engineer with a sharp mind and wide-ranging interests, but opinionated and stubborn — was concerned about the connection that was developing between his eldest daughter and me.

The big problem for him was that I was uneducated.

I hadn't gone to university (yet.)

I was not a doctor.

Not an engineer.

And being a fighter pilot is fine, but doesn't really count...

In order to get the green light from Yaakov, I was put through two serious tests.

The first was playing a game of chess against him, probably meant to test my quick-wittedness and competence. Luckily, I knew how to play chess very well.

The second was much more complex and difficult.

One of the famous delicacies of Jews from Poland is calf's foot jelly. A lot of work is invested in its preparation, and it was considered by Polish immigrants to be a dish fit for kings. But whenever I see this quivering meat jelly, I shudder. The mere thought of having to taste aspic was revolting.

At one of our dinners, Jakob served calf's foot jelly. Of course, I also got a plate with a generous portion of the "delicacy." And while I stared at the vibrating dish placed in front of me, everyone watched me, probably to examine the depth of my seriousness and determination and to see if I was suitable for the family.

I marshaled all my mental strength — and I ate.

It was terrible, but I somehow met the challenge.

However, it turned out that wasn't enough for me to get a stamp of approval.

I had won over Anat's mother, Renia, a beloved and charming woman, but Jakob's mind was still not at ease with me.

Privately, he engaged Anat in a serious conversation and explained to her that he was very concerned about the gap that would emerge between her and me. She was studying medicine, she would advance significantly; I, on the other hand, was still stuck in the military — a pilot, granted, but that didn't particularly impress him...

Where would that leave us?

Grandpa Jakob's version is a little different from Anat's. According to him, Anat came of her own initiative to consult with him.

Either way, our family, our children, and grandchildren testify that somehow we all got along...

• • •

Seek advice, listen, but never forget that you alone determine and decide what is good for you.

The choice is yours and yours only, not anyone else's, with all that implies, for better or for worse.

82.

Idiot?

When I began serving as CEO of El Al, one of the things I was struck by was the mistrust and suspicion among the company's employees, at all levels, toward the senior management and the board of directors. This had an adverse effect on the company's business aptitude, its ability to pursue paths to productivity, and the capacity of its people — as good and professional as they might be — to express themselves and make an impact.

From my very first day at the company, I tried to change the situation, but it took a year until the opportunity for a significant breakthrough arrived— when we finished the year with a profit and I received a bonus in accordance with my contract.

That bonus allowed me to come up with a program aimed at changing El Al's atmosphere and organizational culture, promoting initiative and excellence, inspiring enthusiasm among the employees, and encouraging them to think outside the box and take action.

My idea was to establish a special fund for excellence and personnel.

I decided to invest half of the bonus money I received, as these were resources that the company itself found difficult to invest, for various reasons.

My wife said (and still says...) I'm n idiot. "A person should not invest his private money in a project of the company at which he is employed, however important and valuable it may be, even if he's the CEO. Such a move should be funded from the company's coffers, not our private money," she said.

"And besides," she added, "no one will appreciate the extraordinary steps you're taking."

Despite her objections, I was completely at peace with the decision.

I put 5.7 million shekels of our own money into the fund (half of the bonus I received) and an additional 2 million from another clause in the agreement signed with me — a total of NIS 7.7 million.

The idea was to invest the money in the company's employees for three years, a little over two-and-a-half million shekels a year.

To spearhead the project, I selected Ilan Avishai, director of El Al's air service division and former colonel in the Air Force, a great man and a superstar with a unique ability to penetrate impermeable walls, get complex projects off the ground, and deal with difficulties and challenges in an extraordinary way.

At the outset, I emphasized the following principles:

1. The purpose of the fund is to encourage excellence, unique thinking, action, and execution with proven results.
2. The plan must include values-based activities with our employees that emphasize that El Al is not only a business entity but also a corporation of national importance.
3. The fund must be invested in people only and not in the construction of "monuments."
4. All El Al personnel must be eligible, except for members of management.
5. Everything must be aboveboard, transparent, and monitored.
6. After I defined the principles, we sat down to formulate an individual plan for the use of the fund's monies.

On the moral level:
We commit to send all the members of the company in Israel and around the world — about six thousand people — on educational

tours in Jerusalem, including Yad Vashem[10], the Western Wall,[11] and the City of David.[12]

In the business sphere:

We commit to encouraging, rewarding, and incentivizing talented, creative, and enterprising people to raise ideas and lead processes of improvement and growth, regardless of their role and status and unconfined to their areas of responsibility. The goal is to encourage initiatives that increase the company's revenue, reduce an expenditure, or improve a service — from the idea and initiative stage, through planning and execution, to achieving the result.

Before embarking on the big move, we decided to conduct a pilot program in order to learn, debrief, and draw conclusions.

We chose an employee who had spearheaded a creative process in the technical field, leading to savings of hundreds of thousands of dollars, and we decided to award him a prize of NIS 36,000 and to fund his engineering studies.

We posted it in-house to make it clear that we were serious.

To our great surprise, we were roundly criticized.

Where did this come from?

Why did he deserve it?

What about the people who worked with him?

And also statements like "Shkedy always looks out for his friends."

The only "friend" who had any part of this was my wife — the money was her money too — and she had warned me in advance that not everyone would welcome my initiative, then repeatedly told me that I was an idiot...

We realized there was a problem. But that's exactly why we launched a pilot program.

---

10. Israel's official memorial to the victims of the Holocaust.

11. Also known as the "Wailing Wall" or the "Kotel" in Hebrew is the most religious site in the world for the Jewish people. Located in the Old City of Jerusalem, it is the last remaining outer wall of the ancient Jewish temple, and an incredibly important site of modern Israeli history.

12. An archaeological site in the Old City of Jerusalem. About 3,000 years ago, King David turned the city into a political, religious, and spiritual capital for the entire Jewish people.

WHO THE F*CK IS MICHAEL?!

We sat down, thought it over, and formulated a plan whose main points were the following:

1. Everyone is eligible to compete.
2. No manager can prevent their subordinates from submitting proposals.
3. Significant prizes and plaudits will be given to the "supportive environment" in which the winner works.
4. The team to examine the proposals and recommend the winners will be made up of El Al personnel who are admired and about whom there is a consensus throughout the company regarding their character, integrity, and professionalism.

We chose the team and called them "the saints." It was very important to us that the employees felt that everything was being done fairly and transparently, without any politics. One of the people chosen for the "saints" team was Ayelet Oren, a lawyer from the office of El Al's legal counsel, an honest woman who is valued on a personal and professional level. At first, she refused out of fear that she was going to take part in something "crooked." I explained the rationale to her, and she was convinced of the fairness and significance of the process. In the end, Ayelet became a great supporter of the project, convincing people of its importance and demonstrating the purity of the process through her involvement.

The project ran for three years, until I finished my tenure at El Al.

It started with several dozen proposals and reached hundreds of proposals each year. All sectors participated in the competition, even the most jaundiced and cynical people.

Each year, ten contestants won.

The prizes awarded were very respectable, worth making the effort for:

- First prize — 100,000 shekels
- Second prize — 75,000 shekels
- Third prize — 50,000 shekels
- And everyone else — 25,000 shekels for each winner.

252

In addition, each of the winners received a specially designed sculpture, created by a famous artisan, and a personal certificate of appreciation that was no less important than the monetary prize.

In order to stifle objections from the winners' colleagues, and in recognition of the importance of the people around them and the importance of teamwork, we also awarded the supportive environment of the winners a significant monetary group prize. This allowed the winners to feel comfortable around their co-workers and showed the group members that we appreciated their contribution. We also gave them a massive, bright poster marking the award and expressing appreciation for the department and all its people.

The proposals reaching the final stage were selected by a committee that included the entire "saints" team; the company's legal advisor, Attorney Omer Shalev; the company's auditor, accountant Gil Ber; the financier, Ariel Schwartzberg; the external director, Prof. Shuki Shemer; Avishai the project manager; and me.

The committee's discussions were public and took place in a large hall where the participants, their friends, and managers were present; from the second year of the project on, we also made sure to broadcast the session live to all the employees of the company. In this way, everyone could be a partner and see with their own eyes the purity and fairness of the process.

Many were surprised to learn that I, as the company's CEO, had only one vote on the committee, just like the rest of its members.

We made sure the event got its full attention.

The day on which the winners were selected and announced was a holiday in the company, and the prizes were given out in an impressive and moving ceremony in the presence of the families of the winners and the other employees.

The positive results were not long in coming.

The return-on-investment ratio was 8.64:1 — that is, for every dollar invested (from my money and from my wife's money) there was an increase in income or a reduction in expenditure for the company of $8.64.

That was fantastic, but no less important were the positive dynamics created within the company and among its employees and the atmosphere of excellence, partnership, and collaboration at all levels. The foundation touched everyone, in one way or another, just the way I wanted.

At one point, they asked me if I was willing to include people who work at El Al but were not directly employed by the company, such as members of the security department who were civil servants, or cleaning staff employed by an external company.

Of course they're eligible, I said. Anyone who has a direct influence on the company, even if they are not directly employed by it, is invited to participate in the excellence project, innovate, and win accolades and awards, and they would of course also participate in the educational and values part of the tour in Jerusalem.

Here is one story that demonstrated to the company's people that each and every one of them could bring about change:

Three aircraft cleaners came up with an idea to save money by resizing the plastic bags used to collect garbage after flights. They did not shy away due to cynical reactions and attempts to discourage them, tried out the idea themselves, and proved that it could significantly reduce costs — hundreds of thousands of shekels a year. It was exciting to see them, their proud families, and co-workers who honored them with thunderous applause as they took the stage to receive their certificates of appreciation and respectable monetary reward.

One day, when I left my office, an elderly man named Nissan, with white hair and a wrinkled face, was waiting for me at the door. He ran a large team of cleaners and was completely dedicated to the work and his staff. He was emotional, tears streaming from his kind eyes.

Nissan said that he had been in Israel since the 1990s and had never been to Jerusalem. It was only thanks to the project that he finally got to visit it. I was excited to see and listen to him.

Despite the tremendous response, there was one group that had a hard time emotionally with the move: El Al pilots. At first, they didn't want to participate in the project or the tour to Jerusalem.

But little by little, the investment also ripened among the pilots. From the second year on, they participated in the project and even won prizes; and in the third year, most of them also participated in the tour of Jerusalem.

I was delighted.

The extent to which the project has succeeded can be seen from the fact that Assuta Medical Centers fully adopted the excellence project. The person who decided on this was Prof. Shemer, chairman of Assuta and a man with a big heart, who was part of the selection committee as an external director of El Al.

I was thrilled.

I'm glad I had the courage to make the move and I'm completely at peace with it even today, looking back.

83.

"Dad, Can I Have Your Credit Card?"

Omer was a teenager, he came to me one day and said, "Dad, I want you to give me one of your credit cards."

"What? Why?" I asked.

Omer answered: "My friends got credit cards from their parents, and they can withdraw money whenever they need to. I want one too."

I said, "There's no way you're getting my credit card.

"You get pocket money. Manage your money.

"Want more money? Work and earn it."

He was salty, to say the least...

He whirled around angrily and walked away with a sour face.

To his credit, after a while, he came to me and said, "Dad, I get it. It would have been much easier for you to give me a credit card, and whatever amounts would have been charged because of me, I guess wouldn't have been a huge deal for you. But not giving in and doing what you think is best for my education is much harder."

I was moved and delighted to see that, despite his young age, Omer understood implicitly the importance of education, as well as the difficulty in instilling it.

84.

"Yekke"[13]

My friend Doron is a *"Yekke"* in the deepest sense of the word —
orderly, organized, strict, and punctual.

He is mentally unprepared to ever be late and is never behind
schedule. Indeed, he arrives ahead of time, under all circumstances
and in all locations, before everyone else, waiting somewhere in the
vicinity to make his entrance right on time, "on the dot."

I really like Doron, but whenever I'm around him, this aspect of
him makes me feel uncomfortable.

One day, I was supposed to meet Doron and a third party at a
restaurant in Tel Aviv.

I arrived a little ahead of time — God forbid I be late — so I sat
down and waited for them.

The time for the meeting arrived — and Doron was not there.

Time passed, the seconds ticking by.

Another five minutes.

Another ten minutes.

Another fifteen minutes.

Doron was running late?

It couldn't be.

After seventeen minutes, he arrived, all upset — sweating, panting, apologizing, and utterly at his wit's end.

And so I sat back, smiled, and told him with great relish, "It's all
good my friend. I'm fine. I'm in a much better mood now..."

---

13. A "Yekke" is a Jew of German-speaking origin, often perceived in Israel as having attention to detail and punctuality.

•••

It is enough to make a mistake once for the "message" to fade away.

85.

"Shkedy, You're Still Alive?"

As a young pilot, I got to the Skyhawk squadron at Hatzerim Airbase just after finishing my operational training course. The commander of the squadron at the time was Yuval Noyman, a sharp and understanding man. I really liked his personality and the way he thought.

Shortly after arriving at the squadron, I was assigned to go up against him in a dogfight, practicing one-on-one aerial combat.

Facing off against the commander was something to thrill and challenge any pilot in the squadron, certainly one as junior as I was, even more so when it came to an esteemed and experienced aviator like Neumann.

It was clear to me that I had to do anything and everything to beat him.

We engaged in a series of dogfights, and I was very pleased.

Surprisingly, the results were in my favor.

There was only one problem: I blew right past every imaginable flight restriction, so I was dreading the debriefing.

We landed and I headed to the squadron commander's office for the debriefing.

We debriefed the flight in detail, in a matter-of-fact and in-depth manner. To my surprise, not a single word was said about my disregard for the restrictions.

I was very relieved.

Then, on my way to the door, Neumann asked me, with a small smile at the corner of his mouth:

"Shkedy, could it be that you were at zero speed???"

The minimum speed we were allowed to fly at was 120 knots (about 140 mph). At zero speed, you lose control of the aircraft, and it can get into a spin that is difficult to pull out of. If you manage to avoid that, the aircraft simply falls until it reaches some velocity, and then the airflow over the wings resumes, and control returns to the pilot.

Another characteristic of zero speed in a Skyhawk aircraft is a large cloud of fuel that comes out of the aircraft and envelops it. You can't miss it...

"Yes," I said, "I was at zero speed."

I waited for a ringing slap, but then Neumann told me something I didn't expect to hear:

"Very well, keep it up, take the plane to its limits."

I'm not sure he meant it; in fact, I'm pretty confident he didn't... But I took his words seriously and quite far, and I really pushed the envelope in my flying, to the limits and sometimes well beyond them.

It certainly took me places, and my performance was not bad at all — but it was very risky too.

At some point, I switched to flying Mirages.

Then, when the Mirage retraining was over, it came time to decide who would be selected to fly the F-15, which at the time was the most advanced aircraft in the IAF. Although objectively I was an excellent pilot, it was decided that it would not be responsible to entrust an F-15 to me.

Today I know it was a justified decision. But in real time I took it hard, and since I had nothing to lose — at least I thought so then — I continued to fly wildly and dangerously.

One day I flew against Yehuda Koren, commander of the base our squadron belonged to, a quiet and purposeful redhead who was an excellent pilot, with an impressive record of having shot down ten enemy planes.

I was very pleased with the results of the dogfight.

We landed and went to the debriefing.

Koren did not say a single word about the results of the flight. He referred only to the wild way in which I had flown and decided, without hesitating, to ground me. The amount of time I was grounded seemed like an eternity to me. It was just awful.

But apparently, he saved my life.

A few years later, when I was walking in Tel Aviv one day, I met Yoske Tzuk, a veteran reserve pilot. We had flown together in the same Mirage squadron. He looked surprised to see me and asked, "Shkedy, you're still alive?" The words were said with half a laugh, but there was also a grain of truth in them.

When I returned to the air after being grounded, I flew in a much more mature and responsible way. Surprisingly, this did nothing to harm my skills or my results.

I learned that behaving responsibly doesn't impinge on your professional performance.

* * *

Balance is critical in any area of life.

Finding a balance between two approaches at different points in my life has been significant.

Neumann and Koren balanced out my professionalism, personality, and motivation. They played a meaningful role in the way I developed and flew, wherever I went in the Air Force itself or in life in general.

And in my staying alive...

86.
You're a Star

One day I was invited to speak at a large conference of senior medical professionals, leaders in their respective fields in Israel. Sitting in the audience was Prof. Emmie Hodak, an internationally renowned dermatologist who was my father's doctor.

To her great surprise, in the middle of the lecture, I called her to the stage. I said that she was a real star, and I described in a few words her humanity and her professionalism.

It was amazing to see Prof. Hodak's reaction. She was moved to the depths of her soul when I called her to the stage, and after I complimented her in front of her colleagues, including the chairman of the Israel Medical Association, Prof. Zion Hagai, she barely managed to make it off the stage because she was so overwhelmed.

It was also amazing to see and feel the "vibe" that passed through the crowd.

One of the most important things for a person is recognition and appreciation. External symbols, such as money and titles, are important to people because they express, at least in their eyes, an appreciation for them. But positive reinforcements can be just as significant, and perhaps more...

There are two types of reinforcements: positive and negative.

Positive reinforcement: When you want to say something good about a person, wait for the opportunity with the greatest audience, call that person up, and praise them in front of everyone.

Such a gesture is of great importance both for the person receiving the positive reinforcement and the people who hear the words. As far as the recipient of the compliment is concerned, there is a huge difference if you tell them in private or in front of an audience, while the audience would do anything to have that same feeling.

Every time I give positive reinforcement in public, I see the excitement, the energy, and the motivation that it arouses — both on an individual level for the recipient of the reinforcement and on a group level.

Before I meet with a group or organization I'm unfamiliar with, I look for a broad consensus as to who among them is a real star, both in personality and professionalism. Then, to illustrate the meaning of positive reinforcement in front of a large audience, I call that person to the stage, right in the middle of the lecture, just to tell them what a star they are.

It's fascinating to see the reactions, both theirs and the audience.

Negative reinforcement: When someone needs a reset, call them to your office, shut the door firmly, and make sure no one else but the two of you can listen in. Put things on the table in the clearest and most poignant way.

Do everything so as not to insult them personally, but hold a mirror to their face. Make it very clear to them what they need to correct in their behavior or function, and what you expect from them.

One thing must be clear to both of you: not a word of what is said in the room will ever be released, certainly not by you.

When such difficult things are said face-to-face, they have the potential to be corrected and improved. When spoken in public, they cause that person to be withdrawn, defensive, bitter, or aggressive and blame others. In such a case, the potential for change and improvement shrinks to nonexistent.

Some of the people who worked with me, who went on to become famous, had occasion to sit in my office and hear harshly critical things from me. Some of them were crying bitterly at the time.

Under no circumstance would I reveal, in speech or in writing, who they are and what I talked to them about, and they know it very well.

I would never have told the following story either, were it not for the fact that the person in question recounted it at his El Al retirement party, as an example of something that changed his life — and, of course, had I not received his permission to include it in this book. He undoubtedly underwent a profound change and felt strong enough and confident enough to tell the story.

The man I am talking about is Shali Zahavi, who was VP of Cargo at El Al during my tenure as CEO.

Shali is a person with a heart of gold, authentic, creative, and smart, who knows how to read the map and deal with complex situations; a true professional and a first-rate operator.

There was only one problem: inside he was a volcano roiling with lava, and he couldn't help but erupt frequently. When things were not going in the desired direction, he threw unpleasant tantrums in public.

With all my love and appreciation for him, that was completely unacceptable to me.

One day, after a discussion during which he lashed out bluntly at one of the other VPs, we walked down the hall and then I hissed quietly at him, "Shali, come into my office, now!"

He came in.

I said, "Shut the door, all the way."

He shut the door.

Without dawdling, I told him in the simplest and clearest way, "The next time you have an outburst, I'm going to land a kick in the middle of your face. (Metaphorically, of course...) There is no way that I can accept such behavior, and I expect and demand that you immediately and substantively change your behavior."

I made it clear to him exactly how I required him to behave and concluded, "What I told you now will remain between the two of us."

Shali looked totally shocked.

He did not expect that things would be said so sharply, clearly, and unequivocally.

And he also did not expect that my words would remain confidential.

From that moment on, his behavior changed completely, and he did his job superbly, without tantrums.

Later on, Shali became El Al's VP of Commerce, and I have no doubt that the profound change he underwent enabled him to carry out the complex and sensitive role with great success.

Shali was and still is a good friend of mine.

• • •

Reinforcement has tremendous importance.

87.

An Urgent Phone Call

The F-16D "Barak" (Lightning) squadron that we established won
almost every competition and every possible prize in the IAF.

Almost...

One of the competitions was called the Maintenance Level
Competition, and the technical sections of all the squadrons at
Ramat David Airbase participated in it.

We attended our first competition as a squadron and enthusiastically cheered on the excellent team of technical personnel who
represented us.

But we didn't win first place.

At the end of the competition, I approached our teammates,
shook their hands, and said that I trusted them and was sure that
we would win the next time.

We debriefed, learned our lessons, and figured out what we would
do next time to improve and win.

For the next competition, we were well-prepared in accordance
with the conclusions of the serious debriefing we conducted.

We invested in practice and training and arrived rested and ready.

But that time, too, we didn't win first place.

At the end of the competition, I approached the members of the
team. They were crestfallen.

I encouraged them, told them that I trusted them, was proud of
them, and that I knew we would win in the future.

Again an in-depth debriefing was carried out. We decided what
we would do differently the next time.

Yitzhak Nahum, the excellent technical officer of the squadron, could no longer stand the situation, and as the next competition neared, he arranged a dedicated training camp for our team...

We came more prepared than ever...

We competed...

But once again, we failed to win first place...

I approached, encouraged, hugged, and told them I knew we would make it to first place in the future.

We continued to win almost all the competitions across the entire Air Force, but we couldn't win the maintenance competition at our home base.

More than a year had passed since the end of my tenure as commander of the squadron. I was already the head of the IAF's operations department when one day my secretary told me:

"A soldier from your squadron really wants to talk to you. He says it's urgent."

"Okay," I said, "put him through, and we'll talk."

When I received the call, there was a huge shout of joy from the other side of the line.

"Shkedy, I had to tell you: We won the Maintenance Level Competition."

●●●

It is very important to convey to your people that you believe in their abilities.

They will do anything to be proud of themselves.

They will do anything to make you feel proud of them.

They will do anything to prove you right, even when you are no longer there...

Itzhak Shkedy

88.

Meir Would Never Believe It...

I've got to admit: fashion has never been my forte. Either it never interested me much, or I'd defiantly do the "wrong" thing to piss people off.

When I was a child, this issue was not given any particular importance at home, though they made sure that we were always clean and tidy. Even though we never had much money, my father always managed to look somehow at his best with what he had.

My wife Anat has an outstanding description of her impressions of the clothing in which I arrived for our first date. I'll spare you...

The Air Force, and the IDF in general, has an advantage when it comes to clothing: the uniform.

But even there I somehow managed to stand out — for the worse...

Ramat David Airbase had a legendary master sergeant by the name of Meir — a strict but gentle man with a great soul — and whenever he met my wife, they complained about me together. He would teasingly say of me, "I don't know why, but he always looks like a *schlumper*" — a bum.

That's why, as the commander of the base, before I entered an auditorium or went on stage to talk to the troops, I would stand in front of Master Sergeant Meir, and he would take care of me, adjusting my uniform so I looked presentable.

When I arrived at El Al, I could no longer rely on Meir to fix me up before an event or meeting. Also, I had to deal with civilian attire, which makes a powerful and significant statement. After all, I was CEO of one of the largest and most important companies in the economy. So I needed an appropriate and presentable wardrobe — i.e. clothing my wife found reasonable...

Still, I could never have dreamed about what would happen at the Superbrands event, which was designed to choose the most prestigious brand names from the leading corporations in the Israeli economy, at which I represented El Al as its CEO. The airline won not only the rank of "superbrand," but the even more exclusive title of "brand of brands" — one of only three companies in Israel to do so. That didn't surprise me, from my familiarity with the company and its people. But who, out of all the CEOs, was named "Best Dressed" by the newspaper that covered the event?

You can already guess...

Meir would never have believed it.

It's not that I've become a fashion icon since then... Quite the contrary. As soon as I finished my tenure at El Al, I returned to my usual attire.

• • •

Even when something seems impossible and even counterintuitive - there is still hope.

89.
A Perk?

Who wouldn't want to be treated to a flight in a fighter jet?

It sounds like a remarkable, particularly sought-after experience, something to tell the grandkids about.

But the truth is that for a person whose body is not accustomed to being in extreme situations, with extraordinary stresses in high G, flying in a fighter jet is a dubious pleasure that usually means throwing your guts up...

I have flown with non-aviators several times, some of whom were courageous warriors on the solid ground of the battlefield. They quickly realized that flying in a fighter jet was far from a fun experience.

Once upon a time, they allowed non-aircrew members to join pilots in two-seater fighters. Today that it is a very rare occurrence, usually done to introduce this world to people who are involved with aviation on a professional or operational level (such as an aviation physician or the commander of an infantry or armored brigade who may need to call in air support, et cetera) — not as a perk.

I particularly remember one incident. I was a young Mirage pilot at the time, and I was asked to fly with a technician who had been selected as an outstanding member of our squadron — and so was to be given the "perk" of a Mirage flight.

The young man was round and bespectacled, all smiles and pleased as punch.

Until we got into the jet...

Even as we taxied towards the runway, I felt, as we talked to each other over the radio, that he was very apprehensive about flying.

It wasn't supposed to be a particularly complicated or difficult flight, but as we took off, the tech burst into tears and said he wanted to go back.

I tried to calm him down, telling him that we'd finish and land soon. As I continued to fly, I constantly checked my rearview mirror to make sure he was OK and that he was still conscious.

The tech vomited and then fell silent...

We finished our flight and landed.

After landing, I stopped the plane on the side of the runway, popped the canopy, and let him recover, breathe fresh air, and clean himself up. And there was a lot to clean up...

We waited in that position, off to the side, until the tech could regulate his breathing, clean himself up and resume talking.

I waited a little longer, to make sure he was in reasonable condition, and only then did I taxi the plane back to our takeoff position, where all the members of the technical section were already waiting to welcome their friend with enthusiastic shouts and thunderous applause.

He raised his hands into the air and produced a huge smile.

"Well, how was it?" the guys from the section asked him.

"Great!" said the tech.

Of course, I told them he handled himself like a real pro...

There isn't always a connection between appearance and reality.

So, if someone offers you the perk of flying in a fighter jet, think twice before putting on that flight suit. The fun is uncertain at best.

90.

I Can't Let You Go Out Like That...

When I was a squadron commander, I was chosen to join the IAF delegation to the Paris Air Show. The problem was that it was scheduled during an intense period of training flights, and I had no intention of leaving the squadron for a few days. That's why I announced that I would pass on the trip.

My superiors were not convinced. They explained to me politely but pointedly that they were "happy" to hear my opinion, but it was important that I be exposed to what was happening in the world of aviation outside of Israel. So the matter was not open for discussion.

It was decided that I would go.

A few weeks before the trip to Paris, during our "shutdown" week when the squadron wasn't flying and its members went on leave, my wife Anat and I flew to Austria to visit Etty and Doron, a couple of good friends of ours who lived in Vienna.

Because of his occupation, Doron's wardrobe was always meticulous, impeccable, elegant. Just the opposite of me.

When I told them I was supposed to fly to the Paris Air Show, Doron shuddered.

"Are you going to dress like you usually do?" he asked, and then quickly answered his own question: "No way. I can't let you go out like that. We're going to a special store here in Vienna, and I'll get you set up."

Now it was my turn to shudder... But I realized he was probably right.

We went to an exclusive store in Vienna where Doron bought his fancy clothing.

I told him, "Do your thing. Choose whatever you think is best. I won't get in the way."

This strange event ended with some serious purchases: a suit, shirts, shoes, and ties. The climax was Doron asking them to bring me the last word in men's fashion — which, at that time, meant a plaid jacket that struck me as neither suitable nor stylish...

But I didn't interfere. I trusted him and went with the flow.

A few weeks later we went to the Paris Air Show. The delegation was headed by a senior officer from the Air Force with the rank of brigadier general; there were a number of other senior officers with the rank of colonel; finally, I, the youngest of the participants, the lieutenant colonel, brought up the rear of the delegation.

Our first meeting was with senior executives from a huge American aircraft conglomerate.

The year was 1992. The Internet was still in its infancy, Google hadn't been born yet, and it was difficult to know who was who and what each executive looked like.

All the members of the Israeli delegation were dressed, as expected, in their *bar mitzvah* suits — except for me, in my fancy outfit chosen by Doron, headlined by the tweed jacket.

To my great surprise, the American executives went straight to me. They were sure I was the head of the delegation.

I got it.

In American culture, a person's attire is of great significance. As far as they are concerned, whoever is dressed in the most elegant and meticulous way is probably the most senior.

•••

Each culture has its own messages and symbols, and it is worth getting to know them.

91.
The Power of Transparency

As the commander of Ramat David Airbase, I took every opportunity to tour the base's squadrons and units, meeting all of the personnel — men and women, enlisted, NCOs, and officers — and talking to them about what was on their minds.

One of the issues that came up regularly was the unfairness, biases, favoritism, and manipulations concerning the duty rosters.

This struck me as utterly unacceptable.

During "Command Group," my weekly meeting with the commanders of the squadrons and the commanders of the units on the base, I declared unequivocally and clearly that this had to stop immediately and that all concerned had to deal with the problem resolutely.

However, the problem was not resolved.

My firm demands on the subject and all the actions taken by the commanders to remedy the situation simply did not help.

The base personnel understood that I had no intention of compromising on the matter, but apparently, that wasn't enough. The hard feelings would not go away, certainly not at the pace I wanted.

I realized that I had to pull it all up, root, and branch.

One day, a young officer named Dikla Hertzog came up to me and told me quietly and with a shy smile, "Sir, I have an idea of what to do about the duty rosters."

"What is it?" I asked.

Dikla replied, "I think we can prepare and distribute a master

274

list with the names of all officers and enlisted, writing down next to each and every name what shifts they've taken and when. That should allow us to tackle the problem of unfairness."

The idea sounded interesting to me.

I told her, "Regardless of your position, you need to attack this matter with everything you've got. I'm giving you full backing, with total authority and responsibility to lead the process.

"As you propose, put together this master list, from the most junior soldier all the way to me as commander of the base, along with what duty shifts we've taken and when."

Dikla tackled the challenge with all her heart and soul. She invested all her energy and free time, saw to every detail, and composed a living document that was updated on a daily basis. The master list was available and accessible, in various ways, to all the base's personnel.

The change for the better was immediate.

It was amazing.

The feeling of resentment gave way to a sense of deep partnership.

Dikla's idea had several aspects that led to the rapid change:

— Everyone saw and understood the full picture continuously and immediately, which reduced objections and gossip.

— It was clear to everyone that fairness and equity had a deep and moral import for me as commander of the base.

— From the moment the master list was open and visible to all, the people who used to evade their duty shifts or arrange "discounts" for their buddies could no longer afford to behave in that manner. They understood that they, too, were bound to a purity of ethics.

And all thanks to the courageous young officer Dikla.

● ● ●

Transparency has tremendous power and can quickly lead to change.

92.

Annoying and Hard to Hear?
So What...

When I was a young Mirage pilot at Eitam Airbase in northern Sinai, near El-Arish, our squadron had an excellent, professional, and experienced pilot.

There was only one problem: all of us, young and older, really didn't like him. His behavior and conduct aroused in us deep disgust and harsh antagonism. He yelled, lashed out, couldn't control himself, and insulted people without even understanding what he was doing.

We tried to avoid any contact with him whenever possible...

After a short time in the squadron, I realized that even though I really didn't like this pilot, to say the least, it was still worthwhile to listen to him and learn everything I could from him in the field of aviation. Despite his problematic personality, he had a rich understanding of flying, pushing the envelope in the cockpit.

Every time he spoke and explained about flying, I made sure to be present. I sat as far away as possible, but I listened attentively to what he said. And indeed, his professional explanations were instructive, fascinating, comprehensive, and informative.

Unlike my comrades, who continued to keep their distance from him, I realized that it doesn't matter who the speaker is, or how much they may be liked or disliked; what matters is the bottom line of what they have to say.

There's no doubt that it's nicer to listen to someone you love and appreciate, who is pleasant to be around. But sometimes you need to know how to isolate your disapproval of a particular person from their capacity to teach you important things in their field.

I learned a lot from this pilot about what to do in the realm of aviation, and I learned a lot from him about what not to do in the realm of interpersonal relations.

Later, when I was El Al's CEO, I decided to hold monthly discussions and debriefings with employees on topics essential to the company, from aircraft to fuel, commercial policy to regulation, safety, and more. The aim: to learn, improve, and move forward.

One of the topics we discussed once a month was customer service. I decided that each such discussion would begin with a guest speaker, someone from outside the company who would allow us to see things through their eyes. In other words, help us really understand the client's point of view.

The people who took us up on this were very serious and accomplished individuals from diverse fields such as business, high-tech, academia, medicine, sports, education, etc. These were people who really knew us in-depth, flew with us a lot, and saw things that we, from inside the corporation, could not see.

At the beginning of each discussion, I would tell the guest, in the presence of the company's personnel — first-class professionals — not to embellish or refine anything, but to say things in the sharpest, most poignant, and clearest way, even if it was harsh criticism. This was the only way we could learn and improve. And if they saw fit, they could also talk about the good things they'd observed that were worthwhile and appropriate to preserve and enhance.

Our first guest speaker was a complex man, a superstar in his field, and the owner of a well-known high-tech company who flew a lot and who knew the world of aviation in general and El Al in particular. Shortly after he started talking, some of the employees sitting in the room interrupted him with hisses and boos, accusing him of saying things that simply were not true.

He really pissed them off.

I told them, "I suggest that we let our guest speak. We'll hear him out, without any interjection, and only when he's done we will complete the picture from our perspective and decide if and what further action ought to be taken."

Only after six such meetings, over the course of about six months, our employees learned how to hear the guest speakers out, without interrupting, interjecting, or objecting. They finally figured out how to accept criticism, think it over, and be open to changes. The truth is that we made important changes thanks to the things we heard in those meetings.

• • •

Even if someone is personally annoying, or the difficult things they express are irritating or even hurtful, it is worthwhile to listen to them and learn.

93.
Terner's Criteria

Toward the end of my tenure as an instructor at the Hatzerim flight school, I began to think about the next stop on my journey.

I loved the Air Force. I loved aviation — the challenge, the competition, the comrades, constantly pushing the envelope. I had an in-depth understanding of what it meant to serve as a pilot in the IAF.

But I was still young, and I wasn't sure that this was what I wanted to do in life.

After much deliberation, I came to the conclusion that I had to develop a broad perspective for the future by venturing into the halls of academia. I put in my papers to be discharged from active service and enrolled in university classes to study mathematics and computers.

Not long after, the person who was then the head of the Air Force Personnel Division, Brigadier General Yaakov Terner, called me in for a chat. We had known each other from the time we both served at Hatzerim, Turner as the base commander and I as a young Skyhawk pilot.

I arrived at his office.

Terner, without any special preamble, in his direct way, asked, "Shkedy, why do you want to be discharged?"

I replied, "I've decided I want to go to university now. I feel that studying is important for me at this stage of my life."

"Why can't you do that within the framework of the IAF?" Terner asked.

"That's impossible," I replied. "Only someone who has served as a squadron commander can pursue a degree without leaving the IAF, and I don't meet that criterion."

Terner's response was completely unexpected, certainly in those days, "So from now on, you do meet the criteria. I have decided to allow you to go study."

I was surprised and said, "If it's possible, I'd like to go to university within the framework of the Air Force."

Nowadays, this is quite commonplace: young officers are sent to university, combining their academic studies and their pilot training. But then, in 1982, it sounded completely delusional. It is hard to describe today the significance of such an unusual, unconventional, and groundbreaking decision as Turner's at the time.

Later on, when I was appointed commander of the Air Force, one of the first to call to congratulate me was Terner, then the mayor of Beersheba. He said to me simply, "You see, Shkedy? I was right."

94.
Run, Eli, Run...

After I learned with great difficulty to swim, they recommended to my mother, who did not know and does not know how to swim to this day, to sign me up for the Hapoel Ramat Hashavim swimming team.

There was only one swimming pool in the area, and it probably wouldn't have met the Olympic standard either. It was originally built as a water reservoir, with diagonal walls, and had to be converted into a swimming pool.

Despite this, the team, managed by the legendary Ruchke Bogin, was large and very good, comprising children from the surrounding communities.

We trained several times during the week, but on Saturdays, we competed across the country. I was a weak swimmer, and I felt bad about myself and my abilities, but I didn't give up and continued to train.

Because of my father's work, it was hard for him to drive me to competitions as other parents did. But when it came to particularly important competitions, he would make an effort and take me.

Such was the case on that Saturday when the semi-finals of the Israeli Swimming Championships for Children and Youth were held at Kibbutz Maayan Zvi in the north.

Swimming has four main styles: butterfly, backstroke, breast-stroke, and front crawl.

You usually start by learning to swim the breaststroke.

That was the only style I somehow managed to learn, so it was the one I competed in. The result, as expected, was not something to be proud of.

I completed my heat, sat on the grass, and began licking a popsicle.

Then suddenly I hear my father shouting:

"Eli, run quickly..."

"What? Where?" I asked.

"They announced the backstroke, and no one showed up to compete," Dad answered.

I looked toward the pool and saw to my surprise that it was truly empty.

There was not a single swimmer.

I began running.

I threw away my popsicle.

I jumped into the water.

I swam alone.

I almost drowned.

But I finally won first place in a swimming competition...

I started to develop my backstroke ability and compete in that style, and I achieved decent results.

I learned that it is important to understand what your advantage is. If it is a relatively "empty" field, in which there are few contenders and competitors, then naturally you will have a greater chance of success.

When competing among two or more competitors, it is important to analyze your and your opponent's (or opponents') advantages and disadvantages, and to dictate the direction you want to take the competition.

If you find a way to utilize your advantages and match them to the opponent's disadvantages, then even if in the overall concept of total ability the challenger in front of you is better than you, you'll win.

For example, in a tennis game, you may have the advantage in agility and as a volleyer playing close to the net, while your challenger is more of a baseliner, hitting groundstrokes from the back of the court, but not quite as agile. In this case, you want to avoid trading groundstrokes, because you will lose for sure. Instead, you need to get inside the service line, close to the net, as fast as you can and try to win by playing to your advantage — i.e., with the help of your net game.

• • •

Understanding the relevant areas in which you have a relative advantage and grasping your and your opponent's strengths and weaknesses are important conditions for victory.

95

Connecting Through the Screen

In late 2018, the family of Lieutenant Colonel Emmanuel Moreno, a member of Sayeret Matkal, the IDF's elite intelligence-gathering commando unit, who was killed in an operation in Lebanon, contacted me and asked me to participate in a seminar to be held in his memory and in the memory of Colonel Dror Weinberg, who fell in battle with terrorists while he was a brigade commander in Hebron.

The least I could do for the families and in memory of the fallen was to come to the seminar and speak, so I did.

The event took place at the Wohl Center adjacent to Bar-Ilan University, before a large audience, including the cadets of the IDF's Officers Training School, otherwise known as Training Base 1.

A few days later, a friend sent me a link to a lecture on YouTube.

"Look familiar?" he wrote to me.

I was surprised.

I didn't know that my lecture was filmed at the seminar, and I certainly didn't know it was uploaded to YouTube.

And then... I saw that something completely unexpected was happening:

The lecture, about half an hour long — quite lengthy by the standards of social media — went viral and reached hundreds of thousands of views within a short period of time.

I'm far from an expert in social media and the Internet, but this intrigued me, and I tried to study it, crack the case and understand: What happened? Why did it happen? What could I learn from it?

That is, do an Air Force-style debriefing.

I came to the conclusion that it was not the lecture per se, but something else.

This encounter, along with the authentic stories told in a direct way and in relatable terms, made the viewers think about themselves — to be open, to listen, to feel, to think about their beliefs, their values, their truth, and what they would do in my place in the situations I described or in similar situations from their own lives. They personally connected to each story and every topic I discussed, thought about similar events that had happened to them, and felt that my words were relevant to their lives, even if they came from completely different worlds.

They were active viewers who talked to me — and, mostly, to themselves — through the screen.

To a great degree, the decision to write this book, and the ways in which it is written and presented to the readers, are the result of the debriefing carried out following that lecture and the insights I attained.

96.
"Dad, Without the Materials"

I have been blessed with three wonderful and talented children: Nimo, Maya, and Omer. Each of them with their own character and temperament, each one and their preferences, each a whole world.

On the one hand, it is a great source of pride when you have such children. On the other hand, this presents no simple challenge: How much do you intervene? Are you just trying to convince, or are you coercing? When do you let go and watch from the sidelines? When do they feel comfortable asking for your advice or help on their own initiative? And what is the stage when they become your best advisors?

Maya, my daughter, is very, very special and talented in many areas. When it came time to choose an academic track in high school, she consulted with me.

My suggestion was to focus on three essential subjects that would open up all the possibilities for her in the future: mathematics, physics, and English at an advanced level.

Beyond that, she ought to study whatever speaks to her heart, whatever she wants and enjoys.

She listened, thought about it, and decided a little differently:

She would indeed study advanced English and math, but she would pass on physics.

Maya preferred to invest her time and energy in other things, which she found much more meaningful than studying physics.

Then it came time for Maya to begin the military enlistment

process, which usually occurs in 11th grade; her grades were excellent, allowing her to do whatever she wanted.

Almost...

One day, she called me — I was then commander of the Air Force — and said, "Dad, I want to serve in the Air Force as an instructor on the flight simulator, but they won't let me. I never took advanced physics, and they say I need that..."

I said, "If those are the prerequisites," (though, by the way, that changed a while later) "then that's what they are."

"But, Dad, they sometimes make exceptions to allow..." Maya replied.

I said, "There's no way I'm going to intervene to make this happen. I won't do favoritism."

Silence on the line.

Maya entered the IDF and was trained as an operations room administrator in the Air Force.

One evening I came home and found her decked out with her training uniform, boots, and rifle.

"What happened??" I asked.

She replied, "I'm going to the officer's training course."

She basically said to me, without words: "Dad, I'm doing fine on my own..."

I had the great privilege of awarding Maya her officer's bars.

Since then, whenever she has chosen a direction or taken on a significant task, she has studied the subject in depth, not taking it lightly but preparing herself well.

She has always been daring, never being afraid to surge ahead. This has made her very successful in her work and in fulfilling her dreams.

Maya has the ability to understand the deep meanings of things by listening sincerely and thinking openly.

When I started writing this book, I told her what my intentions and goals were.

I told her that the stories in the book should be, as I saw them, the catalyst for all my readers to find themselves. The words ought to be relevant and touch the lives of everyone, arousing thoughts about themselves and about situations in their own lives.

WHO THE F*CK IS MICHAEL?!

I also told her that I would attach letters and pictures from my life relating to the story in each chapter. By the time I began writing, I had already started collecting and organizing that material.

Maya listened to me very attentively and then said, "Dad, I think it's a mistake to attach visualizations to your stories. They'll detract from the text and prevent readers from using their own thoughts about how the stories relate to them — exactly the opposite of what you want to happen and your deeper purpose in writing the book."

I thought about what Maya said.

I realized that she was right and that I was wrong.

She showed me the light.

I removed all the materials I had planned to use in the book.

97.

The Bond

In every interaction between people — spouses, family, friends, business partners, et cetera — different types of decisions are made.

Concerning each decision, two aspects must be examined:

The first is the nature of the decision.

The second is the dynamic, the energy and the mutual feelings created among the people involved, during and after the decision-making process.

Over the years, I have learned that in decision-making, several main types of situations tend to arise.

In the first situation, I must decide, and it is within the scope of my authority and responsibility.

In this case, I consult, I listen, I consider — and then I decide.

Even if I do not accept the recommendations of whomever I consulted, I emphasize some aspect of their advice which has proven good and helpful.

If I accept their recommendations, I do not hesitate to give them real and public credit.

It doesn't diminish me. Rather, it enhances them and greatly strengthens the dynamic and the bond between us.

In the second situation, someone else has to decide and it is within the scope of their authority and responsibility.

In that case, I'm not in the center. What matters is the other and the decision they have to make.

I only offer advice (assuming they asked me to...)

If my advice is not accepted, I don't broadcast it as an insult or disappointment. I'm not supposed to be in the center and not everything revolves around me...

More than that: Even if my advice is accepted, I don't expect public acknowledgment and credit. It's just a bonus, and some people have a hard time doing that.

I know and they know that I have wholeheartedly given advice to someone whose best interests I care about, helping with an issue important to them.

In the third situation, responsibility is undefined, so it is actually a joint decision.

When the issue is important to me, I declare it as such calmly but clearly, and I lead the process in a spirit of cooperation and thoughtfulness.

If I feel that the subject is more important to the other person than to me, I let them make the decision and go with the flow sincerely, without making faces...

If they ask, I tell them.

If they don't ask? That's fine too.

If they insist that I be a partner in the decision, I ask the other person to choose three alternatives that are good for them, and I help them make the choice.

Often, the dynamics between people are more important than the quality of the decision.

For example, what type of sofa to buy, which restaurant to go to, or where to go on vacation.

The color of the sofa does not matter that much, nor how nice it looks — what is important is that we sit on it to enjoy ourselves and have fun.

In the fourth situation, the other person makes an important and significant decision that concerns me without taking me into account, contrary to my clear and unambiguous position, without consulting me at all.

When it comes to an issue that is important and significant to me, and the decision makes me feel so bad that I cannot make my peace with it, I will live my truth and just not be there.

In some situations, only listening, empathy, and identification are required. To really listen to the other, to feel what they're feeling without expressing an opinion, merely reflecting the other's words and being with them. Sometimes it is important for them to say their piece, to know that I hear them, I'm with them, and I understand them.

They'll reach the necessary conclusions on their own.

• • •

Listening is the greatest gift you can give, and the greatest gift you can receive.

98.

If You Refuse, I'm Leaving

My sister Yael decided to seriously study goldsmithing, a field she has loved from an early age.

She completed her studies, worked in a prestigious jewelry workshop, and then began teaching goldsmithing at Beit HaLohem[14] in Tel Aviv.

Towards the end of the first year of studies, preparations began for the annual exhibition, in which Yael's students, wounded warriors from the IDF and other security forces, would display their works and creations as well.

They were very excited and invited family and friends to the exhibition.

My sister, who wanted to empower her students, demanded that the name of each creator be mentioned next to their work so they'd receive the respect they deserved.

Sounds obvious?

Not really, as it turns out.

The answer Yael received from the organizers of the event surprised her:

"That is unacceptable for us. The works will be presented under the title 'Yael Shkedi's Class.' This has been the case for years, and the same applies to the students in your course."

Yael, who always lives her truth, immediately replied:

---

14. Beit HaLohem (The Warrior's House) is a rehabilitation, sports and recreation center for injured soldiers and members of Israel's security forces and their families.

"I'm not prepared to accept that. All rights belong to the students who created the jewelry, not me. They are the ones who put in the work and demonstrated talent, ability, diligence, and perseverance. Therefore, their names ought to appear next to their creations.

"If you refuse to let me do what I believe in and know to be right and proper, I'm leaving."

In the end, after extensive struggles, and after the powers that be made quite a few faces to express their displeasure, they complied with her demand. The works were displayed in the exhibition alongside the names of the creators, exactly as she wanted.

This struggle made Yael realize that she had to do things her own way.

A short time later, she left Beit HaLohem without a second glance and committed to establishing a private school for goldsmithing.

Thus, "Yael Shkedi Jewelry School" was established in Kfar Saba, a private school for jewelry-making and design that has become one of the leading such establishments in the country.

At the end of every year, at the gala opening of the lovely exhibition, I always enjoy seeing Yael, her team of teachers, and the apprentice artisans.

I enjoy seeing how happy she is, glowing and flourishing, how the staff is happy and proud, and how the people who learn in the workshop are excited and full of satisfaction from having been able to fulfill a dream, to express themselves and no less importantly, to be appreciated for their work.

• • •

When you feel that significant decisions are being made about things that pertain to you and are important to you contrary to your beliefs and worldview — just don't be there, leave.

When you follow your path — with your dream, ideas, and your faith — and succeed, the sense of satisfaction is tremendous.

99.

Packed a Suitcase, Said Goodbye, and Left

My daughter, Maya, married a man we liked very much.

Some time passed and I saw that Maya's demeanor had changed.

You never really know what happens behind the closed doors of other relationships, even if they are the people closest to you.

But I saw that she was dispirited and out of sorts. She didn't smile and I felt that something bad was going on with her.

Professionally, she was flourishing; the problem lay in her personal life.

I met with her, we spoke several times face-to-face, and I realized that the situation was really no good for her.

She tried — really tried — to get things back on track, but it was to no avail.

From week to week, the situation deteriorated.

Maya was very hesitant about the right course of action.

Then came COVID-19.

The uncertainties of lockdowns and quarantines turned the family unit into a pressure cooker.

One day Maya took a suitcase,

Packed some clothes,

Said goodbye,

Left the house just like that, as she was,

And came to our house.

We told her:

"We love you.

"Whatever is right and good for you,

"Whatever you decide,

"We are here with you and for you."

During the period she stayed with us, she debated, weighed, debriefed, and pondered the situation.

It was undoubtedly no easy move, with no simple feelings involved. It was complex to cope both with her surroundings and her inner world.

Despite this, I felt a considerable weight had been lifted from her.

I was happy to see her relax more and return to smiling.

After about a month, Maya rented an apartment for herself.

The change she had undergone was amazing.

It was impossible to mistake what we saw — her brothers, her mother, and me.

Her energy was restored, her joie de vivre returned, the internal and external dynamics changed, and she simply beamed.

Does the termination of a relationship, whether familial or in business, signify capitulation or failure?

Is a person who chooses to persevere as if things are normal, motivated by the right things?

Because of social conventions, should a person stay for a long time in a place that is bad for them?

Is "What will they think?" or "What will they say?" more important than how a person feels?

To analyze the issue, one must start with the most important question:

What is the goal?

Is it to live in a relationship dictated by norms, or is the goal to live a life imbued with meaning, happiness, and a sense of satisfaction?

Which is more correct: to preserve the relationship at all costs, even when it stifles you, empties you, and exacts a heavy toll, mentally and emotionally, or to dissolve the relationship, especially when there are still no children, and allow yourself to embark on a path that can lead to happiness, joy, and light?

To me, parting is not a failure. Very far from it.

Maybe it is the end of a dream that has not come true.

In some situations, separation is the way to achieve a better life, even if in a different form, and actually staying in an unsuccessful relationship is a failure that removes you from the goal.

Parting does not erase or eliminate the good things from the past.

The shared experiences and beautiful moments will remain.

It is important to do this without blaming yourself or the other party, but only to debrief, learn, and decide the right thing to do.

Life is here and now.

Sometimes we confuse our goal with the question of success or failure.

A relationship is not an end but a means.

To feel good about yourself, that's the goal.

If it is bad for us, but we stay in the relationship regardless, we might have gotten a little confused...

If you have reached a point of mental suffering and do not feel like seeing and living with your partner, if it's not beneficial long-term and things are not going in the right direction, it is probably not a relationship that is good for you.

You have not failed.

You've made a choice.

Apparently, your eyes were opened, and you boldly decided to follow a different path.

Embarking on a new path is always accompanied by uncertainty. People tend to stay in the place they know well and create the illusion of stability and security in a place that may not be good for them.

But in my view, temporary uncertainty that can lead to a better and happier life is far superior to the certainty of a bad situation.

After you have decided, it is right to commit purposefully, to resolve the issue as quickly as possible, even if you compromise on material things. Just hit the road and move forward.

And that's exactly what Maya did.

It moved me to witness her inner strength and the relief she felt

ELYEZER SHKEDY

after deciding to leave a place that was bad for her, even though it meant compromising on material things. She was driven by her goal, which led her to embark on a new path to a better place.

100.

Put It in the Safe

My wife, Anat, contracted Parkinson's disease at a very young age, thirty-two. I was then the commander of HaEmek Squadron at Ramat David Airbase.

We didn't tell anyone about the disease and decided that we would deal with it together.

It was important to me that Anat came with me to all the events I attended and so, despite the demanding roles I filled, we had time together.

Anat was a true partner in everything that was happening, hence we were less preoccupied with her illness.

We developed different methods of coping with the situation, especially when the drugs had a diminished effect, and we did not allow the disease to take over our lives.

As commander of the Air Force, I tried to keep my flights abroad on duty as short as possible; if possible, Anat would join and not stay in Israel without me.

My guideline was I would fully pay out of pocket all expenses related to Anat.

It was simple when I flew on a civilian airline like El Al, and so I did. But as commander of the Air Force, some of the flights, especially those of shorter range, were in the IAF's planes.

I talked about it with my team, whom I loved. It was important for me to listen and hear the opinions of young, sharp, savvy people, coming from different fields with a sensitive and broad perspective.

I made it clear to them that I wanted to pay for Anat on those flights as well, if she joined me.

"Why?" they asked. "After all, the flight is happening either way."

I said, "That has nothing to do with it. I want to pay for her anyway. In such a situation, call El Al or another airline that flies to the same destination, find out how much a flight like that costs, and I'll deposit that amount in dollars in the safe."

"But no one will demand payment for it," they said.

"If anyone does ask," I replied, "tell them that Shkedy already paid for his wife, and the money is waiting in the safe."

Then one of them said, "The other generals won't appreciate this... They'll be on the hook too."

I said, "We won't tell anybody."

"And what do we do if no one asks for the money you deposited in the safe?"

"When I finish serving here, we'll donate the money to a good cause."

When my service as commander of the Air Force ended, there were several thousand dollars in the safe. I decided to donate the money to the children of the Etzion School in Kfar Saba, which was admirably led by the legendary principal Yisrael Lenchner, a man who was all about giving and many of whose students were the daughters and sons of Ethiopian immigrants.

The gift was accepted with tremendous joy.

Some time later, when stories about the flights of politicians and their families blew up publicly, they asked me, "How did you know?"

"I didn't know anything," I said. "It was important for me to live my truth. Regardless of the law or procedure, as a leader and commander, I had to do the right thing, so the people around me could understand that this is what is expected of them. That's why I did it."

●●●

It is important to always live your truth.

Go the extra mile to avoid the appearance of wrongdoing.

Anything and everything is a personal example.

101.

Send Her to Us

One day, when I was the commander of the Ramat David Airbase, my friend Raz, who was then the commander of the flight school, called me. It was shortly before the winging ceremony, and among the graduates of the pilot's course was also the first female combat navigator in Israeli Air Force history, Sari.

Raz was upset. "I'm very worried that they'll sabotage her down the road just because she's a woman. What do you say?"

I said to him, "Send her to us to Ramat David. We'll put her in HaEmek Squadron, which we both know very well, and we will make sure she is well taken care of."

A few years earlier, I had spearheaded the re-establishment of HaEmek Squadron as an F-16 squadron, and Raz was one of the first pilots to serve in it. (Before becoming a pilot, he had served in Sayeret Matkal, first as a soldier, then as an officer in the unit.)

A few minutes after our conversation, I received a call from the commander of HaEmek Squadron, who asked to speak with me urgently.

"Come on over," I said.

The squadron commander and his deputy, who was a navigator, were both excellent officers and airmen. They immediately began with an impassioned speech about how much they were in favor of integrating women, how genuine and meaningful a process it was. But...

They thought it was very wrong for Sari to join their squadron.

This was a squadron with complex and difficult missions, they explained. Why set her up to fail?

I listened to them very attentively without saying a word, and when they finished I said:

"She will come to HaEmek Squadron, and your mission is to do everything to help her succeed.

"You know me. Under no circumstances will I compromise on quality, and I am convinced that she can do her job."

Silence in the room.

The squadron commander and his deputy understood that I was determined to move this along, together with them, and that we would succeed.

Following the meeting, I decided to clarify the message, my intentions, and my approach to the subject. I gathered all the base's personnel — enlisted, NCO's and officers — and told them that the first female combat navigator would soon arrive at HaEmek Squadron, and that I was convinced it was the right decision.

Usually, I told them, it was quite comfortable and pleasant to be around me. But there ought to be no misunderstandings: sometimes it is very, very worthwhile to steer clear and not mess with me.

If I heard that someone, in any way, stood in her way, treated her improperly, or tried tripping her up for no good reason, he would answer to me directly, I said.

And that would be an example of a situation in which it would be best not to cross my path at all...

Roger that. Message received, loud and clear.

Sari, a tiny and determined officer with a penetrating gaze, arrived at the squadron, was integrated, and quickly became an aircrew combatant in every sense of the word. She participated in combat missions, including sorties in the Second Lebanon War, and performed very well.

To the credit of the squadron's officers and enlisted personnel, it must be said that they really treated her as an equal among equals, but the credit for the breakthrough goes first and foremost to Sari herself.

• • •

About fifty percent of the population is female, so statistically about half of the State of Israel's finest ought to be women. It is right and necessary to allow women to express themselves in every field of life, and this is also true of the Air Force. Not only for the sake of equality of opportunity, which is important in its own right, but because integrating high-quality and talented women, selected from twice as broad a group, leads to better results.

The IAF reserves the right to choose the best and most suitable from among all draftees to participate in the pilot's course, in recognition of the importance of air power and its centrality. Naturally, aircrew members perceive themselves as an excellent team — and quite rightly so. The decision to add women to this male group was not easy, to put it mildly. And even after the decision was made, its full realization was far from self-evident.

Unfortunately, there are those who try to prevent the inclusion of women in significant roles. And they do it using different methods, overt or covert.

The first method is simply not to allow them in the door.

On this issue, Israel's High Court of Justice said its piece, and today in Israel there are excellent women in every field of pursuit.

The second method is to allow one woman in and fail her during training, then say, "We really tried, but it doesn't work. Here's proof they're unfit."

And the third method is not to invite them to tryouts like the men (despite the court's decision to the contrary), but to wait for them to apply on their own accord.

I found out about the third method by chance as commander of the Air Force, when I discovered that those responsible for summoning draftees to screen for the pilot's course never called in women who met the statistical criteria, even though they did call in men who met the very same standard.

When I heard about it, I announced that it was completely unacceptable to me and demanded that the procedures for summoning women to screening exams be equal to those for men.

Various and sundry objections were then raised, but I didn't care, and they had to do exactly what I demanded. Indeed, this was the impetus for a complex shift within the IDF; nowadays, whoever meets the statistical criteria is summoned to screen for the pilot's course, girls just like boys.

Self-evident? Obvious? Sometimes, people are completely oblivious to the obvious.

• • •

When I was appointed commander of the Air Force, I wanted to open up all the positions in the IAF to women, including in the elite commando units Shaldag (Kingfisher) and 669. I held discussions on the subject with the relevant officials in the IDF and eventually concluded that we would open all the positions — except for a very limited number of positions over which the Manpower Directorate and, surprisingly, the chief of general staff's advisor on women's affairs, raised particular objections.

I also stipulated that in each of the professional tracks in the Air Force, our goal was to reach a defined, significant percentage of women within two years, not as a supplement to current staffing but as an integral part of it.

In some quarters of the corps, there was strong opposition to this, but the Air Force is the Air Force, which means that once a decision is made, implementation is not long to follow. In fact, we reached most of the targets I aimed for within a year instead of two.

• • •

Beyond the fact that equality is an essential right, I believe that ensuring it is very much the right thing to do, from a broad perspective: for women, for men, for the Air Force, for the IDF, and for the State of Israel.

102.

The Ego Beneath the Surface

When it comes to decisions on special and sensitive issues, those that involve organizational or personal changes, you often run into a wall in the form of ego.

In retrospect, there were two main issues in the Air Force in which ego played a particularly large role in the context of decision-making. This applies to the egos of the aircrew members, pilots, and navigators, as individuals and as a group.

And let there be no doubt, I do not exclude myself. I had to go through a process within myself that enabled me to make decisions and launch significant and necessary initiatives pertaining to these sensitive issues.

The first topic was the inclusion of women in the pilot's course, their training, and their placement as aircrew combatants in every sense of the word, as I detailed in the previous chapter.

The second issue was the use of unmanned aerial vehicles (or by their new name, remotely piloted aerial vehicles).

The operational potential of UAVs is enormous. But the thought that a UAV can replace you, an aircrew member, is an affront and very emotionally difficult to accept.

It will always be draped up in serious, substantive, and operational arguments, but one thing will always remain in the background, beneath the surface: ego.

Ego is a completely human thing, but it must not have any weight in decision-making. Your role as a leader is to make decisions based solely on substantive considerations, even if they pluck at your heartstrings or those of your personnel.

Believing that the processes you want to advance are important and justified is only half the battle. The other half is making things happen.

To make things happen, especially when it comes to complex and sensitive issues, it is important to explain to your people, at every opportunity, the rationale behind the decision, convince them of its importance, and emphasize how determined you are to implement it.

Accurately define your expectations and give direct instructions as to the who, what, and when of the implementation process.

It is important that you make sure to execute and track the progress of each mission by receiving status reports. And even then, in the same discussions throughout the process, you must repeat the messages over and over again, never holding back.

When your people see your determination and believe like you in the importance of the process, they will be able to overcome the ego barriers and become true partners with you.

103.

I Was a Colossal Fool

When I was a cadet in my pilot's course, there was a screening stage called "Check 8," which involved eight test flights in a Fouga — a French two-seat jet trainer. Those who successfully passed this initial stage would continue the course and begin a structured process of learning aviation.

After the screening flights, several flights would be made with an instructor and then the cadet would be sent to do a "solo" — that is, to fly on their own, to shore up their skills and confidence, and advance to the next training phase.

In the first solo, the task is to take off, make one pass over the runway, and land safely.

After the first solo circumnavigation of the runway, the learning process continues with some of the flights being with an instructor and some being solo flights near the runways.

In the next stage, the cadets are sent to "solo areas," flying to a designated location to practice on their own, without an instructor.

I had an instructor from Ramatayim named Licht — a smiling, caring, orderly, and strict person. Licht decided to send me very early in the process on my first solo of flying around the runway and landing.

I got through it safely.

After a few days, Licht decided to send me first to the "solo area."

Before the flight, he briefed me thoroughly: "Go to the area, do exactly what is defined in the flight syllabus, execute some very basic flying maneuvers" (he went over them extensively) "and return safely."

My plans were completely different...

I decided to perform some aerobatics, which of course went well beyond my capabilities at the time.

I set out on my flight, did some basic exercises as planned, and then started going off script. At that stage of my life, my skill for such stunts was negligible.

And then... I found myself diving toward the ground at tremendous speed.

I pulled on the stick with all my might and got out of it.

But when I looked at the accelerometer, I saw that it had reached 8G.

The jet's limit was 4.5G.

Exceeding the stress limits can cause massive damage to the structural integrity of the aircraft, to the point of disintegration.

Big mistake.

I realized that my time in the pilot's course was probably over, so I stayed in the practice area and made a few more turns to wring the final moments out of what I presumed to be my last flight of the course.

I landed back at the runway, reported what had happened, and received a pretty serious punishment. But to my great surprise, I was not kicked out. To this day I don't know why.

In today's Air Force, they'd toss me out so quickly I wouldn't need a plane to break the sound barrier.

I was a kid and a colossal fool.

104.

They Caught Shkedy's Kid...

In fourth grade, it's time to choose which youth movement to join. When I reached this age, my father told me, "You can go to any youth movement you want, as long as it's Hashomer HaTza'ir..."

All my friends from school in Ramatayim picked a different youth movement.

Since they needed to assemble a minimum number of kids for activities, they had to recruit from all kinds of places and a wide range of ages. Apparently, those kids' parents had also told them they could go to whatever youth movement they wanted, as long as it was Hashomer HaTza'ir...

At first, I didn't know any of them, but I soon connected with two kids from the group, little punks like me, and we became good friends.

Before each activity, one of our gang, a boy who was kind but something of a troublemaker, brought a pack of Royal cigarettes he'd pocketed from his father, a famous director. We would climb the roof of the clubhouse, lie on our backs, and smoke for fun.

We really liked the activities for fourth-graders, but we liked the part that preceded them even more: smoking leisurely on that roof.

One day, the youth leaders decided to hold a scavenger hunt, and as part of the preparations for the activity, they went up to the roof to hide the treasure, a watermelon.

To their great surprise — and to our even greater surprise — they caught us red-handed, smoking away.

It was a huge scandal. Did you hear about Shkedy, the principal of the children's institution? They caught his young kid smoking on the roof of the clubhouse.

They dealt with us fittingly...

In retrospect, joining a youth movement made me feel mature and independent, but as a child, I didn't always fully understand the meaning of things, and sometimes I got confused between what was allowed and what was forbidden. One of the manifestations of this was smoking.

• • •

Children are constantly checking their limits. The role of the parents is to straighten them out when necessary, which is what my parents did.

105.
The Hitchhikers

When I was a captain and commander of the advanced combat course (the last stage of training fighter pilots) at Hatzerim Flight School in the south, my wife Anat and I went to a wedding in the center of the country.

We returned home to the family housing quarters at the base, very late at night.

In the Ashkelon area, I saw four young men in uniform hitchhiking, and I stopped to pick them up.

To my great surprise, they were four cadets from my course: Yavneh, Gutman, Aroeti, and Harlev.

Of course, they were not supposed to be in that area at all, and at that time in particular.

Anat and I drove a Peugeot van. Up front, the driver could sit alongside two passengers; in the back, there were two benches against the sides. There was a partition between the two compartments, with a window set in it.

Aroeti was sent by his friends to sit up front with us. From Kfar Saba, he had been in Anat's class in high school, and I really liked and appreciated him for his determination. He'd fought with all his might to get into the pilot's course, making it when he was already an IDF officer.

The rest of the cadets sat in the back.

We drove off.

Silence in the car.

Aroeti — who was usually peppy, smiling, full of joie de vivre, talkative — said nothing. His gaze was serious, and his face drooped. He must have felt that I was going to explode.

I was quiet.

Silence.

Anat didn't understand what was going on.

We arrived at the base and dropped all four of them off near the cadets' quarters, without saying a word.

Although I was furious, I slept on it and decided that I would not share the matter with anyone from the senior command of the flight school, as the verdict would be clear.

The next morning, when the four of them were positive that their time in the pilot's course had come to an end, I called them to my office.

They filed in.

Frigid silence.

I looked at them and said, "We all understand very well what happened yesterday and what it means."

"Yes," the four of them said sadly.

They were excellent people, generally well-behaved, and I thought it was wrong for them to be dismissed from the pilot's course because of their stupid act.

I said, "You're confined to quarters on the base for the rest of your time here off-duty, and everything stays between these four walls."

They looked at me, disbelieving their ears, and left the room stunned.

All four completed the pilot's course and later became leading aviators and senior officers in the IAF — squadron and base commanders — and went on to significant positions in military and civilian life.

• • •

Those who are tough, demanding, and uncompromising can sometimes make a completely different decision than expected.

106.

Whoever Didn't Want Me...

At the beginning of my journey in the IAF, it was decided to send three young pilots, including myself, from the Skyhawk squadron to the Mirage squadron. After a brief period of retraining, the most suitable aviators would be sent to the F-15 squadron, which at the time had the most advanced aircraft in the IAF.

As a young pilot, I was very wild and reckless. I violated flight restrictions time and time again, often by a wide margin.

At the end of the retraining period for the Mirage squadron, when it had to be decided whom to send to fly an F-15, I wasn't chosen.

I was informed about the closed-door discussion, where it was stated that "it would be irresponsible to put an F-15 in my hands."

I was offended to the depths of my soul, but I picked myself up and went back to flying recklessly and wildly.

A short time later, the decision was made to ground me because of my safety violations. I had a very hard time with the decision, but I got the message.

When I went back to flying, I flew in a much more mature and responsible way. Surprisingly, it did not impact my abilities or my results.

A few months later, a discussion was held in preparation for another retraining course for the F-15, as well as a retraining course for the first F-16 aircraft that arrived in Israel at the time.

In the F-15 squadron, which had given up on me a few months earlier, they realized that maybe I did belong there, so they reached out. I decided that I had nothing to look for in a squadron whose commanders had previously dismissed me as irresponsible and unworthy of being entrusted with an F-15. The insult still stung.

I told the commander of the base, who represented me at the meeting, "Either they send me to the F-16 squadron" (and prove to those who need it how wrong they had been) "or I'm staying in the Mirage squadron. I'm not setting foot in the F-15 squadron. No one can force me to extend my service and switch to a more advanced jet."

To my delight, it was decided that I could transfer to the F-16 squadron.

Zevik Raz, the commander of the squadron I joined and who a year later led Operation Opera to attack the nuclear reactor in Iraq, was pleased with the fact that I had said I wanted to fly only F-16s and not F-15s.

I'm not sure he knew the real reason...

It was the best thing that happened to me in the Air Force.

I came to a great squadron — the 1st Jet Squadron — with people like me and a squadron commander, Raz, whom I liked and appreciated a lot. The F-16 system was of high quality, young, dynamic, and energetic, and it allowed junior pilots like me to develop, take the lead, and express our abilities.

The circle was made complete when, in retirement, I started playing golf with the commanders of the F-15 squadron from those days, those who said (at least I thought so at the time) that I was not responsible enough to be entrusted with such an aircraft.

Unexpectedly, in one of our conversations about the past, they emphatically told me that they had nothing to do with the statement and the decision. On the contrary.

Perhaps...

The truth is that I like them very much, which does not prevent me and my good friend, Shani Boy (Meir Shani) also a former Air Force pilot, from giving them the business, that is, tearing them to pieces on the golf course, as they deserve...

You never know in real time if a bad thing happening to you may turn out, in retrospect, to be the best thing that has ever happened to you.

And the truth?

In those days, it would have been really irresponsible to hand me an F-15...

107.

A Jammed Sprinkler

I was chief of staff of the Air Force when the decision came up as to who would be the Air Force's next commander. There were three very good candidates, of whom I was the youngest.

The IDF's chief of general staff then was Moshe "Bogie" Ya'alon, and the minister of defense was Shaul Mofaz.

The tension was immense.

At that time, a large event was held at Mann Auditorium[15] in Tel Aviv, hosted by the Air Force Association and attended by members of the IAF throughout the generations. Ya'alon and Mofaz were there as well.

My seat, as the chief of staff and deputy commander of the Air Force, was next to the defense minister.

We had a good relationship. I appreciated his understanding and vision of operational matters and liked him. And I felt it was mutual.

At least in normal times...

But on that occasion, Mofaz's head was pivoting like a jammed sprinkler, never quite reaching me. In other words, at no point, throughout the evening, did he exchange a word with me or even turn in my direction; only to the other side.

The meaning of this behavior was immediately clear to me, and I told my wife, "They didn't choose me. Could there be a clearer sign?"

We got home, and that same evening they called from the office

---

15. The largest concert hall in Tel Aviv and home to the Israel Philharmonic Orchestra.

of the chief of general staff, Ya'alon, and asked me to come the next day early in the morning for a meeting.

Now the reality was undeniable: Ya'alon was going to inform me that he and Mofaz had chosen another candidate.

I was mistaken.

The next morning the chief of general staff informed me that I had been selected to serve as the next commander of the Israeli Air Force.

My explanation for what happened at the event at Mann Auditorium — though I don't know if it's true, I never talked about it with Mofaz — is that sometimes, precisely when you don't want to give something away, which in this case was something positive, your body language conveys the opposite message.

108.
The Speech...

"Air Force Southward" was a groundbreaking vision requiring far-reaching organizational changes, creativity, and thinking outside the box. This was not just an internal organizational endeavor by the corps; this was a Zionist and national mission to strengthen the Negev Desert in southern Israel and the periphery.

Thanks to the commander of the Air Force at the time, Dan Halutz, who understood the profound significance and courageously initiated the process, and thanks to many partners in the corps and outside of it, the vision became a reality.

The central component of the "Air Force Southward" program pertained to Nevatim Airbase.

The airbase in the city of Lod was about to close, and Nevatim in the south was supposed to absorb a major portion of the IAF's heavy transport fleet, as well as fighter squadrons.

As commander of the Air Force, I had to decide who would be the first commander of the unified Nevatim Airbase.

I struggled with the decision. Whomever I chose would not only have to run the base but also spearhead the complex process of relocating the transport array from Lod to Nevatim. In other words: rebuild the Nevatim base.

All the candidates were excellent people and fine officers, pilots head and shoulders above the rest. However, it was a decision in principle, not just a personal one:

Would it be better to appoint a superior combat pilot or a superior transport pilot?

Until then, every base with fighter squadrons had commanders who had been fighter pilots themselves.

One thing was clear to me: this had to be successful — no room for error here.

With these facts in mind, could I make a revolutionary decision and appoint a transport pilot to serve as commander of a mixed airbase? I could expect fierce opposition to such a move, both from within the corps and across the IDF. Or should I play it safe and pick a combat pilot?

I made my decision.

I invited all the candidates for the position to inform each of them personally of my decision.

One of them was Eden Attias, a transport pilot who had previously commanded the Flying Camel Squadron, the Elephant Squadron, and the Sde Dov Airbase.

He came into my office and took a seat.

I felt from his body language that he was tense and anxious, but I didn't know how much or why.

Without any unnecessary preamble, I told Eden that I had decided to appoint him to command Nevatim Airbase, promote him to the rank of brigadier general, and put him in charge of the complex and important integration process of the heavy transport array.

Despite my struggles to reach a decision, I was wholeheartedly committed to the conclusion I'd reached.

Eden was an excellent transport pilot with a strong personality, whom I loved and appreciated as a commander and as a true professional.

Then, after I told Eden that I had selected him, the following inconceivable thing happened:

Eden launched into a speech that he had prepared in advance. I listened, surprised. I realized that he might have heard me, but he hadn't really understood what I'd said. He simply could not digest the fact that I had chosen him as commander of Nevatim, so he gave the speech he had prepared for the seemingly expected scenario that I'd choose a fighter pilot, not him, to lead the united base.

At some point, I stopped him and said, "Eden, I've chosen you."

He looked at me and remained silent. I saw in his eyes that it
finally dawned on him, but he still could not believe that he had
been selected for the position.

Eden was emotional and thrilled. He understood the deep meaning of choosing him, and as I expected and anticipated, he turned
out to be an excellent base commander.

•••

*Sometimes, when locked into what you think is expected, it is difficult
to comprehend any other reality, even if it is simple, unambiguous, and
clear.*

109.

Superhighway to Change

I'm a big believer in change.

Advancement and development are deeply linked to the ability to change. Everyone with their own motivation and their own pace, the main thing is to move forward.

The problem is that people don't like change.

One of the things that stops us from developing and changing is uncertainty.

There is a great fear of exiting our comfort zone.

The transition from the familiar place to something new, unknown, and uncertain, produces butterflies in the stomach.

Moreover, the good feeling we get from success is ephemeral, while bad feelings that stem from failure tend to linger.

I've experienced this as well.

I debriefed the topic in-depth and realized that with every change I've made, there have been several stages:

The first stage: Bubbling
I'm not quite aware of my situation, yet I feel that something isn't working properly, even though I don't know what yet.

Things sink in gradually.

At this point, I'm mostly trying to convince myself that I'm doing fine overall. But it preoccupies me nonetheless.

The second stage: Thinking and maturing
I reach a point where I'm more aware of my situation and take deep

stock of myself. I consider the situation and understand it, but still postpone dealing with it.

The more difficult, problematic, and serious the situation, the stronger the feeling that I need to do something, especially when I get smacked in the face because I can't believe something like this could happen to me or my people.

In such a situation, I have to deal simultaneously both with rational analysis and with emotions such as anger and fear... which had been dominant.

Both ideas and feelings are active players, and I have to find ways to deal with both and still move forward.

There are also situations in which something burns in my bones, and I have a profound feeling that I need a change. Still, I am afraid.

The third stage: deciding

I'm finally ready; I reach a decision and say — initially to myself — that I am going to make a change.

The fourth stage: planning

I realize that without a plan of action on the way to the goal, there will be no change.

Planning is the "backbone" of change. I build a simple and clear plan of action: who takes action, what they do, and when they do it.

If the plan is not simple, it will simply never be.

The fifth stage: action

After I formulate a plan, I take the first step toward implementation, without which nothing will happen.

And I set off...

The sixth stage: preservation

To make a real change, success must be preserved. For this to happen, we have to prepare an action plan to assimilate the change, experiment, practice, and create positive reinforcement.

Positive reinforcement can spare us from falling. And I've had falls.

I don't see them as failures.

If you don't act, you don't fall and you don't fail.

I debrief myself critically, learning what I should have done differently. Most importantly, I realize it's better to enter a state of uncertainty that may yield something good — even if not in the immediate term — than to get stuck in the comfort zone that leads me nowhere.

I realize that I cannot continue to behave passively and that I have to be proactive.

The change depends on my ability to let go, to open up from the inside, and to act. Without that, nothing will succeed.

Along the way, I discovered that the transition from one stage to another (from permeation to thinking, then to deciding, planning, taking action, and preservation) is particularly difficult. These transitions required a lot of energy and sometimes gave me regrets, but they didn't make me falter.

Once I set out with the action plan, I felt close to getting on the superhighway to change.

Merging onto the superhighway meant facing difficulties and challenges. It required altering past patterns and being determined.

It was important to understand when I was drifting toward the shoulder, so that I could purposefully and proactively get myself back to the center lane, staying on the superhighway and not flying off the road.

I've always tried to have people by my side whom I appreciate and trust to accompany me through the process and point things out to me when necessary.

This was true for me personally and also as the leader of a group or organization.

Even when things seemed impossible — and I've experienced situations that seemed impossible — change was possible.

It depended on my attitude and my motivation.

•••

Change depends on me.

322

110.

My English Bug

English was a sensitive issue for us at home.

My parents didn't know English, and neither did my sister and I.

My father, who was self-taught, decided to learn English on his own. He invested a lot in the endeavor and reached a medium level of proficiency — which was still much higher than the rest of the household.

In high school, I was an excellent student, especially in math and science, but I had a bug when it came to English.

In the end, Dad took it upon himself to do my homework in English. When he finished, we would go through it together in case they surprised me in class with a question.

That's how I managed somehow.

At that time, a student who had earned "very good" marks in a certain subject for two years in a row was exempt from taking the matriculation exam in that subject, and that was their matriculation grade. It was possible to do this in only one subject, and I debated among several subjects, including English.

My father, who knew very well what my skill level was, told me: "Obviously it has to be English," and so I graduated from high school with a "very good" matriculation grade in English.

That is, Dad finished with a very good grade.

He really did make good progress...

This "bug" accompanied me down the road in the Air Force, and I always found some way around the problem. But I realized that I couldn't avoid it forever, and I came to the conclusion that to finally fix the bug once and for all, I needed to study in the United States. Eventually, my superiors decided to send me to pursue a master's degree in America.

There remained only one problem: how to pass the Test of English as a Foreign Language. TOEFL measures the English proficiency of applicants seeking to study at universities in the United States. It was a precondition for enrollment.

This time, I couldn't rely on my father as I had in high school. I had to deal with it on my own. I realized that there was no choice and that I had to tackle the issue, buckle down, and do everything possible to get past the obstacle that threatened my plans to study abroad.

At that time, I was the head of the IAF's Operations Department, a difficult and demanding position in which I was responsible for the corps' operational planning. I decided that no matter when I got home and how tired and exhausted I might be, every day I would study English and prepare for the test for at least an hour.

Although there were preparatory courses for exams of this kind, I didn't have time to take them, so I made an independent study plan.

I bought books, developed study methods, and every evening, at home, I did four things:

I studied the theory and methods.

I took similar tests.

I watched movies and television in English, covering up the Hebrew subtitles until I could listen and understand quickly.

And I read a few pages from an English book to prepare for the reading comprehension section of the test.

Just like planning and prepping for a military operation.

It was crazy.

I put my heart and soul into the project and wouldn't give up.

The combination of being the head of the Air Force's Operations Department, a 24/7 position, and preparing for the test late at night was brutal.

Then the day of the test arrived.

324

It was administered not far from Air Force headquarters in Tel Aviv. I took a two-hour break, went to take the test, and returned to the office.

I passed with flying colors. I was accepted to the Naval Postgraduate School in Monterey, California, and we traveled there with the whole family.

The study material itself was no problem, but since everything was conducted in English, it complicated the matter a bit, especially when it came to taking tests. Here, too, I developed a method for myself: I read each question several times to make sure I understood correctly, and then I could handle the answering part...

I'd gone through some obstacles and challenges in life, so I knew I would get through this too.

The person who really "helped" me contend with English in front of an audience was the lecturer in the course on the Arab-Israeli conflict, Dr. Glenn Robinson, who was no fan of Israel, to say the least (Chapter 33, "Battle Scene on a Pastoral Campus"), and made sure that all the students knew his opinions.

I knew I had to give him a "fight." I felt that I represented not only myself but also the State of Israel, the IDF, and the Air Force.

In each lesson, I gave an impassioned speech to refute his claims one by one.

I invested a lot in preparing for each "battle" and practicing my rebuttal.

I didn't care about anything else, and I fought him with all my meager strength in English, which was growing and growing.

Nowadays, I lecture in English to huge audiences in Israel and around the world, and I make sure to do it off the cuff, without notes.

Dad would never believe it...

111.
Somethings You Can't Explain. Unless...

I was invited several times to participate in Prof. Yoram Yovell's *Heart to Heart* talk show, and I declined.

In the meantime, my father's health was declining, and I realized the end was near.

Just then, I was contacted by the program once more.

I decided that this time I would participate and talk about my father and how he had influenced my life. I asked them to air the show as soon as possible so that my father would have a chance to watch it on TV.

The production staff promised to do everything possible ahead of the broadcast. And they did. But shortly after the show was filmed, even before it aired, Dad passed away.

The program was broadcast on March 30, 2015, the very same day as the funeral.

I felt that Dad was watching the program and listening to my words on the way to heaven.

112.
Vertigo

As a flight school instructor, you bear a huge responsibility — for the fate of the cadets and for the human and professional quality of the Air Force. You are constantly facing dilemmas: Are you acting correctly? When should you intervene? Are you too strict? Not strict enough?

These dilemmas throughout the training process are dealt with by using a variety of instructors and assessors, so that each person may instruct, observe, and test the candidate from their own perspective.

I had the privilege of being an instructor at the flight school.

As the commander of the Advanced Combat Course, the last stage of the pilot's course, I made sure that at any given time, I was personally training two cadets: one who was highly valued, an obvious talent in the field of aviation — to strengthen them and help them bring their abilities to the fore and surge forward; and another whose achievements in aviation came to them less naturally than their comrades but whose personal fortitude I admired and whom I believed had tremendous potential — to allow them to have a breakthrough, shore up their confidence, complete the course, and get on the right path with my mentoring and guidance.

There have been many examples of people who completed the pilot's course, even though they were no great shakes in the air, only to surge forward later on, become daring combat aviators, and even lead the Air Force.

Danny was a handsome guy, tall and admirable, whose kind eyes testified to his inner depth and character. He was a cadet who I thought had great potential, but aviation did not come naturally to him.

I decided to guide him, encourage him, and do everything I could to bring his potential to the fore.

I invested all my efforts in Danny, and he really developed, advanced and achieved a good level of proficiency in flying.

In preparation for the final exam of the pilot's course, I asked the commander of Hatzerim Airbase, Asher Snir, to assess him personally to get an impression of him and evaluate him. It was important to me that an experienced officer and pilot like Snir, whose wisdom and character I greatly valued, give me his opinion. Of course, I didn't interfere. The test was based on the standards set by Snir, formerly the commander of the flight school.

Danny passed with flying colors. Snir was so impressed with his flying abilities that he gave him a high score.

I was delighted.

After completing the course, Danny went on to an operational training unit (OTU) in a squadron for combat pilots.

I continued to monitor his progress.

In the middle of the training period, Danny called me and told me it wasn't going well.

I decided to come to the squadron where the operational training was held, to fly with him and try to help him cope with his difficulties.

I flew with him.

I didn't recognize a particular problem. He probably felt safe with me and displayed good flying ability.

Danny continued his operational training, passed more tests of various kinds, successfully completed his training, and was assigned to an operational Skyhawk squadron.

A short time later, Danny was killed on a night flight.

It was probably due to vertigo, a physiological phenomenon manifesting in a mistaken sense of your spatial orientation. For example, a situation in which you're flying right side up, but you still feel, really feel, as if you are flying upside down.

Many pilots and navigators experience this firsthand. I have experienced brutal spells of vertigo a number of times in my life as well.

Unfortunately, in the history of the Air Force, there have been several accidents caused when pilots suffering from vertigo could not snap out of it and were killed. A well-known case in the IAF was when the commander of a Phantom squadron, an excellent and experienced pilot, was struck by vertigo. He was unable to control the aircraft with the help of his instruments and instead dove toward the ground. At the very last moment, his navigator took control and saved them both and the plane from crashing.

However, Danny was flying in a single-seater plane, without a navigator.

He really was a wonderful and special person, a talented officer with tremendous potential. I felt terribly sad.

Unfortunately, accidents can happen to anyone. And they do happen.

From my knowledge of Danny's character and abilities, I estimate that if he had safely completed his initial term as a pilot, he would have reached a very significant position in the Air Force and in life in general.

Danny's death has occupied my thoughts ever since, and I know that his face will accompany me until my last day.

113.

The Blessing...

While I was deputy commander of the 101st Squadron at Hazor Airbase, they decided to send us a junior navigator, fresh out of the pilot's course, with honors.

Integrating an inexperienced navigator in a squadron operating the most advanced fighter aircraft at the time — two-seater F-16s — and executing the most complex missions available was a dramatic undertaking, far from being a given.

The navigator selected was Nir Barkan.

Since the squadron did not have a designated retraining protocol for a navigator coming directly from the pilot's course, we decided to throw him in the deep end by attaching him to various types of flights, including very complex ones. Ideally, this would allow us to learn how to integrate and train junior navigators in the future. A "pilot program," as it were.

Shortly after he arrived at the squadron, Barkan and I set out for particularly complicated dogfight training.

During that flight, we had a close call with another aircraft — the closest of my life. That is, we almost had a mid-air collision that would have disintegrated us in the sky. We passed unimaginably close, about thirty feet between our plane and theirs, at a tremendous passing speed (combining the speeds of the two aircraft) of almost 1,000 MPH, completely uncontrollably.

The dogfight was immediately halted; we caught our breath and returned to the landing strip.

Complete silence in the cockpit.

We landed, climbed out of the plane, and walked to our squadron. Then Barkan, who in light of his youth and inexperience did not fully understand what had happened, innocently asked me:

"Say, Shkedy, is that what it's always like?"

Barkan, a man of impeccable quality and an excellent officer, has gone far in the corps since then. He has served as commander of HaEmek Squadron, commander of Ramat David Airbase, commander of Hatzerim Airbase, head of the air division, and head of the air operations division. At the time of this writing, he is serving as deputy commander of the Air Force.

There is no explanation for the fact that we are still alive, except for unimaginable luck or a higher power.

I went to a synagogue to recite the *Birkat Hagomel*, the blessing to express gratitude for surviving a lethal situation.

114.
If and When...

Ever since becoming a junior pilot, and throughout my journey in the Air Force, I have lost friends and warriors on missions, crashes, and training accidents — aircrew, officers, NCOs, and enlisted soldiers.

It was hard for me, and far harder for the family and relatives of that person. I make sure to speak to as many of them as I can before Rosh Hashanah and before Passover, to chat and meet during the year, and to attend every Memorial Day service at Ramat David and Pilots' Mountain, west of Jerusalem.

Grim thoughts would occupy my mind at times, especially once my children were born:

What should be done if the unthinkable befalls me and my family?

What would be my last request from my wife Anat were I to be killed on duty?

And this is what I asked her to do:

If it happens in a training accident, never blame anyone for my not coming back. You must know that I could just as easily have been guilty of the death of another.

And if it happens on a combat mission, however sad and difficult it may be — unfortunately, this is the terrible price of war.

Do not in any way engage in searching for culprits, I asked, even if someone has made a serious mistake. Just don't do it.

Let the Air Force debrief, study, and deal with those who need to be dealt with, if necessary.

Even if things do not happen at the pace you want, and even if the systemic and personal findings are not as you believe they should be, let it go.

This is the way I would like you and the children to go on with your life.

This is my last request and my only request.

Take care of the family and the children.

Take care of yourself.

Move on.

I made sure to repeat this and tell it to her every time.

It was very hard for her to hear these words, and whenever I talked about it she had tears in her eyes. But she said she would do as I asked, if and when...

This helped me remain serene about my family's future every time I embarked on a flight or went on a mission.

I didn't do it to protect the system, but to protect my wife and children. I felt that dealing with death and guilt, which is very natural and even essential in certain situations, squeezes tremendous energy out of the survivors, occupies their hearts and souls, and greatly diminishes their ability to cope and look ahead. Such a struggle would never bring me back but would take a very high toll on the mental and physical health of those I love, making it very difficult for them to embark on a path leading them back to the light.

There is no right or wrong here, and it's not feasible to be judgmental about this difficult, complex, and delicate issue.

I don't know what Anat would have done.

But that was my request.

115.

An Iron Weight on Our Foot

El Al is no ordinary airline. It has unique characteristics, and its history is deeply connected to the history of the State of Israel since its inception. The Israeli flag symbolizes a great deal, and that's how it's been since the first flight, on September 29, 1948, taking Foreign Minister Moshe Sharett to Geneva and bringing the first president of the State of Israel, Chaim Weizmann, to Israel.

In 1991, El Al played a central role in Operation Solomon. On one flight, it filled a 747 with 1,088 Ethiopian immigrants, including two babies born during the flight. This is probably a world record for the number of passengers on one flight, but above all, it was a national and Zionist mission of the first order.

The State of Israel is in many ways a kind of island, and access to it in times of emergency is almost exclusively by air. It is no coincidence that the state has a golden share in El Al, with all that this implies.

One of the main issues that I was required to address when I took on the role of CEO at El Al was the security of the company's aircraft and the safety of its passengers and crew.

The security of an Israeli airline is an extremely sensitive and important issue that cannot be taken lightly. Naturally, the issue is dealt with by state authorities and falls under their purview. The Shin Bet security agency directs and manages how security protocols are implemented on the ground and in the air, in Israel and around the world, and the matter must be financed by the state.

For years, Israeli airlines were required to cover forty percent of security and safety expenditures. For El Al, this meant a huge outlay of about $40 million a year. Arkia and Israir — two smaller Israeli airlines — also spent large sums, proportional to the volume of their business.

This was a very heavy financial burden, especially for Israeli airlines intensely competing with international airlines flying to and from Israel, whose security issues are largely subsidized by their home countries.

I'm all for competition. That's what I've believed all my life, wherever I've been. In the business world, competition leads to the utilization of resources, initiative, creativity, excellence, and the ability to cope with changing situations. However, it is important that competition takes place on conditions that are as fair and equitable as possible.

You cannot have two swimmers compete if one has an iron weight tied to their ankle.

I mean you can, but the results would be quite predictable...

In addition, security costs are not under the airlines' control; rather, they are determined by the Shin Bet's definitions and directives. The CEO of El Al has no discretion on the matter, even if he understands security matters well...

Therefore, I believe that even if it is a private commercial company, the state must act fairly and enable it to compete on fair and equitable terms against the competition. Certainly in the field of aviation, which is so significant for the State of Israel.

I decided to go to battle to correct this injustice.

For me, the struggle was both righteous and imperative. But when I talked about it for the first time with the company's management and board members, the responses were:

"It's a waste of time..."

"We've tried it many times before..."

"There's no one to talk to..."

"They have other political agendas..."

"They are much stronger than us, so even if we're right, there's no chance..."

We held an in-depth discussion on the subject together with

some of the leading lawyers in Israel — and they also explained that we stood no chance. Only Tami Mozes, a member of the board of directors and controlling shareholder of the company, a special woman whose wisdom and personality I love and appreciate, said very courageously that despite the risks of going to war, she thought I was right and she is with me in the battle.

I told the board members that I would do everything and anything to achieve success, even if it cost me my seat.

We set off.

The struggle was hard and long. I recruited everyone who could help, rolled up my sleeves, and realized that along the way I would also have to take my licks.

Believe me, I did...

But I wouldn't give up.

At the same time, I asked that we prepare a petition against the State of Israel in the High Court of Justice. I believed then and I still believe in the judicial system; I felt and knew that we were right; and I was willing to go all the way in the face of forces that were dozens of times stronger than us, with all the risks that entailed. Our petition before the High Court of Justice was ready to go, but just before it was filed, we decided to shut the company down for two days. That was a stage I really didn't want to reach, but there was no choice. We had to demonstrate to the decision-makers how serious we were and make it clear to them that if the situation didn't change, the very existence of El Al was in danger.

It was do or die from the company's perspective.

When you fight for something, you usually encounter two types of responses:

One type comes from those who relate matter-of-factly to the subject.

The other type, which is unfortunately more common, comes from those who do not have substantive arguments and reasons, so they engage in ad hominem attacks on the person opposing them.

When they came out against me personally — as they certainly did — I knew that the attackers had no substantive arguments and reasons for their conduct and decisions, so the solution was inevitable, whether I would get to see it through and enjoy it or not.

The struggle was exhausting and lasted about three years.

But in the end, we achieved our goal, without resorting to the court.

The state reached a conclusion for immediate implementation: instead of forty percent, Israeli airlines would have to pay only two-and-a-half percent of the security costs.

The significance for El Al was a reduction in annual expenditures of about $38 million in a multi-year agreement with the Ministry of Finance, i.e., about $380 million over a decade. Most importantly, this allowed El Al to survive and compete on equitable and fair terms with foreign airlines.

• • •

When you believe that your struggle is right and just, go with your truth.

Fight with all your power and don't give up.

There is no guarantee that you will succeed, but there is always a chance.

116.

You Have No Approval

When Anat and I decided to get married, we faced the question every young couple must: where to hold the wedding.

The Givat Hod institution in Ramatayim, which my father ran for many years and where I grew up, felt like home to me. I felt more connected to it than anywhere else.

We decided that we wanted to get married there, on the institution's grounds.

There was something much more exciting and special about it than a wedding in a hall or other venue.

My father contacted Avraham Schwartz, his successor as director of Givat Hod, and asked him to let us get married there. Of course, he stressed, we would pay the same rate as the most expensive place in the country, which then was Gan Oranim.

Schwartz agreed immediately.

But my father, who was more righteous than the Pope, also sent a letter to inform the Tel Aviv municipality, which officially owned the institution.

We got ready for the wedding and sent out invitations; everything was arranged and ready.

What could possibly go wrong?

At least that's what I thought...

One Thursday, shortly before the wedding, I got home late at night and saw my mother sitting in the living room waiting.

"Did something happen?" I asked.

"You won't believe it," she said, "but the Tel Aviv municipality won't approve holding the wedding at Givat Hod."

Wait.

What??

And why were they mentioning it only now???

I was shocked, but I wasn't going to give up. "Don't worry," I told her naively, "tomorrow morning I'll go talk to Cheech."

Shlomo "Cheech" Lahat was the mayor of Tel Aviv at the time.

Mom burst into bitter laughter and said in despair, "It doesn't work that way. There's no chance that the mayor will meet with you, certainly not if you just show up; and there's no chance he'll agree to change the decision."

I never wore a uniform when I was off duty to achieve anything, but I realized that this time, I had to make an exception.

In the morning, I would put on my uniform and drive with Anat to meet Cheech.

Early the next morning, Friday, we headed for Tel Aviv.

We parked outside city hall.

We went up to the top floor, where Cheech had his office.

We went up to his secretary and told her we wanted to talk to the mayor.

"You have an appointment scheduled?" she asked.

"No," we answered.

"Then you can't meet with him," said the secretary with a stern face. "You can't just drop in like this. You have to schedule a meeting well in advance."

"We have a very urgent problem, and we have to talk to him today," I said.

"That's impossible," the secretary pronounced again in a sullen voice, demonstratively lowering her gaze to the schedule that was on the desk.

We moved to the side silently.

What could we do now?

One thing was for sure: We would not give up.

We thought about it, discussed it, and concluded that if we sat on the bench in front of the secretary and waited until the mayor left to go home, no one could stop us from talking to him on the way to the elevator.

We sat there for a few hours, the secretary busy with her affairs and not looking in our direction. We were totally ignored.

Then suddenly, I realized that she was peeking at us from time to time, her face softening a little.

Maybe she felt sorry for us. Maybe she realized that we were not going to move. Either way, eventually she came over to us and asked, "What's the urgent problem you have to see the mayor about?"

We told her.

"Well," she said, "I'll try to talk to him or get you in anyway."

"Thank you very, very much," we told her.

A short while later she came up to us and said simply:

"The mayor has approved holding your wedding at Givat Hod."

• • •

When faced with a serious problem, ask yourself how you would act if there were no restrictions. Do not rule out the right solution in advance just because you anticipate difficulties. Deal with them in any way you can, avoid the landmines — and you will succeed.

117.

I Need an Answer Today

Before assuming the position of CEO El Al, I did a "doctorate" on the company — an in-depth research project with the goal of understanding its economic and financial position to the last decimal point. But after about three months on the job, I realized that we were facing a very big problem, whose intensity and severity I hadn't been aware of.

El Al had signed with Boeing to buy large-body 777s a few years earlier. The date of the next payment, approximately $80 million, was approaching.

El Al's situation when I took office was very precarious because of the global economic crisis at the time. In the past, payments to Boeing had been somehow deferred, but this time there was no way we could defer the payment.

Omer Shalev, our legal counsel and corporate secretary, was utterly downcast. Nissim Malki, El Al's CFO, was upset too. Reuven Virovnik, VP of Human Resources, was equally concerned. These three senior officials — all of whom were smart, experienced, and esteemed professionals who'd dealt with quite a few crises in the past — fully understood the seriousness of the situation El Al faced.

The concern was that unless exceptional and immediate measures were taken, the company could find itself in a very dire financial predicament.

A dramatic scene.

In the small conference room across from the CEO's office, our "war cabinet" convened "The Executive" — a group of board members well versed in the key financial issues the company was facing.

We put everything on the table.

Silence in the room.

The atmosphere was very tense.

The members of The Executive were well aware of the significance of the matter.

I looked at them, saw the concern on their faces, and told them that I had to think carefully before convening the entire board of directors to make difficult decisions with potentially far-reaching consequences for the company and its personnel, customers, investors, and shareholders.

Our meeting concluded with a heavy sense of unease.

I left the conference room and went to my office.

A short time later, the door opened. In the doorway stood Tami Mozes, the controlling shareholder of El Al. She came inside, all upset.

Tami is on the ball and talks to everyone at eye level; beyond that, mainly, she is a real warrior.

I felt that she realized her life's work might go down the drain.

I told Tami that I would do everything I could for the good of the company. I had faced some very difficult situations in my life, and I had dealt with them.

Tami calmed down a bit.

In such situations, when the pressure around you is enormous, the most important thing is to take a deep breath... drink some water... count to ten, keep your cool, and think of out-of-the-box solutions, even if they seem impossible in the moment. Do not be afraid, and act with a sense of purpose.

I told Tami that I had an idea.

"What is it?" she asked.

"I'll fly to the States and try to meet with the president of Boeing's civilian arm, Jim Albaugh, to persuade him to cancel the deal."

It really seemed to be an impossible mission.

How could we get to him?

Why would he agree to meet with me immediately?

Boeing is a large and substantial company, publicly traded on the New York Stock Exchange. The deal had been signed, and we had already paid a down payment of millions of dollars.

There seemed to be no chance in the world that he would cancel the deal.

But what did we have to lose?

Tami was having a very hard time and my heart was with her, but I began to see a little glimmer of hope in her eyes.

I asked for Jim Albaugh's personal email.

I wrote him an email and asked to meet with him urgently.

You never know when the people you've met in the past can help you in the present.

As the CEO of El Al, I hadn't had the chance to talk to Albaugh yet, but I'd met with him several times previously when I was commander of the Air Force and he was the CEO of Boeing's military wing (which produced, among other things, the IAF's cutting-edge F-15 fighter jet and advanced types of armaments).

Jim read my email and responded immediately, rolling out the red carpet for me.

For an American executive of his caliber, it was a highly unconventional move.

I wrote back that I'd be there the next day.

"See you then," he answered.

I got myself organized to fly to Boeing headquarters in Seattle.

I wrote down bullet points for myself.

I decided to take Stanley Morais with me. He was an El Al company man who had emigrated from Canada. His English was of course excellent, and I had been impressed with him during my short time at the company. I valued his keen intuition and interpersonal sensitivity.

The truth is I wanted to practice the speech I was planning to give to Jim Albaugh with Stanley during our flight to the United States, along with the conversation I anticipated.

We set off. A long flight to New York, and from there a connecting flight to Seattle. Then a few hours of sleep, and first thing in the morning — the meeting with Albaugh.

I practiced during the flights, and I continued to run my lines in the hotel with Stanley, all the time fine-tuning my message, my requests, and my English. The essential aim was to keep everything clear and unambiguous.

There would be no second chances. I had one bullet in the chamber.

The next morning we arrived at the Boeing offices.

It began as a one-on-one meeting, and Albaugh later invited Bill Daley, who was responsible for Boeing's civilian aircraft sales worldwide, to join.

I gave an impassioned speech.

I detailed the severe challenges that the company faced.

I explained that the global financial crisis and the security situation in the region had worsened El Al's economic situation.

The company's cash was on the line as collateral for the hedges made on fuel the previous year.

At this stage, I declared, we were unable to meet our commitment to buy the planes. Unfortunately, I couldn't say when things would change.

I emphasized to him that had he not approved my urgent request to meet with him, we would probably have been forced to take drastic measures.

Such measures, I emphasized, would be bad not only for El Al, but also for Boeing. A true lose-lose situation.

I reminded him that El Al was a long-standing and very loyal customer of Boeing and had been flying their planes exclusively for more than sixty years. El Al was a public company, and we were committed to transparent and proper conduct.

In the end, I said in the simplest and clearest possible way:

"I am aware of the far-reaching implications that this issue has on El Al and Boeing. But I ask that the transaction be canceled, without any penalties."

The fines imposed in such situations could be heavy, and I knew we had no chance of meeting those costs.

344

I promised him that as long as it was up to me, I would not leave El Al until it got back on the right path and returned to its position of prominence and strength in the business world.

I also said that I would do everything in my power to allow us to purchase narrow-body aircraft as soon as possible, the price of which was significantly lower than that of wide-body planes.

Albaugh — tall and distinguished, a silver fox who hunched a bit with a stern expression — waited until I finished speaking, then stared at me and said, "This is crazy. It has far-reaching implications."

Still, he promised that he would think about it, consult with his people, and decide.

I said, "OK, I understand that, but I need an answer today. I came specifically to meet you face-to-face, and I'm flying back to Israel this afternoon. If we don't find a solution we'll probably have to implement drastic measures in the coming week."

"I got it," he said. "I'll think about it, I'll consult with my people, and we'll meet again for lunch, when I'll let you know my decision."

We met for lunch and then, without unnecessary preambles, Albaugh informed me that in view of the unusual and critical situation, he had decided to approve my request and cancel the transaction.

I thanked him, and in my *hutzpah*, I asked for a refund of the deposit we had paid to Boeing, $12.6 million.

Albaugh looked at me in disbelief, but said without blinking: "You know what, this down payment" (which was supposed to "evaporate" if the deal was canceled) "can be put toward your next deal with Boeing, if there ever is such a deal."

I called Tami and told her that the deal had been canceled. I would have been able to hear her shout of joy from seven thousand miles away, even without the phone...

I updated Amikam Cohen, chairman of El Al's board of directors, and we both felt very relieved.

• • •

It ain't over 'til it's over.

118.

Boeing at a Bargain Price

One of the rules I have set for myself in my professional life is that I only assume a given role for a specified period of time, no more. This was true for me in the military, and it has been true for me in civilian life as well.

Another important rule that I set for myself is that after I have completed my tenure leading an organization, I never remain in an operative position in the same place. It's not good for the organization, not good for my successor, and not good for me.

I am happy and proud of what I've done, and now continue moving forward, on to another mission and to a different field.

It was very difficult for people who grew up in the business world to understand and accept this way of thinking: that it's possible to say "no" to a significant job and position or a substantial financial offer.

After more than four years, I decided my time as CEO of El Al was at an end.

I appreciated and loved El Al and its personnel at all levels, including the board members and controlling shareholders.

When I finished my role as CEO, I told Tami Mozes, who was then the controlling shareholder of the company:

"Whenever you're having doubts, when it comes time to make weighty decisions, you are welcome to consult with me. I promise to do everything to help you or anyone else at the company, but I am not the CEO or the chairman of the board, who will have the authority and responsibility. I don't have a personal agenda. My only agenda is the welfare of the company, the welfare of the people working there, and your welfare.

"If you want, I will offer comments and critiques from my perspective on important matters.

"I will invest as much time and energy as it takes to study the subject, and I will tell you and the executives of the company my opinions and my recommendations.

"Of course, you don't have to accept them. Listen and decide.

"As a matter of principle, I'll do it for no compensation, on a volunteer basis.

In one of our conversations, Tami told me that an offer had come from Boeing to purchase pre-serial 787 Dreamliner aircraft at a "bargain price" and that El Al was seriously considering going for it.

I looked at her. I couldn't believe it.

I always try to study a subject in depth before I express an unequivocal opinion or make a decision about it, but on this subject, I had a lot of experience and knowledge from both the Air Force and the world of civil aviation.

I told her that in my opinion, it was a minefield that should be avoided. I strongly recommended avoiding a pre-serial aircraft "deal" at all costs.

"Why?" Tami asked. I saw on her face that she was relieved and that the offer hadn't sat right with her either.

I replied, "A pre-serial aircraft is produced even before the company develops a serial, uniform line of aircraft of a certain model. With pre-serial planes, various tests are carried out, adjustments are made, and experiments are done; and at the end of the process, when the serial production line is inaugurated, they try to get rid of them."

In my experience, I explained, usually the weight of the pre-serial aircraft is different, which is significant in terms of flight ranges and fuel consumption. Its systems are not uniform and the interactions between them are more problematic. Maintenance is also a thorny issue because these are often non-standard systems.

From the business perspective, a pre-serial aircraft does not have a "list price" for buying and selling — the way you might find a car's Kelley Blue Book value.

For all these reasons, I believed that a relatively small, vulnerable company like El Al ought to avoid such a venture, which could turn out to be a serious error. It was too great a risk to invest huge sums of money in a product with no guaranteed future value — either in terms of efficient operational utility or in resale, which is sometimes required in civil aviation.

A serial plane, on the other hand, is a completely different story.

I told Tami, "I suggest you invite the world's number-one civilian aircraft expert. I'll have him over at my house. I'll ask him a few questions in your presence — and in the presence of a few others who know their stuff — and then you make whatever call you think is right. No doubt, this is a major decision."

Tami thought about it and said, "That's what we'll do."

They sought out a prestigious expert in the field from America, brought him over to Israel on short notice, and accompanied him to my home.

We sat on our balcony: the expert, Tami, and a few other prominent people with knowledge in the field.

The expert gave a brief overview of the subject.

I asked him a few probing questions about pre-serial aircraft. Tami and the others listened attentively to my questions and the expert's answers and understood the problems with the proposal that was raised.

In the end, the company's board of directors decided not to purchase pre-serial aircraft. Instead, they bought the excellent serial 787s.

• • •

We err all the time. The trick is not to make big mistakes and not to make the same mistake twice.

When you head down to the bargain basement, you'd better watch your step. In most cases, the great "deal" is for the seller, not the buyer...

119.

The Real Estate Shark

One evening, shortly after I was discharged from the army, I got home and saw my wife, Anat, sitting in front of the computer.

"What's so riveting?" I asked.

She replied, "I'm looking at a Hever[16] construction project in Tel Aviv, combined with a Gindi[17] civilian project, and I'm checking it out."

For a while, we had been talking about how when the children were grown up, we ought to move to Tel Aviv. But it seemed quite hopeless from an economic point of view.

I said, "How do you think we'll be able to afford an apartment in Tel Aviv?"

Anat replied, "Why don't we try to buy a small three-room apartment as an investment?"

"If you really want to," I said, "go check it out..."

She delved into the topic and analyzed it painstakingly, day and night: plans, prices, reports. Eventually, she met with a sales representative for the project.

She came back and told me, "This Friday they're holding a lottery for apartments at the Tel Aviv Fairgrounds."

My son Omer and I responded with smirks we didn't try to hide,

16. The "Hever" Consumer Club provides tax consultancy services free of charge, as well as accompanying services at significant discounts for standing IDF personnel, retired army personnel, IDF Workers' Organization, employees and retirees of the various security agencies, members of the IDF Disabled Veterans Organization – and their families.
17. Gindi is an Israeli and international real estate developer.

and at that moment we gave her the title of "Real Estate Shark." But Anat was not moved by our cynical and dismissive response; on the contrary: it only amplified her motivation and determination.

"No problem," I said. "I'll take you to the Tel Aviv Fairgrounds. Do whatever you want, but I'm not going to mess with it."

Friday morning arrived.

I dropped Anat off at the Tel Aviv Fairgrounds and drove away immediately.

After a few minutes, she called me.

"Yes?"

"Listen, it's a mob scene here. People are starting to line up now. One line is gigantic, and the other is not quite as long..."

"Okay," I told her, "I got it. So get in the slightly shorter line."

"All right," she replied, "but you ought to know, that's the line for bigger apartments, four rooms and up."

"Alright," I told her, and to myself I thought, *We'll see what happens.* She had no chance of winning that lottery and the issue would be off the table.

After something like an hour, another phone call from Anat.

"Listen, I got a number in the lottery," she said excitedly. "It gives me the right to choose an apartment from the unclaimed ones — if there are any left."

After another hour or so, another phone call from Anat: "OK, it's my turn now," she updated me. "All the apartments have been claimed already — everything except the penthouse."

I almost fell out of my seat, even though I was in the car...

What were we doing buying a penthouse in Tel Aviv?

Where on earth would we get the money from?

I said to Anat, "Put the guy in charge on the line."

I talked to him.

He said to me, "Listen, how's this: you pay ten thousand shekels now, think it over for a week, and if you decide it's not for you, we'll give you back nine thousand."

I said to myself: A week of thinking about something this big ought to be worth a thousand shekels.

We paid the ten thousand.

We thought it over.

This was during the severe economic crisis of 2008, and the bottom had fallen out of the real estate market. The rock-bottom prices meant that once we sold our house in Yehud, the deal was manageable.

From the time of Anat's initial deep dive into researching the subject, up until the lottery at the Tel Aviv Fairgrounds, all of four days had passed.

Then, a week after the "lotto" drawing, we made our fateful decision.

It took us barely ten days to take the most important and significant financial step for our family, the biggest of our lives.

To this day, Anat refuses to admit that she lives in a penthouse...

We laugh about it, but in the end, Anat turned out to be a true real estate shark.

•••

If you have an opportunity, seize it.

120.
Nothing Like the Samba?

Shortly before I arrived at El Al, a new direct route was opened from Tel Aviv to São Paulo, Brazil.

That was great news.

Opening a new route is always a joyful event, inspiring, and exciting for the airline's personnel — all the more so when it opens up a new region to direct flights from Israel, in this case, South America.

El Al invested a fortune in the Brazil route, flying its most expensive and newest aircraft, the only one that could handle the direct flight: the Boeing 777.

But already in my first few months as a CEO, I realized there was a problem. The route was special and might very well hold serious long-term potential, but from a business perspective, it simply never took off.

The results for the company were only getting worse. All the attempts to improve the situation failed, and we were losing money on the route hand over fist.

I decided to make a very unusual move and immediately sent Izzy Cohen to Brazil. At the time, he was El Al's representative in Paris, doing a wonderful and professional job there.

I cannot express the depth of my sorrow over the tragedy which occurred while I was writing this book, as Izzy and his wife Barbara were killed in a cable car collapse in Italy.

When I presented the Brazil challenge to Izzy, he accepted it without hesitation. He quickly got organized, relocated to Brazil with Barbara — who also understood that they were being sent on an emergency mission — and set to work, trying with all his might to improve the situation.

I decided to go to Brazil myself to understand the problem up close, see what could be done, and give Izzy some backup.

I went there and got an impression of the situation. We made decisions and took purposeful action, but the situation did not improve.

I asked for a comprehensive and quick economic analysis in order to understand in depth the current situation and the outlook for the future.

The bottom line was that we were losing millions of dollars on the route. The company was already in a deep economic crisis, fuel prices were skyrocketing, and the Brazil line exacerbated the situation, causing great concern.

One of the suggestions put on the table was to shut down the route, even though it had been opened only a short time earlier.

I realized that I had to make a decision. I convened deliberations on the matter and listened attentively to the pros and cons of each option.

For any airline, shutting down a route is difficult — certainly such a special line we had just invested a great deal in. The decision could not be made lightly.

I told myself that I had to study the economic data in depth before I made my decision.

I took all the materials they had prepared and presented to me, and over three consecutive weekends, I sat alone at home with the data and crunched the numbers. I read, delved deeper, analyzed, deliberated, and decided to shut down the route.

In retrospect, did I make the right call?

I believe so.

I could have given the Brazil line another chance; when you have to decide, a non-decision is also a kind of decision. But in the reality that lay before me, I realized that keeping the route running would have further undermined El Al's strapped financial situation. I had to make the hard call in the immediate term for the company to survive in the long term.

121

An Elephant on My Desk...

As commander of Ramat David Airbase, I used to meet frequently with the troops. In addition to the meetings I initiated myself, every soldier, NCO, and officer on the base had the opportunity to request a meeting and talk to me about any topic that was important to them without it being considered going over the head of their immediate commander. This was our "open door policy."

Anyone could write down the topic they wanted to talk to me about, and we would schedule a time to speak face-to-face.

In some cases, the people who asked to meet me had written that they wanted to talk about one topic, but when they came to my office they talked about something completely different.

That's how it was the day an officer entered my office and told me to disregard the subject she'd penned, and that she needed to confide in me that her commander was embezzling money.

I asked her how sure she was.

The officer replied that she was completely sure, and even gave detailed examples that sounded credible to me. She was a determined and outstanding officer whose performance I greatly valued.

I was horrified by the very serious allegations against an officer who was directly subordinate to me, who commanded a large group of people, and whom I personally liked. He was in daily contact with me, we lived opposite each other in the family housing complex at the base, and we often drank coffee together.

It was hard for me to digest the story, and I hoped it wasn't true.

354

There was now a massive elephant in the room, and I felt like it had sat down right on my desk.

It was undoubtedly one of the greatest challenges I faced — ethically, as a commander, and on a personal level.

I decided to deal with the matter with the highest level of sensitivity, with purpose and impartiality, however difficult it might be.

I called the chief of CID (the Criminal Investigative Division of the Military Police) directly. I told him about the officer's suspicions and asked him to personally wade into the thick of it, immediately.

If the senior officer was innocent, it was important to me that this be determined quickly and clearly by a high-level investigator after examining the issue in depth. This was the proper and fair course of action. And if, heaven forbid, the senior officer was guilty, he had to be dealt with decisively and without any compromise.

I would do whatever it took for the truth to come to light — whether that truth was a painful one or a relief.

"I understand," replied the CID chief. "I'm on it. I'll launch an investigation and get to the bottom of it."

He asked me not to talk about it with anyone.

In the meantime, life at the base continued as usual.

Other people from the same unit came to me on their own initiative — through my open door and other channels — and independently told me their perspective on that senior officer. They knew nothing about the investigation being conducted against him.

I listened and wrote everything down but said nothing.

I felt that they were having a hard time with the fact that I was just listening and writing, but not saying anything or doing anything.

I saw the disappointment in their eyes.

At the same time, I felt good about the fact that they were not aware of what was happening and did not even know about each other's reports.

I continued to work with the officer under suspicion as if nothing out of the ordinary was going on. Not a hint, not a gesture, not a word. I was very careful to maintain a businesslike and decent relationship with him, even though a cloud hovered over us, glowering at the edge of my mind.

Quite a challenge...

I was anxiously awaiting the results of the investigation.

And then it happened: a phone call from the CID chief, informing me that "the suspicions against the officer are well-founded." He was ready to come to the base and make an arrest.

I told him I'd get back to him right away.

I realized that from that moment on, my main task was to minimize the damage so that the base would continue functioning with as little impact as possible.

It was a terrible feeling. If the allegations against the officer were indeed true, it would severely damage the trust of his people, damage the entire organization, and damage me personally.

It was just a few days before the memorial service commemorating the fallen soldiers of Ramat David Airbase, a significant, sensitive, and moving ritual held every year with the participation of the bereaved families and the troops, past and present. As if that were not enough, the person in charge of the ceremony was none other than the senior officer who was about to be arrested for embezzlement.

That was when I had to bring the commander of the Air Force up to speed.

I called Major General Dan Halutz, who was the commander of the corps at the time, updated him on what was happening, and said that despite this delicate matter, I intended to do everything the right way, with purpose and determination. Halutz was as clear on the matter as I was.

I called the CID chief and asked him to come as quickly as possible and do whatever he saw fit to do.

I understood what kind of challenge we were facing. I knew I had to make sure that the officer under suspicion, who had not yet been proven guilty, and especially his family, would be treated with the utmost sensitivity. His wife and children lived in the family housing complex at the base, and they were about to find themselves in a very difficult and embarrassing predicament through no fault of their own.

I would never wish any commander or manager to be in a situation similar to the one I was in.

At the same time, I had to make a quick command decision: who would take over the unit of the officer under suspicion, and who would lead the memorial ceremony in the spirit of the long-standing tradition of Ramat David Airbase.

In my view, the commitment to the bereaved families is deeply meaningful.

I decided to take an unconventional step and appoint a senior officer from another field, not from within the suspected officer's unit. I had faith in his unique character and ability to cope with difficult and complex tasks on short notice, and I knew he would be able to handle this as well.

Indeed, he deftly took the reins and rallied the subordinates of the arrested officer, who managed to scrape themselves off the floor. Everyone understood the importance of the event and did their part professionally and in an exemplary manner.

I also shared the story with the beloved TV personality Dalia Mazor, who for years, on a volunteer basis, hosted the memorial ceremony at the airbase and played an important role in its success. Dalia immediately understood how complex the situation was, and she led the ceremony with all her heart and soul, with tremendous love and sensitivity, in a way that honored the fallen and their families.

I was very proud of everyone.

That things turned out the way they did should not be taken for granted, and ought to be fully appreciated.

• • •

In such cases, one must be decisive, unequivocal, and uncompromising. The way you act sends a clear message to the people you're leading — not just the specific person in the eye of the storm.

122.
Dumpster Juice

When the Yom Kippur War broke out in October of 1973, I was an 11th-grader at Katznelson High School in Kfar Saba. Our class focused on the sciences, and the students had a very high view of themselves...

Our studies continued in one format or another. We went to school from time to time, but our heads were in a completely different place.

We tried to do everything we could to help the war effort.

In the afternoon, we worked in the supermarket, replacing reservists who had been called up; at night, we took the wounded, who arrived in ambulances, to the emergency room of Meir Hospital.

One morning, during school, we suddenly heard from the loudspeaker on the wall of every classroom — which we called "Big Brother" — the voice of the principal, Gedalyahu Lachman, a professional educator and a special person. He addressed us and said:

"The workers from Qalqilya have stopped coming," he said, referring to the Palestinian laborers from the nearby Arab town. "The city is looking for volunteers to man the garbage trucks and pick up the huge piles of trash that have accumulated all around Kfar Saba."

Silence in the classroom.

I looked at my friend Doron and said, "Do we have anything better or more important to do? Apparently, they really need us. Let's do this."

So, we went to work as garbagemen...

I suggested that Yacob, a good friend of mine from a different school, might want to join us.

He immediately answered the call.

Dressed in pants, long-sleeved shirts, and rubber boots, with large bucket hats on our heads to soak up the dumpster juice, we went on our daily mission.

The garbage truck driver picked us up very early in the morning. Two of us picked up the trash cans and lifted them into the truck, while the third stood inside, amid the refuse, to dump out the contents of the cans and hand them back empty.

Even though I knew we were contributing and doing something important, I felt very uncomfortable over the looks that were directed at us, the "garbagemen."

But my mother, the one who washed my clothes every day and "enjoyed" the odor of the garbage, was really touched by our actions. She implicitly understood the situation, told me we were doing the right thing, and that we should ignore the looks in our direction.

When I saw how touched my mother was and heard what she said, I stopped being ashamed of our work and felt good about myself.

In many ways, garbage suddenly started smelling a bit different...

123.

Emotional Support

While she was still in high school, my daughter, Maya, who has a fiery personality, decided to open a jewelry design business and sell her work weekly at the bazaar in Kfar Saba.

I thought about what I could do to help her feel confident, break through, develop, and bring her talent, energy, and creativity to the fore.

I told her, "Live your dreams. The expenses are on us, the income is yours. We have your back, anything and everything you need. We love you and we are with you all the way. Have no fear. Seize the day."

Maya listened, smiled, and tackled the challenge. She made jewelry and sold it, but she refused to take a single cent from me for her business — then and down the road. She chose the emotional support of her family.

Maya broke through and evolved, first as an architect and then as a jewelry designer. She took a chance and developed a very successful jewelry brand called YAMA. Throughout the process, as a matter of principle, Maya refused to accept material help from us for the business. She knew she had emotional backing and a kind of safety net, even if she never used it.

And she did it on her own. Her dream, talent, initiative, courage, investment — everything.

I am proud of her, believe in her, and love her.

• • •

"Emotional support" is as important as material support. Maybe even more.

124.
Apropos or Ad Hominem?

Major General (Res.) Johanan Locker is a man who shatters boundaries.

Locker was the first navigator in the Air Force to be appointed squadron commander, and he performed the job in an exemplary manner.

Time and time again, when I had to choose an officer for a vital position in the corps, I chose him. I knew I could trust him fully.

Locker held senior and prominent positions, including commander of Hatzerim Airbase, head of the Air Division, and chief of staff of the Air Force, leaving his mark on the corps for many years.

In his last position in uniform, he served as the prime minister's military secretary.

About two years after his retirement from the IDF, Prime Minister Benjamin Netanyahu appointed him to head a committee that would examine the defense budget in depth.

When Locker submitted the committee's conclusions, some senior members of the defense establishment were, to put it mildly, less than thrilled.

The defense minister and the ministry's director-general invited several former senior officials — chiefs of staff, generals, and directors general of the ministry — to hear their opinions on the Locker Report and how to address his findings.

I was invited to the meeting, too.

After we were presented with the report, the participants were asked to respond to its conclusions, but instead of a professional and substantive discussion of the committee's recommendations, the discussion turned into a personal attack on Locker.

I asked for permission to speak and said that in my view, the committee's findings should be analyzed matter-of-factly:

— Accept and implement the findings deemed correct and that demand action.

— Discuss the findings which require further thought and decide what to do about them.

— To declare, simply and clearly, which findings the defense establishment has substantive objections to and cannot accept under any circumstances.

In any case, I emphasized, personal attacks on Locker were beyond the pale. He was a man of many accomplishments, whose integrity and decency I put implicit trust in, and who had performed the task assigned to him to the best of his professional understanding and the understanding of his fellow committee members.

In other words, our discussion had to be apropos, not ad hominem.

Unfortunately, that was not how things turned out.

A few days after the meeting, Yohanan called me and asked to meet.

I heard in his voice that he was upset.

We met.

Johanan spoke from the bottom of his heart, especially about the personal attacks and being condemned as a "traitor" to the defense establishment — the same body to which he had dedicated his life and held in high regard.

The looks directed at him by some of his colleagues and comrades-in-arms, the accusations hurled at him, stung him particularly harshly. He felt excommunicated from the Air Force family. It was a terrible feeling for him.

I had no doubts about Yohanan's integrity and decency. I knew how much he cared about the State of Israel, the IDF, and the Air Force. He would not have done anything that could harm national security. That would have gone against the values on which he was raised and had reinforced in the Air Force throughout his decades of service.

He had no reason to be ashamed of the report he had submitted or its findings.

It was hard for me to hear Yohanan's words and see his pain, sorrow, and frustration. Then an idea came to my mind.

"The corps is holding a large conference at Hatzerim," I told him. "Are you planning to go?"

Yohanan replied that he'd feel very uncomfortable and would rather not attend.

I said, "You know me, I don't usually go to these events and conferences; but this time, I'm going. And so are you."

He understood where I was headed.

"OK, I'll go," he said.

We went to the conference. There were thousands of people from the Air Force, both regular and reserve. We took our places in the front row and then I said to him, "Yohanan, let's stand up and turn toward the audience so that everyone can see us standing together and chatting calmly."

The message was: "I'm with you."

I felt that the whole audience was staring at us, but it achieved the goal. The message that I conveyed to the crowd without saying a word, standing with him during his time of difficulty, engaged in intimate and friendly conversation with him, could not be mistaken. The large crowd realized the great appreciation that I had for this decent and brave man, and that I would not tolerate anyone who denied that.

I don't know if it's true; we've never talked about it. But I feel that in those moments, Locker felt great relief.

125.
Alpha, Zero Drops, Maximum Shootdowns

In 1990, I was assigned a unique mission: to establish an F-16D Barak two-seater squadron at Ramat David Airbase in the Jezreel Valley. This was HaEmek Squadron, which had a distinguished history and had been closed six years earlier as Kfir squadron.

The establishment of the squadron was undoubtedly one of the most amazing experiences of my life. How a squadron is established is of tremendous importance when it comes to its future activities and operational capabilities. Alongside good examples, there are many bad ones.

From the very beginning of the process, it was important for us to connect with the squadron's people and its former troops and pilots, and to embrace all the bereaved families of the squadron — all of them.

And so we did.

It was fascinating to see how in two-and-a-half years we transformed the squadron from an embryonic state to full combat readiness: determined, powerful, with impressive operational capabilities; and no less important — with spirit and soul.

I had the great privilege of choosing a special group of people from the "Major Leagues" of the aviation, technical and administrative worlds;

To enable them to express themselves and turn them into a cohesive, resolute, focused, and superior team;

364

To create synergy and true partnership between them;

To lead them to the highest summits of achievement;

And to build a solid foundation with them for decades to come.

In hindsight, the establishment of the squadron made me feel that even the sky is not the limit.

"Alpha,
Zero drops,
Maximum shootdowns."

In other words, hit the bullseye, survive, take the offensive.

This is the motto that I repeated every day, at the end of each briefing for training flights or operational flights, a motto that kept us all focused.

And this has been the motto of the squadron and its people ever since.

I have no doubt that this approach goes with them wherever they find themselves.

It excites me time and again to see the team that established the squadron and the next generation that grew up within it sharing the same spirit and soul. These wonderful people are leaders not only in the Air Force but also in the civilian world.

Many successful startups have emerged and developed from HaEmek Squadron. This is not surprising: these are genuine superstars, by their nature determined and goal-oriented, who believe in their abilities and who are not afraid to take risks.

It is no coincidence that I made my last flight as a fighter pilot, at the end of my term as commander of the IAF, at HaEmek Squadron with my family, friends, and squadron mates with me.

For me, HaEmek Squadron has been and will remain a combination of honorable tradition, great people, and excellence in every field.

Establishing the squadron and building it from the ground up was a dream come true for me. It allowed me to express the things

WHO THE F*CK IS MICHAEL?!

I believed in while creating a true partnership among our people on the ground and in the air, who performed earnestly, with all their hearts and souls.

...

I'm proud of you,
I believe in you,
And I love you.
Then, and now.

126.

The Chosen One

"You have chosen us from all peoples."

"A treasured people."

"A light unto the nations."[18]

I believe these phrases are closely linked and connected by one strong thread — from being chosen to being a light unto the nations.

They convey an important message that has nothing to do with one belief or another or one creed or another: "chosenness" means a commitment to giving and ethical behavior, not being granted privileges.

And from society to the individual: A chosen people should be a light unto the nations, and what is true for an entire people, is also true for those people chosen to lead.

Leaders in every field — in education and society, in culture and business, in the military and religion — should be a light for their followers and to all those who draw inspiration from them, to chart a path for them and to set an example for them.

The thought that chosenness gives the chosen one the right to behave in an inappropriate manner and to abuse their position to obtain privileges such as power, money, and prestige is utterly unacceptable to me. On the contrary, those who are "chosen" are obliged to do more, in every field.

---

18. Isaiah 42:6 - The term originated from the prophet Isaiah, which is understood by some to express the universal designation of the Israelites as mentors for spiritual and moral guidance for the entire world.

In my view, these are the four moral "obligations" incumbent on the chosen person, by virtue of having been selected to lead.

The first commitment that comes from chosenness is **totality**.

There is no such thing as a part-time leader.

Leader and commander are all-encompassing roles, 24/7.

This is an unparalleled personal responsibility and commitment.

The second obligation that comes from chosenness is the **understanding that a title or appointment is not the essence**.

People follow leaders and trust them for their character, conduct, action, and inner strength, things that do not arise from a rank on the shoulders or from the title of "commander" or "executive." Title and rank are just names and symbols that represent the fact of chosenness.

A person who bases their leadership on title or rank, motivated by the drive to acquire privileges of money, power, or prestige, is no leader.

Power, money, and prestige can change a person's character and personality, and when it comes to a person chosen to lead and manage, this can be a real danger.

The third obligation that comes from chosenness is to set a personal example.

A **personal example** in anything and everything you do, top to bottom, no exceptions.

You can talk, communicate, explain, and utter beautiful words in an impressive way, but what really matters is how you behave and what you do.

The conduct and actions of the leader speak louder than their words. People at all levels see and understand very well what the leader does and how they behave, in every area of life. Especially when the leader thinks people are not paying attention...

I remember myself as a young pilot, looking at a senior commander and saying to myself: Does he really think I'm dumb? That I don't see or understand what he's doing?

Just as the leaders behave, so will the people under them.

If they behave and act in a proper, correct, ethical, and professional manner, their followers will do the same. And if their conduct is bad, corrupt, or inappropriate, their people will consider it a legitimate norm, regardless of laws or rules.

The fourth obligation that arises from chosenness is **responsibility for the whole**.

A great leader cares for his people (for everyone); a small leader takes care of their denomination (or their associates).

This is true at all levels — for a small or large group, for an organization, for a city, for a state, and for a people.

In each group, there are those who have grown up in the same environment as you, and those who have not.

There are those that you like more and there are those that you like less.

That's legitimate.

But as the leader of a group, you must take care of everyone and really accept whoever is different from you — in their views, origins, and the culture from which they come. You must not only accept the other but also convey it in your behavior so that each of your people feels it. This is significant for each and every member of the group, and it is important for the cohesion of the group.

This is a tremendous commitment and responsibility. It's not simple by any means, but critical.

You are everyone's "father" equally.

To me, these four obligations express the moral significance of choosing a person to lead and manage. They are obligations, not privileges.

127.

It Seems You Don't Trust Me

When I was the commander of HaEmek Squadron, we launched an attack in the area of Janta in the Beqaa Valley.

I led the formation while Khen, one of my deputy commanders, was flying alongside me.

Khen and his navigator were unable to release their armaments on the first overpass.

Khen asked me to do a 270, i.e. to turn around and try another run at the target.

I authorized it.

Another pass, bombs away — but no hits.

A difficult experience.

As a commander, I knew it could happen even to the best. And Khen, a talented pilot with a babyface whose abilities I appreciated and whose personality I loved, was one of the best.

Some time after that incident, Operation Accountability was launched against Hezbollah in Lebanon.

I did not assign Khen to a mission.

He took it very hard. He came into my room, stood in front of me, and told me quietly, angrily, almost insulted, "You didn't assign me to a mission. I guess you don't trust me."

I looked him in the eye and said, "Khen, I trust you one hundred percent. I am waiting for a complicated attack mission to come up, with an anti-aircraft threat like we faced in Janta, and then I will send you."

Khen stared at me for a long time, turned around, and left the room without saying a word.

I didn't doubt his abilities, not for a moment. I trusted him and waited for an opportunity to allow him to prove himself. Indeed, during that operation, an equally complex and dangerous mission came up, in a similar area and at a similar threat level.

I sent him to carry out the attack.

Khen got a second chance to prove himself. He attacked, hit his targets, did very well, and came back safely.

The tremendous relief he felt was palpable, as if a huge stone had been removed from his head and shoulders.

I had no doubt that it would affect him later in life, in the military and in the civilian world.

And so it was. Years later, Khen wrote me an amazing, moving letter. He wrote about the second chance he got, about being able to give people under you the feeling that you believe in them and their abilities, and about the self-fulfilling belief in your people and in yourself.

Khen has become one of Israel's leading figures in the field of green architecture.

If he had not been given another chance to prove himself, he would have been living with the feeling of failure to this day.

•••

When you have to let go of a sense of failure, no matter what field you're in, the best thing is to confront the situation once more, despite all the fears, and show yourself and everyone else that you can do it.

Then, you're ready for takeoff...

128.

Things Have a Life of Their Own

Throughout my life, I have initiated and led quite a few processes related to change and the creation of new things. Together with my people, we turned dreams into reality.

My wife, who is my biggest critic, has two main critiques, mainly regarding "soft" subjects — those related to the heart, soul, motivation, and values.

First note:

Who appointed you?

"Why do you think it's permissible for you? Who has given you the right to do things that deviate, in many ways, from your role?"

The second note:

"A minute after you finish your job and go, the processes you have led will be stopped; it is natural that your replacement will not want to continue the things that are identified with you. There can be different reasons for this, relevant or emotional, but that's human nature."

I think differently.

Let's take the first critique, "Who appointed you?"

When you lead a large group or organization, your task and duty is to lead and achieve excellent results in any legal way, even if it is very unconventional.

Although these things are not always measurable, the "soft" subjects are of great importance. They make the group a group, strengthen its members as human beings, and I am convinced that they improve its abilities and results.

Therefore, if you believe in the importance of those "soft" subjects — go for it, do not be afraid, seize the day.

I have never encountered a legal impediment to the processes I've led.

Values-based processes change reality, change the environment, change ways of thinking, and lead us all to a better place.

Now, let's take the second critique: "Won't your successor pause or halt whatever you set in motion?"

My conclusion is this: if the processes I lead bear out and succeed at least twice, they'll have a life of their own. They will then continue and no longer be dependent on me.

The leader, the commander, and the manager have an interest in things succeeding during their term of office. Therefore, it does not matter to them who set the wheels in motion and who dreamed of things in the past. What really matters is what happens here and now.

Beyond that, even if a project is paused or halted, it is very possible that the seeds sown among the people involved will germinate and flourish in different ways in the future.

And if the process continues even after the end of your tenure, it will probably go on and evolve into new areas, with great intensity, under the leadership of your successors.

"You need not finish the work, but you are not free to abandon it."
(Ethics of Our Fathers)

I am happy to see things I dreamed of and that we set out with, succeed and develop in positive directions, even if my successors enjoy the fruits of my labor without knowing that I sowed the seeds or that I'm connected to things in any way.

To me, the question of whether things are recorded in my name or not is meaningless. I'm just glad to have had the privilege of dreaming, believing, initiating — and taking action.

373

129.
You Wouldn't Want to Live
In The Past...

When you have completed a significant chapter of your career, let it go.

You were entrusted with a position, you took it on, you were pro-active, and promoted the organization and the field you worked in, but now you just return the deposit.

It's not yours.

Your name is not the title and position you once held, but your own name.

Don't be fooled...

> *Greater than the title of "master" is "my master."*
> *Greater than the title of "my master" is the title of "our master."*
> *Greater than the title of "our master" is one's own name.*
> *(Tosefta, Testimonies)*

One of the most psroblematic tendencies is to be in the grip of past memories, past titles, and past roles, living in them.

The past is a great place to visit, but you wouldn't want to live there...

Be happy and proud of what has been, and then move forward.

Insofar as it is up to you, retire at your peak.

There is no meaning to one year less or more in your office.

Much more important is how you finished your tenure and the

feelings you leave with. This has tremendous meaning, accompanying you for the rest of your life.

If after retirement you must continue to make a living, that's your top priority. Do it with all your might. It is your duty and responsibility; any work ennobles the worker.

If you can afford it financially, take a break. One of the most fascinating, important, challenging, and satisfying stages in life is the respite after the end of one chapter before the beginning of a new chapter.

A breather allows you to think, look inward, wrestle with yourself, and make significant decisions about how to proceed, which is difficult to do during periods of intense activity. There is a deep process of incubation, curiosity, wondering, and deliberation in such a period, without disturbances or external noises.

What can interfere with the interval is your fear of losing the stability and security provided by a set schedule, usually determined for you by others...

As I see it, it is far more important to strive toward the places you've dreamed of, you're curious about, passionate about, that you feel have meaning, value, and purpose, and that you want to engage in them not because you have to but because you want to. Security and stability will come later.

•••

Twice in my life I finished a significant chapter and moved on to a new one: when I finished my service in the Air Force and when I ended my time at El Al.

The respites I took led me to the realization that the most significant resource a person has is time.

Time passes and cannot be reclaimed.

Life is here and now.

You only live once. Think carefully about what you want to do in your life and with your life.

The route, the road you go down, is determined in one of two ways:

Either you use your principles to carve out the path and to figure out your actions — or the sequence of the actions you take paves the way for you.

In my opinion, it is always better to make a principled decision on where to go and use it to determine your actions and the stops along the road.

I made a number of fundamental decisions that were significant for the rest of my journey, both when I finished the Air Force chapter in my life and at the end of my time at El Al.

The first decision was that I didn't want to deal with weapons in my civilian life.

I was an expert in the field and my military background gave me a significant advantage that was worth a lot of money. But I said to myself: I dealt with weapons as a military man for a clear and meaningful mission, the defense of the state, and I don't want to deal with that in my civilian life.

The second decision was to integrate into the business-civilian world and not mix security matters with civilian life.

There is no doubt that these two fundamental decisions guided me and my conduct.

I made the third important decision when I finished my work at El Al. I decided that my main occupation in the next chapter of my life would be in the sphere of society, education, and values — and that I would do so on a voluntary basis.

No matter how much money might be offered to me in the business world.

That's what's important to me.

This is what I want to do at this stage of my life.

And that's what I'm doing, here and now.

• • •

The period between the end of one chapter and the beginning of the next chapter usually includes three stages:

The first stage — Everyone praises you for the plans, the trips, and the time-out you took.

The second stage — Those who do not like you mumble, "He couldn't find a new job."

The third stage — Even those who love you, family and good friends, begin to get upset and worried.

Go with your heart, but be aware of the three stages.

To me, the really important things are:
- To wake up in the morning with joy, anticipation, and excitement for a new day;
- To be around people you love and feel good with;
- To do something that you feel is meaningful to you and allows you to shine;
- To open the mind, heart, and soul, and to learn something new every day;
- To be happy and proud of what was.
- Do not live in the past and with the past.
- Go forward all the time.

At the end of each chapter and in each respite there is real potential for growth, change, renewal, and creativity.

* * *

There's something charming, fascinating, and exciting about reinventing yourself.

130.

Courtesy Through Earth and Sky

In preparation for Israel's sixtieth Independence Day, we debated how to mark the special event within the Air Force.

Such a round number obviously required a fly-over by IAF aircraft throughout the skies of the country, not to mention special flights by the aerobatics team, parachuting maneuvers, and other martial and aerial displays. However, as commander of the Air Force, it was important to me that my troops also commit to an ethical, educational civilian project.

Thus was born the idea that members of the IAF would visit as many high schools as possible throughout the country and meet with a wide variety of students from all sectors — religious and secular students, from the center of the country to the periphery. All of them.

I appointed Moshe Edri to lead the project. He had been seriously wounded while he was a company commander in the Golani Brigade, losing an arm. He had gone on to command 669 — the IAF's Combat Rescue and Airborne Evacuation Unit — and direct the special forces headquarters of the Air Force. He was an excellent officer with a great soul, exceptional organizational ability, and an inspiring personality.

Edri started working on the project right away.

His first conclusion was that it was best to join forces with the Ministry of Education rather than launch a program that could be interpreted problematically by the education system and create antagonism. How could outsiders in uniform come into the classroom, talk to students, and assume the role of teachers?

Initially, I thought differently. I wanted the Ministry of Education to be involved as little as possible. But I listened very attentively to Edri's recommendation and accepted it.

The minister of education at the time, Yuli Tamir, and her advisor Alon Futterman joined the project with all their hearts and shepherded it through the ministry. It really couldn't be taken for granted.

This honest and courageous partnership between the Air Force and the Ministry of Education, recommended by Edri, contributed greatly to the success of the project, which was named "Courtesy Through Earth and Sky."

In the first stage, we held meetings with airbase commanders. Education professionals and officials from schools throughout the region were invited: superintendents, principals, teachers, counselors, consultants, and coordinators. The various squadrons and units hosted them, holding fascinating conversations with them about education, management, values, leadership, and command.

It was important to me that any Air Force personnel who were to meet students — officers, NCOs, and enlisted soldiers — volunteer for it. Those who do not really want to cannot perform such a task.

It was equally important to me that we only visit schools whose principals really wanted us to come.

We thought that if we managed to reach 100 high schools, it would be a great achievement.

Then requests began pouring in from all over the country:

- 100
- 200
- 300
- 400
- 450 school principals asked us to come...

These were schools from all sectors: Jewish, Christian, Druze, and Muslim. We prepared materials and presented values and educational content that seemed important to us.

We trained and readied Air Force personnel for the encounters.

This was an extraordinary operation, values-based, educational, and logistical, conducted by Edri, converging over a single day of visits to hundreds of schools across the country.

In the meantime, the other branches of the IDF also got wind of the project and asked to join. We gladly obliged. My condition was that all the activities be coordinated via the Air Force by Edri, that all the participants follow the Air Force's training and preparatory guidelines, and that it would all be implemented in line with the Air Force's spirit in terms of definitions, content, and messages.

More than ten thousand officers, NCOs, and enlisted men and women from the Air Force and other IDF corps went to hundreds of schools, and all of them did so voluntarily.

We didn't talk to the students about the military. We talked to them about the greatest miracle in the history of the Jewish people through the ages:

The State of Israel.

I was particularly moved to hear that Maya, my daughter, who was then an officer in the Air Force, had volunteered for the project. She came home excited and emotional, eyes bright, relating the powerful and exciting encounters she'd had with the students and their reactions.

Everyone who participated in the project did so with all their heart and soul, and I am convinced they were over the moon.

131.
The Ambassadors

At the beginning of my career as an El Al CEO, amid the complex business struggles, I was looking for avenues to integrate the company's personnel in activities with Zionist and moral significance.

In my view, El Al represents "the civilian wings of the State of Israel and the Jewish people" in the deepest sense, despite being a private company.

I knew Alon Futterman, an energetic and talented young man, from my time as commander of the Air Force, when he participated in the "Courtesy Through Earth and Sky" project as an advisor to then-Minister of Education Yuli Tamir.

In Alon's intense mind, an idea took form: Why don't we take the "Courtesy Through Earth and Sky" project, which we initiated in the Air Force for the sixtieth Independence Day together with the Ministry of Education, and do a similar thing with El Al personnel around the world?

We started rolling out the idea.

I appointed Futterman to formulate and voluntarily lead the initiative together with Brigadier General (Res.) Yehudit Grisaro, who would be the "mother" of the project at El Al. Grisaro, who at the time was our VP of customer service, is a woman I love, with an impressive ability to execute, a big heart, and a big soul. And she was deeply touched by such issues.

I knew that with these two, even the sky wasn't the limit.

The project developed, ripened, and matured. We named it "El Al Ambassadors."

WHO THE F*CK IS MICHAEL?!

The designated "ambassadors" were El Al aircrew, pilots, and flight attendants. The idea was that upon reaching various destinations worldwide within the framework of their professional responsibility, they would also visit with various audiences, mainly in the Jewish community. Dressed in El Al uniforms, they would talk to these audiences about our people, our country, their families, and their lives in Israel. They would describe the beautiful and amazing things about the Israeli experience, things that tended to be pushed to the side due to the intense preoccupation with security and politics. They weren't supposed to talk about El Al unless asked. They might be called "El Al Ambassadors," but they represented all of us in Israel.

The meetings, with all the operations and logistics involved, would be organized by the company.

When we started the project, there was a lot of skepticism about it: El Al is a for-profit corporation, after all, and its staff is not obligated to engage in such activities. In my view, this kind of task could only be done by volunteers who were motivated and committed to the idea. But would they even want to participate in this project — all the more so, pro bono — sacrificing the free time they have abroad after a flight, forgoing traveling, resting, and shopping?

I believed so.

We issued a "call for proposals" for the first El Al Ambassadors' course. We wanted to start with a hundred volunteer ambassadors, and six hundred signed up...

We selected a hundred of them to participate in the training, all extremely motivated and with a deep sense of purpose.

They were trained and sent off.

This has been an amazing project with tremendous impact, which has sparked tremendous excitement in Jewish communities around the world and an immense sense of satisfaction among those who have taken part in it, our El Al Ambassadors.

"As soon as your workplace allows you to do something that has moral rather than monetary worth, it stops being a workplace," said Shiran Nakash Baruch, a flight attendant and ambassador. "It becomes a place where you can give of yourself and do something valuable, but you get it back a thousandfold."

382

I haven't been CEO at El Al for many, many years, and Futterman no longer manages this program for the company. But it continues, with great success, empowering the people and inspiring the organization.

Over 700,000 people around the world have already heard the stories of El Al Ambassadors.

This project has a life of its own.

132.

How Much Does It Really Cost?

What is the real price of what we buy?

Supposedly, a shirt that costs around $75 is much more expen-
sive than a shirt "on sale" that costs around $15.

Is that so?

In my view, the real price of the shirt is the price you paid for it
divided by the number of times you use it. In other words, the price
for one use of the shirt.

If you really like the shirt that cost $75 and you wear it 50 times,
that means it cost 75 divided by 50 — i.e. $1.50 per use.

If, on the other hand, you don't really care for the shirt that costs
$15, you probably bought it only because it was on sale. You may not
wear it at all, and if you wear it only once and then leave it lying in
your closet, the true cost is 15 divided by 1 — i.e. $15 for one use.

In my view, the right thing to do — and what I do myself — is to
go into a store where the prices are within the reach of the average
person and the items for sale are not overly opulent, then choose the
item I like the most without compromising. There is a good chance
that I will wear it many times, and so the price per use will be the
lowest and the enjoyment of each use will be the greatest.

When I go to buy clothes with my wife, I ask her only one thing:
to choose the item she likes the most and finds the most attractive,
without any consideration for the price. The first time you see the
price tag ought to be at the cashier's...

My wife listens very attentively to my words and nods her head
in agreement.

You can guess for yourselves what she actually does...
This is the difference between a magnificent theory and reality.

133.

133.

The Wagon and the Lame Horse

After the signing of the peace agreement with Jordan in 1994, we went there on a trip with a group of about twenty people.

In those days, Israelis could only go on such a trip in a group with a constant armed escort.

One afternoon, our group arrived in Petra. After a short walk in the wadi leading to the ancient Nabatean city, the fantastic, unique, and breathtaking sight appeared before us. Truly a stunning vision.

Then it was time to go back.

Making our way out of the wadi was no easy climb.

I walked in the back with my wife Anat, who found the trail very difficult.

The sun was going down. The group was already far ahead of us, as we shuffled along at a turtle's pace, bringing up the rear.

Suddenly, Anat stopped, sat down on the ground, and said simply, "I can't do this anymore."

We were alone in the middle of the desert in Jordan. The group had already moved on, and there was not a soul around.

I told her, "Fine, we'll sit here in the wadi and wait. Once in a while, a horse or a donkey with a cart passes by. We'll rent a cart like that, get in, and make it to the top."

Waiting...

Waiting...

Waiting...

Darkness fell, and still, no one came.

Suddenly, to our great joy, a slightly lame horse appeared, harnessed to a dilapidated and broken-down cart.

I said to her, "Come on, let's get on," grabbing our backpacks.

Then, to my great surprise, I heard Anat ask the carter, "How much will that be?"

He gave her a price.

Anat answered emphatically: "No."

And he, without hesitation, despite his horse's limp, set off at a gallop and quickly disappeared into the distance.

Unbelievable.

Now what do we do???

Sitting down again.

Darkness.

No horses, no carts. Not even a miniature sample-size donkey.

It was clear to us that we would not be able to make it back up. Maybe the next day...

Anat understood the magnitude of the mistake.

Neither of us uttered a word.

Silence.

There was nothing to do as we sat in the dark.

After quite a long time, when we had lost all hope — Fata Morgana!

At the top of the path appeared another horse with a cart, dilapidated no less. I grabbed Anat tightly, sat her in the cart, and told her quietly, "No questions. Not a word."

As we sat down in the miserable wagon, we felt like we were riding in a royal carriage coming down from the sky.

Somehow, we made it back safely.

Everyone has their own Petra story, and sometimes it has nothing to do with Petra...

• • •

There are situations in which you must act first and ask questions later.

134.
Delta Power

Numbers, and their impact on us, can be quite deceptive.

When the number is treated as standing on its own, it can be daunting.

But what really matters is not the number itself, but the difference between it and the number that seems logical to you to invest — in money, in time, or in anything else.

For example: You want to make someone happy with a wedding gift. You consider giving them $250. They would of course be happy to receive $250, but you know they would be moved and much happier to receive $300.

The discussion with yourself is not about $300 — which may seem a frightening number — but about the difference, the delta. In other words, about 50 bucks.

Isn't it worth it to make the happy couple that much happier by adding another 50? They'll feel much better, and you will feel much better about yourself.

Another example: You eat at a restaurant and receive great service.

It is common to give a server a 10% tip, but isn't it worth it to give a 15% tip, which will make them happy and show that you especially appreciate their work? After all, this is their livelihood.

Again, the discussion is not about the 15%, but the five-percent delta, the difference between the minimum acceptable amount and the more generous measure.

An example from another area of life: You are preparing for a test.

You study over the course of three days, devoting many hours to preparing.

The two-hour test arrives.

You finish it after an hour and a half.

You're dying to hand it in and get out of there.

But it would probably be right to spend the remaining thirty minutes reviewing what you've written, catching mistakes, adding things that slipped your mind, and so on.

The difference is only thirty minutes, which is meaningless compared to the many days and hours you spent preparing for the test.

Isn't it worth it?

This is also true for other issues, such as your attitude toward people and investing time and attention in children, friends, love. These things may be harder to measure, but the principle is very similar: understand the significance of the delta, the difference, and relate only to it.

This is also true for smiles...

When you smile, people smile back at you.

When you are generous, they are generous toward you.

135.
The Ties That Bind Us

When I was an El Al CEO, we signed a codeshare agreement with S7 (Siberia) Airlines for connecting flights from Moscow to dozens of destinations across Russia.

The CEO of the Russian company, Vladislav Filev, came to Israel to sign the agreement. I greeted him. A serious man, thin, with sharp features, a military background, and extensive business experience. I immediately realized that he was withdrawn and introverted.

Before the signing ceremony, we sat in my office and talked. During the meeting, several people came into the room.

The face of the Russian CEO fell.

I said to myself, *What's going on here?*

I guess my eye caught something...

Everyone in my office, including me, wore a jacket and a tie, but he didn't have a tie.

I asked him, "Do you want a tie perhaps?"

He immediately said, "Yes."

I had some spare suits and ties in my closet.

I gave him the nicest tie I could find and immediately his face lit up.

We started the signing ceremony. The atmosphere was superb.

When the event ended, I told my Russian colleague to take the tie with him as a memento.

From that moment on, the relationship between El Al and S7 was simply amazing, in all respects and from all angles. They were willing to do almost anything for us.

Of course, there were also business interests; after all, they're both for-profit corporations. But strange as it may sound, I am convinced that the tie incident tied us to S7's CEO, greatly influencing his policy toward El Al and the message he conveyed to his people.

•••

Personal ties and small human gestures are important everywhere and in any situation, even for companies whose bottom line is profit.
A human being is a human being is a human being.

136.
The Best Spice Available

People will forget the things you said,
People will forget the things you did,
But people will never forget how you made them feel.
(*Attributed to Maya Angelou*)

Three short stories from life:

1. When I was the CEO of El Al, the chairman, Amikam Cohen, and I became good friends. Once a week, we would sit down for lunch outside the company headquarters and talk about various topics.

Our permanent place, to the surprise of everyone who saw us, was Doner, a shawarma joint in Yehud. We loved sitting there not only because of the excellent shawarma — really the best — but mainly because of the pleasant and informal atmosphere, without any posturing; because of the beaming faces of the owners, Liraz and Amir, and all their staff; and because of the simple and genuine fare, seasoned with the best spice that exists: love from the heart.

It felt like home there.

2. In preparation for the birthday of our daughter Maya, I made a reservation at a widely-recommended restaurant in Herzliya.

The whole family of eight arrived, dressed to the nines, and strode into the restaurant.

To my great surprise, it turned out that for some reason they had no record of our reservation. In retrospect, I should have checked before we arrived, which of course I hadn't...

It was 8 PM on a Friday. Maya's face fell as we stood by the entrance blinking awkwardly, looking at each other in disbelief...

What should I do?

Obviously, it's impossible to get a seat on short notice, certainly not for eight diners. I checked several other places, without success, and then I called the Coffee Bar in Tel Aviv, which we really liked and used to eat at often.

I knew that on a Friday evening there was no chance of finding a table there, but what was there to lose?

I asked to speak to Pnina, the restaurant manager, and told her what happened.

Pnina listened and told me simply: "Come on over. I still don't know how, but I'll make it work."

I could see her kind face in my mind's eye.

We went there. Indeed, Pnina, like a champ, found seating for us.

Since then, the Coffee Bar has become like a second home for us. And there's always a place for you at home, even if your arrival is unexpected. Especially when you're in a tight spot...

3. We loved playing at the Ga'ash Golf Club, which was first and foremost a social club.

The club's budget was small, the grounds weren't impressive in size, and the restaurant was a kind of food truck with diners sitting in a tent...

Still, the way they treated us was amazing, it felt great to be there, and we enjoyed having a close circle of friends.

The club manager, Gili, did her job with great love, heart, and soul, caring for the members and making every one of them feel welcome and loved, like at home.

Unfortunately, the club was closed for regulatory reasons, so now we have to play golf elsewhere. And the new place is spacious and impressive.

But it's just not the same. Not even close.

It's a golf course, not a social club, and when the guys who used to play at Ga'ash meet up, we always — always, always — start commiserating over the loss of our beloved Ga'ash.

In relatively old age, it's hard to expand your circle of friends, but at the Ga'ash Golf Club, I forged new and genuine friendships with people I love with all my heart — and with their families. Above all is the "Quartet" of Aroeti, Nessis and Moti Sela — a charming person and a beloved friend, who very sadly passed away and whom we accompanied in the last months of his life — and Mali, who with great sensitivity, replaced him in our quartet after his death.

Another family, composed of friends, is a real gift for life, especially at this age.

It really cannot be taken for granted.

• • •

The things that really matter, the ones that make you feel good, are the people, the heart, the soul, and the warm treatment.

137.

Surprise...

One of my favorite things as a grandfather is to pick up my grand-children, Ido and Itay, from kindergarten once a week. They look forward to the day, and so do I. It is very important for me to be alone with the grandchildren for a significant period of time, with-out any of the parents being around. The connection created this way is direct, strong, unmediated, and very, very special. Most importantly — it's between me and them only.

It starts with their running and tackling me with strong, loving hugs, then continues with a shopping spree for all the sweets they dream of and popsicles — in summer and in the winter...

From there, we head to the charming playground in their neigh-borhood in Ramat Gan, and then comes the culmination of our qual-ity time: heart-to-hearts while licking popsicles, wiping faces and noses with sleeves as only Grandpa allows, and eating the sweets we bought. At this point, all the children in the neighborhood gather around to enjoy the sweets that Mom and Dad don't allow them.

For our beloved Iris, wife of our son Nimo and wonderful mother of Itay and Ido, this is tough. But she has learned to overcome... just as I have learned to cool it a bit...

Of course, sometimes there are unexpected events, like the next one, which occurred during the COVID crisis:

I picked up Itay and Ido from kindergarten, we exchanged big, strong hugs and then we walked happily, hand in hand, to the candy store. We more or less bought the ENTIRE shop, got to the playground, gobbled down the candies, sweets, and popsicles, and engaged in our usual heart-to-hearts. Itay smiled and spoke enthusiastically, while the big, happy eyes of little Ido peeked out at me from his popsicle-smeared face.

Then, suddenly, I saw Itay's smile fade as his attention seemed to turn to something very serious.

I immediately understood what it was.

"Grandpa, I need to poop," he announced.

I quickly took him behind the bushes.

He finished his big and impressive business, then said to me: "Grandpa, I need toilet paper to wipe my tush."

Where would I find toilet paper now?

Quite the snafu. I was of course not equipped for this possibility; had Mommy Iris or Daddy Nimo been around, things would be "going down" differently.

I would debrief later and learn the appropriate lessons, but what could we do now?

I started negotiating with him.

"No problem," I said, "you don't need toilet paper. Just pull up your underwear and pants and we'll go right home. There's really no problem..."

But Itay was not so convinced.

"Yes, I do need paper," he insisted, and just like that we were stuck.

Our conversation ping-ponged amusingly, until luckily I found a solution:

As it was the middle of COVID, everyone walked around with paper masks, and I also had one in my pants pocket.

A multi-purpose magic mask provided a sufficient response to the problem, proving itself up to the task at hand...

138.

Small, Crowded Room

In preparation for Hanukkah, my father decided to organize a party for the employees of the institution he ran.

At that time, there was considerable tension between the employees of the school and Tel Aviv city hall, which controlled it, over wages and working conditions. Dad was afraid that some of the employees wouldn't come to the party as an act of protest, and he realized that the room would probably be pretty empty.

He thought about what to do and then announced:

"The event will be for the students, and their counselors and teachers are expected to come and be with them."

And it worked.

Those who were debating whether to attend or thought about boycotting the event understood, with all due respect to their dispute with the municipality, that he was committed first and foremost to the children.

And if someone still decided not to come, no one would notice...

Indeed, the party was a great success, and the room was packed to capacity.

When identifying potential landmines, it's helpful to mobilize people from a place of values and emotions — a place that touches their hearts and souls.

Just in case, the event should also take place in a small and crowded place. Maybe you can arrange it so there aren't enough chairs. That way, people will have to go get them from outside so they have somewhere to sit...

WHO THE F*CK IS MICHAEL?!

• • •

An event in a small and crowded place creates a sense of intimacy. Those who managed to get a spot inside and fill the place up, feel they have the right to participate in the event and are part of a select group. This, in itself, makes the event a success.

139.

Radicalization or Reconciliation

My father used to say: "I can't understand why they keep trying to divide us. In every Jewish house, I feel at home, no matter what denomination it belongs to — Orthodox, Reform, Conservative, Hasidic, or secular."

One of the questions that preoccupies me, and I guess most of us, is the following: What is the right path for our country and our people?

Our people are amazing: long history, unique legacy, profound works by intellectual greats; we have fierce warriors, Nobel laureates, giants of literature and science, and people of action.

Almost two thousand years of exile brought our people to the brink of destruction and annihilation.

The great miracle of reuniting our tribes with the establishment of the State of Israel cannot be taken for granted.

We have different opinions on different issues, but I feel and believe that the vast majority of the population is troubled by extremism and hatred, is anxious that this will lead to a civil war, and is willing to do anything to prevent it.

Even if someone from my family happens to think differently than I do, that doesn't make him my enemy.

Even if I think he is wrong, even if he expresses himself inappropriately, bluntly and antagonistically, even if he says terrible things — he is no traitor or fascist.

We are brothers.

No person, sector, or group has a monopoly on a particular value.

There is no monopoly on truth.

There is no monopoly on Judaism.

There is no monopoly on morality, humanity, and interpersonal love.

There is no monopoly on democracy.

There is no monopoly on Zionism, patriotism, or love of the Land of Israel.

I do not accept that one stream of Judaism is preferable or that one stripe represents "the only real Jew," above all others.

I believe that the ideal situation is one in which different streams exist among the Jewish people, learning to live together in peace and respect for each other; this is far preferable to a situation in which certain streams are cut off or pushed out of Judaism, leaving a segment of our people to simply "evaporate."

A reality in which people see someone who is not like them or who does not think like them as an illegitimate person, a traitor, or a fascist, is very dangerous.

I hear the violent discourse expanding and polluting the airwaves, I see the hatred bubbling up in the public sphere — and I'm horrified.

Extremism and hatred can quickly deteriorate into an uncontrollable situation, and a civil war would destroy everything we've built here. Everything must be done to prevent it and to heal the fracture before it is too late.

Once something has been torn apart, it's very hard to mend it.

This is not a theoretical matter.

Unfortunately, history teaches us that in the past our people have experienced extremism, hatred, division, and civil war.

It always ends terribly.

Each and every one of us, no matter our political position, has the responsibility to act as a human being. But the greatest responsibility is borne by the leadership.

In the end, the people imitate and behave like their leaders.

There is great importance to the personal example any leader sets, and the duty of elected officials is to say loudly and clearly: this is not how we behave, this is not how we talk.

Words lead to actions.

The tongue has the power of life and death...[19]

What comes out of your mouth cannot be returned.

We have to breathe deeply, count to ten, and drink plenty of water before speaking, reacting, and exacerbating the situation.

It is very easy to hate. Radicalization, division, and hatred are rapid and destructive processes that do not require listening, courage, or willingness to reach out to the other — only to go with your positions to the extreme, "unloading" out of a primal conviction that you are right and that the other is an enemy.

Bringing hearts and minds together is a more difficult, longer process. When it comes to reconciliation, you have to give of yourself.

Rapprochement requires seeing the other, listening, understanding, embracing, accepting, not being judgmental, demonstrating generosity of spirit, and finding ways to live together despite disagreements. Sometimes, it also requires swimming against the current of those closest to you to stop the hatred and bridge the gap.

In my opinion, reconciliation is a great *mitzvah* and a task of paramount importance, and it also entails immense responsibility: our responsibility as parents, instructors, educators, managers, and commanders to educate, inspire, and set a personal example.

Education from an early age has a tremendous power that can shape reality.

At the end of the day, it's up to each person to choose which way to go — toward reconciliation or toward radicalization.

True reconciliation requires colossal inner fortitude.

Civil war, meanwhile, is catastrophic.

The late prime minister Menachem Begin, who was a special person and great leader, said, and I paraphrase: After my death, I hope that I will be remembered above all as someone who prevented a civil war. To me, this is more important than my time as commander of the Jewish underground in British Mandate Palestine or my time

---

19. Proverbs, 18:21.

as prime minister, or than signing the peace agreement with Egypt, or the Golan Heights Law.

Begin, who did everything possible to prevent a civil war after the Altalena incident,[20] when the young State of Israel was barely on its feet, realized that there are greater things than one person or another, one opinion or another. Things that are paramount to the existence of a people and state.

He felt and understood what is important for all of us to feel and understand: radicalization can lead to destruction.

Reconciliation is fundamental to the continued existence of the State of Israel as a Jewish, free, and democratic state, and as the center of the Jewish people throughout the world.

I feel and believe that reconciliation is a monumental mission both for our leaders and for each and every one of us, a mission that carries with it a tremendous responsibility.

---

20. The Altalena Affair was a violent confrontation in June 1948, in which the newly created Israel Defense Forces sunk an arms shipment aboard the Altalena earmarked for the Irgun (also known as Etzel), a Jewish para-military force operating at the time that was later integrated into the IDF.

140.

Would You Sit with Him for a While?

One of the most amazing people I ever met in my life was Sefi Udi.

Sefi was wounded during his military service and left fully paralyzed.

Before the holidays, as commander of the Air Force, I used to visit soldiers who were hospitalized because of injury or illness.

That's how we met.

I visited Sefi in the hospital several times, I was excited to see his beaming face, his broad smile, and his optimism.

At the end of one of the meetings, I said goodbye to him and was walking to my car.

Suddenly, a nurse ran out of the hospital and said: "Sefi is asking for you to come back for a moment. He has something to ask of you. Do you mind?"

Of course, I went right back.

Then Sefi told me: "Sir, a few days ago, they brought in a guy in serious condition. He's lying here alone and almost no one comes to visit him. Would you sit with him for a while and talk to him? That will probably make him very happy."

I did exactly that.

Sefi had never asked me for anything before.

It's inconceivable: the only request Sefi made to me in his life was for another person in distress that he didn't even know — not for himself.

141.
The One Thing No One
Can Take from You

What's the one thing you can never take from a human being?

You can take away a person's money, house, car, dreams, memories, freedom, reputation, dignity — even their very life.

There is only one thing that can never be taken away from a person:

Whatever they give to someone else.

What you have given to others always remains yours.

Giving can be of any kind and in any field.

Giving makes the soul happy and is important in its own right. What exactly you give is less important.

Maimonides writes in *Mishneh Torah* about eight stages or levels of giving, in ascending order:

I present them here in my own words, as I understand them:

The first level: To give a little, with a sour face, but to give, nonetheless.

The second level: To give a little, but with a smile. Smiling and empathy are meaningful.

The third level: To give generously after being asked — i.e., to comply with the request.

The fourth level: To give generously without being asked — i.e., the giving comes from the giver.

The following stages concern the relationship between the giver and the recipient.

The fifth level: The giver does not know who the recipient is, but the recipient knows the identity of the giver and may feel a certain degree of discomfort.

The sixth level: The giver knows who the recipient is, but the recipient does not know who the giver is. In such a situation, the recipient will probably feel more comfortable.

The seventh level: Neither the giver nor the recipient knows about the other. The process is completely anonymous.

The eighth level: At this stage, the goal is that the recipient will not have to continue depending on the generosity of others, instead embarking on a different path, a path of action and work and family, a path of self-reliance allowing the recipient to make their own decisions, act in their own interests, stand up for themselves and reach true independence — financially, emotionally and mentally.

For Maimonides, this is the highest level of giving.

However, as I delved deeper into Maimonides' eight levels, I felt and realized that there was another level — **the ninth level** — which I call the "Level of Fire and Flame."

This stage is all about the recipient, with the giver only in the background.

Giving starts a fire in the recipient, and the flame continues to burn even long after the giver is gone. The recipient, having embarked on the path of success and independence, moves to the path of giving and now becomes a giver. This opens up additional cycles of giving and ensures that the circle of responsibility and giving is never broken.

Those who reach true independence, deep independence, are capable of giving wholeheartedly.

• • •

What you have given to others always remains yours.

405

142.

The Ninth Level

When we established HaEmek Squadron, a soldier named Ronen Polovian served in one of the hardened aircraft shelters (HAS), where the planes are parked to protect them from attack.

Ronen, a solid guy with a round face and kind, smiling eyes, came from a large and proud family that faced profound financial challenges. I quickly realized that he was a professional, energetic, determined soldier, smart and driven, able to create a good connection with people and motivate them to follow him. His professionalism, personality, and sky-high motivation spoke to me; it was a combination I believed in very much. So did the technical officer of the squadron, Itzik Nahum, who had a sharp eye for such qualities.

Ronen was a founding member of the squadron, but he wanted to be discharged from the IDF.

I called him in for a conversation, asking him why he wanted to be discharged and what he thought about becoming an officer.

Ronen looked at me sadly and said quietly, "Sir, I was just a soccer player... I don't have a high school degree, and my grades were trash anyway. No one will accept me anywhere."

I said, "Take the entrance exams, and we'll see."

One day, I received a phone call from the head of the IAF officers' department, Yossi Bar.

"Shkedy, are you delusional?" he asked.

"What do you mean?"

Yossi replied: "A soldier from your squadron named Ronen

Polovian showed up here without a high school degree and with poor grades. Why would you even send him here?"

I said, "Yossi, send him to Officer Training School. By the time he graduates, he'll be at the top of his class, trust me."

Yossi, an open and understanding person, thought for a moment and made a decision on the spot, "If you back him, I'll send him."

I believed in Ronen, in his character and capability. I didn't do him a favor. It was clear to me that it was the correct thing to do and that he had to be given a chance to prove himself and get on the right path.

The "system" has a very hard time digesting such things, but that didn't interest me much. To my delight, Yossi took his cue from me.

I called Ronen to my office and said, "Ronen, you're going to OTS. Walk in there with your head held high, as if you've got a suit of armor with the invisible name Shkedy emblazoned on it. Don't let anyone push you around. You're going to be the outstanding cadet of the course, no two ways about it."

Ronen looked at me, stunned, but said, "I got it."

He went to OTS and graduated as the course's outstanding cadet.

After the course, Ronen returned to Ramat David Airbase. After serving as a technical officer there, he was promoted to technical section commander and other significant positions.

In light of his success, he was then promoted to become the commander of an air maintenance squadron at Tel Nof Airbase, a very complex and significant station, with a mountain of responsibility on his shoulders for a large number of aircrew, planes, and helicopters.

He later reached a significant position at Air Force Headquarters, eventually becoming commander of the Technical School, responsible for training personnel in the IAF's technical sector and its branches throughout the country.

The soldier who had been afraid to go to OTS, who thought himself unfit and imagined that no one would even let him through the door, reached the rank of full colonel and a position of great influence.

When introducing young service members to the technical

school, Ronen would tell them his story and say, "Do you see me? If I'm here, the commander in charge of training all the technical personnel of the Air Force, you could be too. It's up to you."

At Ronen's retirement party, I sat alongside Nahum, HaEmek Squadron's former technical officer, and we were excited to see the appreciation and love Ronen received from many, many people and numerous generations of IAF officials.

Many of the IAF's technicians have advanced and reached their potential thanks to Ronen's character, approach, and the inspiration he has given them, undoubtedly related to the path he took personally.

Ronen gave real opportunities to the people he led.

All credit goes to Ronen Polovian.

To me, his amazing story illustrates the ninth level of giving.

143.
The Chain of Generations

When Dad passed away, we accompanied him on his last journey as is customary in Jewish tradition, but we chose to add a special part to the funeral service.

We stood together, embracing each other — our entire relatively small family, my sister Yael and I with our spouses and children — and we all sang together with great emotion, choking back tears, the songs that Dad especially loved, songs we grew up on and that we sang on Fridays at Mom and Dad's house.

We felt that this was how Dad would have liked the people he loved most, those he raised and adored, to say goodbye to him on his way to heaven.

The deep meaning of the phrase "the chain of generations" became clear to me when my older son, Nimo, told me and wrote a story about an incident from the COVID lockdowns.

I share it now in his own words. It is just lovely.

One Friday afternoon, we took the children to Iris's mother in Beersheba.

Before going, we wondered whether we should go or not. The government's guidelines weren't really clear, but the Passover lockdown had already been lifted, and we were allowed to travel to get groceries. Also, we had no intention of coming into direct contact with anyone – not even Grandma. So, we decided to risk it and brought a gift basket for Grandma with pastries that Iris had baked.

After that whole time of loneliness and social distancing, it seemed Grandma Yehudit really needed the visit because she was very excited when we sat on two benches in the yard outside her home.

The children didn't hug her and kept their distance, but Grandma put bags of chocolate and candies on the ground, like she was feeding stray cats. The kids approached carefully (seriously, like a couple of street cats), took the candy and scarfed it down. The kids were super happy and went on to play in the grass next to us. Their joy was the only thing that was infectious.

Then suddenly, out of nowhere, song over loudspeakers. The whole neighborhood could hear it. Blasting Shalom Aleichem. "Peace be upon you, ministering angels, angels of the highest, from the King of Kings' Kings, the Holy One, blessed be He." The children began mouthing the words, which they probably knew from kindergarten (I confess, we weren't the ones who taught them), walking mesmerized, like the mice following the Pied Piper of Hamelin, out of the yard, toward the notes. I went with them, leaving Mom and Grandma on the benches.

The sounds grew louder and louder, and after a minute or two of navigating some apartment buildings, we found an elderly man, a little chubby, with a big beard, just like the illustration from the famous children's book "Eliezer and the Carrot."

The man stood alone, next to his car, in a parking lot between the buildings, with a microphone in his hand and a karaoke speaker next to him, singing off-key for his pleasure and for the enjoyment of the entire neighborhood.

After the three of us sat down on a bench on the sidewalk in front of him, he continued to sing: "Shalom Lach, Eretz Nehederet (Hello to you, wonderful land)" and a few other songs. Between songs, there was sporadic applause from the balconies.

Then the man said, "And now, our final song before the Sabbath" and started singing "Oseh Shalom." Ittai and Iddo weren't quite as familiar with this song, but I joined in loudly so that they would learn, "He Who makes peace in His heights, may He make peace for us and for all Israel; and say, Amen."

While I was sitting with the boys on that dilapidated bench in that neighborhood in Beersheba, I suddenly remembered Grandpa Moshe, *how this song encapsulated him, just as the seven-branched Menorah and the flag bearing the Star of David symbolize the country.*

I remembered how Yotam and I used to sit with him, on benches just like those, in Gan HaShalom in Kfar Saba in the 1980s. How much we loved him and were happy to just be with him and how when we were with him, nothing else in the world mattered.

And I remembered how we used to eat on Friday nights, with him and Grandma Nechama and with our parents, brothers, uncles, and cousins, around a table with the whitest tablecloth in the whole country. I remembered how every time Grandpa would pour sweet, heavy wine into the mazal cup, which would overflow and stain the whole tablecloth ("How does Grandma get it clean every week?" everyone would marvel); how Grandpa would recite the blessings; and how we would all sing and pray and observe a moment of silence (we didn't know why yet), and then eat and enjoy and laugh.

All the memories made me choke up a bit, and I couldn't really finish the song.

The man finished singing, put the speaker in the trunk, and drove away.

Ittai, Iddo, and I started walking back to the yard.

On the way, I wiped the tears from my cheeks and told the children that it had brought back memories of Grandpa Moshe.

"Did you love Grandpa Moshe?" Ittai asked, and I replied, "The most in the whole world."

• • •

Indeed, the power and meaning of love, soulfulness, tradition, legacy, and education. The deep messages are passed down from generation to generation.

"He Who makes peace in His heights, may He make peace for us and for all Israel; and say, Amen."

144.

Do You Know Where You Are?

We went on a "Witnesses in Uniform" trip to Poland, a large delegation of IDF personnel and service members from other branches of the security forces. We had bereaved families with us, and we were joined by witnesses who had survived hell sixty years earlier.

The journey was unsettling. Being exposed, face to face, to things I'd only read about, heard of, imagined, and tried to understand was difficult and emotional.

We arrived at Majdanek.

In front of us stood the mountain of ashes. Seven tons of human ashes, the ashes of our families who were murdered and burned on this accursed land.

Unimaginable.

On the way to the death camp, we passed by the house of the former camp commandant, Karl Otto Koch. We walked past it upright, in uniform, bearing the Israeli flag and a Torah scroll.

We continued walking toward the camp when our guide, Yaniv, a former Shin Bet agent whose body language conveyed something formidable, asked us to put our bags on the floor.

We put our bags down and followed him without hesitation.

He told us to go into one of the buildings, not far from the camp commandant's house. We went in.

Inside the building was an entrance to another room. He signaled for us to enter. We went in.

He closed the door and asked, "Do you know where you are?"

We didn't know.
Then he said, "I put you in the gas chamber."
We were horrified.
Sixty years later, when we knew where we had come from and what had happened at Majdanek, they put us in a gas chamber and closed the door behind us without our even fathoming where we were.

145.

A Letter in His Uniform Pocket

When our son, Omer, was training as a flight instructor, he joined a
"Witnesses in Uniform" delegation.

The letter we wrote to him, which is presented here in full, he
received while in the Majdanek extermination camp in Poland:

To Omer, our beloved son.

*You now stand in a place that is inconceivable, insane, and
unimaginable.*

*To be at the extermination camps as a young, smart, sensitive, mature
IDF officer and pilot, and try to understand how such a thing could have
happened — is not impossible.*

*It cannot be done and, in our assessment, you will never be able to
understand, how people with hearts and souls conceived, planned, and
built a factory for the mass destruction of human beings.*

*The rational understanding that extermination was carried out just
because we are Jews is incomprehensible. The thought of our people in
general, and of our family in particular, evokes strong thoughts and feelings. The attempt to imagine what happened in these places seventy-five
years ago and the images you saw in your mind will accompany you
throughout your life.*

*From an operational perspective, it is our job to ensure the continued
existence of our people, our state, and our family, and not to rely on
others.*

*Remember that first and foremost, we are human beings, and we
should behave as human beings toward each person.*

What you are doing and what you have achieved — in values, in practice, and in volunteering — inspires us with great admiration and enormous affection.

We have no doubt that Grandpa Moshe looks at you from above and feels great love and pride as well.

Continue to stride boldly into the future you believe in, with all your heart and soul.

Whatever you choose to do and wherever you go, we are with you and for you.

Sending a big, strong hug
With huge love
Mom and Dad

When I wrote this book and let Omer read it, he told me, "Dad, ever since I came back from 'Witnesses in Uniform,' I've been walking around with that letter always in the pocket of my uniform, so that I remember where I come from and where I'm going."

146.
Silent Melody in the
Nuclear Reactor

When it became known that the Syrians were building a nuclear reactor and it was nearing completion, I immediately understood the urgency of the threat. It was a danger of a different order of magnitude — an entirely different level of threat.

It was clear to me that everything had to be done to destroy the reactor as soon as possible, before it became "hot" — i.e., to address the problem before crossing the point of no return.

From the outset, I felt the weight of the responsibility on our shoulders, a responsibility beyond any other.

The fact that I happened to be the chief of the Air Force at the time meant that I would do anything and everything for the mission to succeed.

This is how we approached the issue in the Air Force, and this is how the political echelon and the entire defense establishment treated it.

There was a tremendous mobilization of all the members of the intelligence, operational, and technological communities, who were secret partners at one level or another.

At first, there were only a few hush-hush accomplices, but as the date of the operation approached, their number grew. Still, this was a tiny fraction of the security establishment through its various arms; beyond this, there was strict adherence to compartmentalization in various areas. Only a precious few knew the full picture.

I decided to give the issue absolute priority over anything else — in the thinking phase, in formulating the intelligence assessment, in planning the operation and in the operational preparations for it, at Air Force headquarters and in the field.

I personally addressed the issue from two perspectives:

The first was businesslike, professional, sharp, and determined.

The second was dominated by the thought that constantly loomed over me: that this was something different from anything we'd known, whose immeasurable significance was greater than all of us.

I remember everything:

—The Air Force operational forum at the end of 2006, the first time the bright red light started flashing in my mind.

— The raw intelligence information that I insisted on receiving, reading, and listening to, which was supposedly unrelated, helped me get a clearer idea of the intelligence picture on Syria's nuclear weapons capability — even if it was only theoretical at the time.

—The intelligence provided by the Mossad in March 2007, which indicated that we were indeed looking at a nuclear reactor in a very advanced stage of construction.

—The decision made by Prime Minister Ehud Olmert to appeal to U.S. President George W. Bush to deal with the threat.

—The idea of the message that would be conveyed to all countries engaged in the development of nuclear weapons worldwide in general, and in the Middle East in particular, if the United States were to act and deal with the threat.

— My unequivocal position that Israel must itself undertake the destruction of the reactor.

— My decision to immediately prepare the Air Force for the possibility that we would indeed be tasked with destroying the reactor, regardless of the appeal to the Americans.

— The US president's decision that America would not take military action and explore the diplomatic channel instead, and Olmert's resolute response to Bush.

— The understanding that Israel would have to act on its own.

— The intensive intelligence and operational preparations and activities.

— The formulation of operational plans for the destruction of the reactor.

— The operational models, some of which I flew myself in the F-15I and F-16I squadrons, in order to form my own impressions, get a feel and see things up close.

— The real fear of starting an all-out war with the Syrians if they responded to the attack on the reactor.

— The completion of the operational plan with an idea presented to me by a young officer named Shai.

— The meeting with Defense Minister Ehud Barak in a small room at Hatzerim Airbase, where I sketched the overall operational idea on a paper napkin. This was the moment when Barak became convinced that we could attack and destroy the reactor without the Syrians realizing in real time what was happening, which would significantly reduce the chances of war.

— The arrangements, planning, and comprehensive preparations carried out simultaneously by various teams within the Air Force, some of whom were secret partners and some of whom were not, both for the attack on the reactor and for an all-out war that might break out immediately after the attack.

— The understanding that if a war broke out, the main burden of the first stage would be on the Air Force until the IDF would be able to mount a response.

— The preparation of the Air Force for war when most of our men, who were not secret partners in the plan to attack the reactor, did not know or understand the real reason.

— The meeting with Olmert, in which I recommended that he carry out the plan I had presented.

— Our face-to-face conversation that was held at my request at the end of the meeting with the heads of Israel's security agencies, when we stood alone on one side of the room and everyone stared at us.

— The firm handshake and the look in the prime minister's eyes.

— The moment when I realized that Olmert was determined to give the plan the green light and that the operation would be carried out soon.

— The words of my wife Anat, who of course did not know

anything but apparently felt and understood with her senses that I was carrying a heavy burden, "I don't know what you are planning, but it's time to move it or lose it..."

— The operational wargame in the "pit" at Air Force headquarters, to which I invited IDF Chief of General Staff Gabi Ashkenazi, and our heart-to-heart conversation.

— The phone call from the head of the Mossad, Meir Dagan, in which he gave the IDF chief and me a significant update from the United States, which actually set the clock for the attack in motion.

— The meeting with the defense minister late that night and the understanding that our fighter pilots would most likely be flying over the Syrian Desert by the next night.— If we had to call it off at the last second, we'd have that option.

—The meeting with the head of the IAF's Operations Department, Amikam Norkin (who later became the commander of the IAF), in which I instructed him to activate the attack command and issue the order to put the Air Force on a war footing.

— The activation of the mission command by the head of the operations department.

— My flight to the airbases in the south to meet the mission pilots and navigators, most of whom had trained with complex operational models without knowing the true target. In this meeting, they heard from me for the first time what target they were going to attack.

— The conversation in which I emphasized to them some significant points that were important to me that they hear from me personally.

— The bright eyes of the warriors after grasping the magnitude of the task at hand, and the strong handshake with each and every one of them.

— Directing the operation from the command-and-control center in the pit at Air Force headquarters, while in the next room sat the prime minister, the defense minister, the foreign minister, the chief of general staff, the head of the Mossad, and other senior defense officials, along with an Air Force liaison explaining what they were seeing on the screens.

• • •

It all converged in those dramatic moments in the air and in the pit, moments when:

— I vigilantly followed the progress of the mission with the people in the command-and-control center, until the climax when we heard the codeword "Arizona," meaning the reactor had been destroyed.

— We made sure that the Syrians did not understand what was happening and that no air confrontation was developing that could spark a war.

— We were preparing for the possibility that we might have to move to another command-and-control center in the pit in order to direct the start of an all-out war, should it flare up.

— We then realized that things were on the right path, as we had planned, and that war was unlikely.

I left the command-and-control center to meet the prime minister and we hugged each other, as we both understood the profound meaning of the mission's success and achievement of the goal.

In my estimation, to this day, the Syrians do not know or understand what happened or why, and it is a good thing that this is the case.

We called the operation "Silent Melody."

This melody cannot be stopped, even if it sometimes plays silently.

If not for the courage, wisdom, determination, leadership, and deep commitment of Prime Minister Ehud Olmert, the operation would not have come to fruition.

It was bigger than anything I knew — that's how I felt all along, and that's how I think all the people involved felt — in the Air Force, the entire defense establishment, and the political echelon.

The destruction of the Syrian reactor is deeply linked to our belonging and commitment to the future of our country and our people.

We are not the story.

There are things that are greater than all of us.

147.

You Don't Understand Anything

One morning, my secretary, Avital, came into my office and said, "President Shimon Peres is hosting a state dinner for the president of Hungary, and you're invited."

As commander of the Air Force, I was invited to many events in Israel and around the world. Not because my name is Shkedy, but because an event in the presence of the commander of the Air Force is perceived, for reasons that are not clear to me, as particularly prestigious.

I don't like to go to events. If I have the option not to, I just don't go.

That's why I arranged with Avital that whenever an invitation to an event arrived, she was to answer politely, "Shkedy is very busy, he has a lot of work [which was always true]. Thank you very much for the invitation, but he will not be able to attend."

When she informed me of the event at the president's residence, I told her, "Avital, follow the usual procedure. Let them know I'm very busy, that I appreciate the invitation, but I will not be attending."

Avital listened and left the room without saying a word.

A few weeks later, Avital and I were reviewing the schedule for the next week. She went over what was planned each day and then said, "On this date, you have the state dinner with the president of Hungary and President Peres."

I looked at her in wonder and asked, "Didn't I tell you to cancel?"

And she, nonchalantly, with her light voice and a small smile at

421

the corner of her mouth, replied, "I thought you were wrong. I didn't decline."

Did she just say that to me? What on earth...

Avital was an excellent, smart, and sensitive officer, but my first inclination was to blow a gasket...

But then I said to myself, "Maybe she's right and I'm wrong?" And after thinking about it a bit I came to the conclusion that, yes, she was probably right and I was probably wrong.

"OK," I told her, "call the president's residence and tell them I'm going, and that I want to bring my father with me."

Avital left the room quickly, called the president's residence, and came back grinning from ear to ear. "Of course," she said, "President Peres will be very happy to host your father as well."

...

My father, Moshe, was born and raised in the village of Tolcsva, Hungary. In March 1944, the Jews of Tolcsva were deported to Auschwitz. My father was the only survivor from his entire family. I knew that a meeting with the president of Hungary would be meaningful to him, but I had no idea how much.

I called him and said, "Dad, President Peres wants to invite you to his state dinner for the president of Hungary. If you go, I'll join you..."

It was quiet on the other side of the line for a few seconds, and then my father said to me, "I'll go."

On the day of the event, I picked my father up from Kfar Saba and we went to Jerusalem together.

Silence in the car.

Nearing the end of my tenure as commander of the Air Force, I was preoccupied with my thoughts and Dad with his.

Before we got to Jerusalem, he asked me, "Do you understand what's happening?"

"Yes," I told him. "We will go to the president's residence, have a state dinner with the president of Hungary, with President Peres and other guests. When we're done, I'll take you home."

My father looked at me and said, "You don't understand anything."

Then he began a recitation, like the songs at the end of the Passover Seder. It was a cumulative chant, each time adding a line, then starting from the beginning again, over and over.

"I, Moshe Mandel Shkedy, am going to Jerusalem, the capital of Israel and the Jewish people.

"I am traveling to meet Shimon Peres, the president of the State of Israel and of the Jewish people.

"I am traveling with my son, who is the commander of the Air Force of the State of Israel and the Air Force of the entire Jewish people." (That's the title my father gave me...)

"I am traveling to meet the president of Hungary when sixty-five years ago the value of our life in Hungary was less than the life of a dead dog.

"I'm going to meet the president of Hungary, who doesn't yet know he's going to apologize..."

Then he added:

"If I had been told sixty-five years ago: 'Dream the biggest and most amazing dream you can imagine,' there's no way I would have dreamed of something that's even close to what I just described to you as reality. And it didn't happen over thousands of years or hundreds of years, but in the lifetime of one person."

Dad was right.

His generation experienced the greatest catastrophe in the history of the Jewish people throughout the generations, and now we are part of the greatest miracle in the history of the Jewish people throughout the generations: a Jewish, free, democratic, proud state; the height of progress, innovation and creativity in fields such as: science, high-tech, medicine, technology, economy, agriculture, literature, military, education, culture, and more.

The greatest miracle in the history of the Jewish people throughout the generations has been shared by our mothers and fathers, our grandmothers and grandfathers, each in their own field.

Now it's the turn of the younger generation, which I believe in very much. The future of the State of Israel and the Jewish people depends on what our young people do.

And if you're asking yourself if the president of Hungary apologized, you probably never knew my father.

The president of Hungary had no other option...

He apologized.

• • •

Even the sky is not the limit. You can ask my father in Heaven.

424

What you have given to others always remains yours.

Thanks

Many thanks to my family and friends, the people who know me very well, who read some of the stories, commented, critiqued, suggested, enlightened, and recommended, and have an important part in the result.

Special thanks to those who worked on and delved into the entire book.

To Major General **Sharon Afek** and Attorney **Omer Shalev**, smart and ethical people I know from my years of service in the Air Force and from my work at El Al and much more, who enlightened me regarding sensitive issues.

To **Motty Habakuk**, a true expert in the history of the Air Force. Whenever I wanted to know what really happened, I asked him...

To **Avital Segev**, a sensitive and charming woman whose opinion I love to hear.

To **Jacob Burak**, an esteemed writer whose advice made me smarter and whose perspective I enjoyed hearing.

To my beloved sister **Yael**; our mother **Nechama** and father **Moshe** shaped her personality just like mine. Some of the stories, from childhood and from the rest of our lives, are shared by both of us.

To my beloved children **Omer**, **Maya**, and **Nimo**, who shared their thoughts and deliberations about whether to write a book at all, who read the manuscript in depth and contributed intelligent, important, and Illuminating comments.

To my beloved wife **Anat**, who was with me all the way, who was involved in the work itself and in writing the book — long before I wrote the first word...

To **Ilan Avishai**, a true friend, wise and broad-minded, who invested his heart, his mind, and his soul, and with whom I spoke at length about each and every story. Avishai was a true partner in writing and did so with great sensitivity and wisdom.

To the editor of the book, **Yoav Keren**, a professional and a real superstar, who accommodated me and my desire that the book be as authentic as possible, who fully understood the depth of what I intended to convey and ensured the text was somehow flowing and readable. (That was a very challenging task...) His fingerprints are visible on everything.

To my friend **Dov Eichenwald**, the CEO and publisher of Yedioth Books, whose family background is similar to mine;

Who for years tried to get me to write an autobiography despite my refusals;

Who understood what I wanted — although it was quite different from his original intention — and accommodated me wholeheartedly.

I have no doubt that the moral education he received from his father — who went through hell but chose to see the good, just like my father — had a huge impact on his life.

To Yedioth's VP of marketing, **Eyal Dadosh,** and his staff, who enlisted their experience, wisdom, and understanding so that the book could reach a wide audience.

To the cover designer **Pini Hamou**, whose creativity is an integral part of the book's content.

To the language editor **Ruthy Hazanovitz**, whose sharp eye, energy and professionalism made a significant contribution.

To the producer of the book, **Kuty Teper,** and his staff, who turned the Word file into a real book.

To **Renana Sofer**, editorial coordinator at Yedioth Books, who accompanied the process of the book's birth.

To **Hila Shafir**, who has not rested for a moment.

Thank you from the bottom of my heart to **Benny Carmi, Tali Carmi**, and **Nave Carmi**, who from the outset believed in this book and in the importance of translating it and bringing it forth to a wider audience. They did so with all their hearts and souls and spearheaded the entire publishing process with wisdom and professionalism, together with the entire eBookPro family.

To **Yossie Bloch** and **Oren Klass**, who translated this book into English with prudence, sensitivity, and a deep understanding of its spirit, my intentions, and the messages I wished to convey.

To **Mathew Berman**, for his keen and professional editing.

To **Ira Cohen**, who has accompanied me for years on matters of the English language... who read, reviewed, and provided insightful, precise, and intelligent commentary.

To **Amir Philos**, who carefullyoversaw the process of preparing this book for its launch to the wider world.

And to you, the readers, for giving me the opportunity, through my story, to be part of your story.

A big thank you to everyone,

Shkedy

About the Author

General (Ret.) Elyezer Shkedy was born in Israel on August 16, 1957. He was the fifteenth commander of the Israeli Air Force. During his service, Shkedy commanded numerous strategic operations, including the now-famous Operation Orchard airstrike on the Syrian nuclear reactor. After retiring from active duty, Shkedy became the CEO of the Israeli flag carrier airline El Al—the largest civilian airline in the country. Today, he volunteers as chairman of over fifteen educational and social startups, and is the President of I Belong Israel, where he teaches the importance of tolerance, leadership, Zionism, and personal values.

Shkedy is married to Doctor Anat Shkedy. They have a daughter and two sons.

9 781632 281159